RELATIVISM AND REALITY

From the early Greeks to today's leading philosophers, the question of how our beliefs and theories relate to reality has been the cause of much fervent debate. 'Realists' claim that reality is independent of our thinking, even if it is up to us how we think about it. 'Relativists' disagree and hold that what there is, and the truth about it, depends on our point of view. Which is right? Is there such a thing as an independent truth? Can we ever capture it in thought and language?

Relativism and Reality: A contemporary introduction examines these crucial questions in a clear and accessible manner which will appeal to all who come to philosophy for the first time. Robert Kirk examines the thought of some of the most influential thinkers of the century, with discussions of Wittgenstein's ideas on 'language-games', Quine's 'holism', Dummett's 'anti-realism' and Rorty's 'postmodern pragmatism'.

The result is a stimulating guide to fascinating and important theories about the relations between thought and reality and will be essential reading for all who seek a thorough yet accessible introduction to one of the most enduring topics in philosophy.

Robert Kirk is Professor of Philosophy at the University of Nottingham.

D0927360

RELATIVISM AND REALITY

A contemporary introduction

Robert Kirk

London and New York

First published 1999
by Routledge
11 New Fetter Lane, London EC4P 4EE

Simultaneously published in the USA and Canada
by Routledge
29 West 35th Street, New York, NY 10001

Routledge is an imprint of the Taylor & Francis Group

© 1999 Robert Kirk

Typeset in Times by Routledge
Printed and bound in Great Britain by
TJ International Ltd, Padstow, Cornwall

All rights reserved. No part of this book may be reprinted or reproduced or
utilized in any form or by any electronic, mechanical, or other means, now known
or hereafter invented, including photocopying and recording, or in any
information storage or retrieval system, without permission in writing from the
publishers.

British Library Cataloguing in Publication Data
A catalogue record for this book is available from the British Library

Library of Congress Cataloging in Publication Data
Relativism and reality: a contemporary introduction/Robert Kirk.
Includes bibliographical references and index.
1. Realism. 2. Relativity. I. Title.
B835.K57 1999   98–43681
149'.2–dc21   CIP

ISBN 0–415–20817–3 (hbk)
ISBN 0–415–20816–5 (pbk)

CONTENTS

PREFACE

Our thoughts about the world are influenced by such things as point of view, temperament, capacities, past experiences, and culture. Of course: that idea was familiar to the ancient Greeks. But some thinkers go much further and maintain that what exists itself depends on us. 'Even reality is relative', the American philosopher Nelson Goodman has said. That is hard to accept when you consider everyday events like rain and burnt toast, not to mention catastrophes like floods. How could they depend on us? (There are philosophical positions you can understand people holding even if you disagree, and there are others you can't.) *Realists* hold that reality is independent of our thinking, even if it is up to us how we think about it. *Relativists* disagree and hold that what there is, and what is true, depends on our point of view. Which is right? How do thoughts and theories relate to the world?

If those questions interest you, this book is for you. It aims to make accessible to non-specialists some recent philosophical work from within the so-called 'analytic' tradition. The ideas to be discussed are usually assumed to be too difficult for an introductory text; I have tried to explain them clearly without oversimplifying. Among other things there are expositions and discussions of Wittgenstein's ideas on 'language-games', Quine's 'holism', Dummett's 'anti-realism', and Rorty's 'postmodern' pragmatism. Although these philosophers' ideas appear to drive us towards sophisticated kinds of relativism, reasons are offered for concluding that in fact they do not.

The book is meant to intrigue you, to help you to see the point of pursuing the philosophical issues further, and to prepare you for reading the literature – not to settle matters. I hope it will serve as a useful introduction to philosophy not only for non-specialists wishing to get acquainted with fascinating and important theories, but for beginning students and also for those wondering whether to study philosophy at university.

It is normal, though frustrating, to find you can't read philosophy like a novel and have to re-read some passages – and that the problems are not neatly soluble like murder mysteries. It takes time to reflect on our unnoticed assumptions, which tend to surface only in philosophical discussion. I have done all I can to make the discussions accessible and have tried not to use philosophical jargon without explaining it; there is a glossary at the end of the book. Further reading is suggested at the end of each chapter.

My thanks to the many students whose questions over the years have helped me crystallize my views on the topics discussed, and especially to James Webber for comments on an early draft. I am most grateful to two anonymous referees for detailed comments and suggestions.

Robert Kirk

Nottingham

1

INTRODUCTION

1 Myths

In the Babylonian creation epic, the great god Marduk fights and kills a
monstrous dragon. Having done so,

He divided the monstrous shape and created marvels (from it).
He sliced her in half like a fish for drying:
Half of her he put up to roof the sky,
Drew a bolt across and made a guard hold it....
As for the stars, he set up constellations corresponding to them.

Later 'He opened the Euphrates and the Tigris from her eyes', and among
other things created mankind from the blood of a slain warrior god.[1] That is
one myth (in the original sense: not just any old falsehood, but a story
significant for those who tell it). In another myth subordinate gods are made
to dig out the channels for those two great rivers. Having worked at it for
3,600 years, 'They groaned and blamed each other, Grumbled over the
masses of excavated soil', and withdrew their labour, complaining 'The load
is excessive, it is killing us, Our work is too hard, the trouble too much...'.[2]
To provide workers who would relieve the gods of these burdens, the mother
goddess created the human race from clay mixed with blood.[3]

Stirring tales – but did anyone ever believe them? Well, why not? There
are people today who claim to believe every word of the Bible. Little children seem to believe that Father Christmas delivers presents to each
household. Perhaps, though, just asking whether or not the Babylonian
myths were believed is too crude. What is it to believe a myth, or any other
story? There is surely no straightforward answer. The fact is that those
stories were *told*. In ancient Babylonia, if you wanted to know how things

---

1 *Myths from Mesopotamia*, translated and introduced by Stephanie Dalley, pp.255–61.
2 Op. cit., pp.9–13.
3 Op. cit., pp.1–16.

1

began, those stories were on offer – and, it seems, they had no rivals. In any case, they didn't have to be taken literally, as we tend to put it. They gave satisfaction quite apart from possibly telling it like it was. They were entertaining. They contained sensible messages (for example, useful material for reflection on labour relations, regardless of whether the gods had really spent 3,600 years digging out channels for rivers). They gave the background against which religious rituals were intelligible.[4] They provided a framework in terms of which people could think about themselves and their world.

Some themes recur in myths from many areas of the world. The theme of a god's killing a great dragon is one. But, often, different stories are told about the same phenomenon, even in the same culture, as we have just noticed: was it Marduk or the goddess who made us? It hardly seems possible to believe that such stories all describe what happened in reality. You must either choose between rival accounts or find something better: incompatible stories can't all be accepted as accounts of how things actually happened. (More on this later.[5]) Apart from incompatibility between different myths, it is hard to reconcile what the myths say happened long ago with the sort of things we see in everyday life.

No doubt that is harder for us than it was for the people who originally enjoyed the myths. Today we are not often invited to take stories like the ancient myths seriously; and our thirst for explanations is typically satisfied by convincing non-mythical ones. True, there may be situations and people where the question of reconciling mythical accounts and the facts of everyday life just doesn't arise. Angela Carter describes the state of mind of a tribe of Siberians, led by shamans, at the turn of the century:

> And even when his eyes were open, you might have said the Shaman 'lived in a dream'. But so did they all. They shared a common dream, which was their world, and it should rather be called an 'idea' than a 'dream', since it constituted their entire sense of lived reality, which impinged on *real* reality only inadvertently.[6]

Still, even little children grow out of the Father Christmas myth. Why is that? It is not that the story ceases to be attractive. It remains attractive, which is perhaps why it keeps being passed on to new generations by unbelieving parents. Children certainly begin by taking it literally – to the extent that they can take any story literally at all. Nor does the story seem to be just some kind of decoration glued on to the surface of ordinary life. It seems to have explanatory power. It seems to explain at least two phenomena: the appearance of Christmas presents in the course of

4 See F. M. Cornford, *Principium Sapientiae*, pp.225–38.
5 See Chapter 2, section 4.
6 Angela Carter, *Nights at the Circus*, p.253.

Christmas Eve, and the fact that Christmas brings numerous pictures of a man dressed in red winter clothes with white furry edging, distributing presents from a reindeer-drawn sleigh. However, when the story is regarded as an explanation of these phenomena, it comes under increasing strain as the child grows up. Some of the things Father Christmas is said to do are very peculiar. How can such a bulky man get down the chimney – even if there is a chimney in the house? How can he get through all the work in one night? How do reindeer fly? What about those characters in the shops, who all claim to be Father Christmas? Clinging to belief in the story gets harder and harder to reconcile with what the child knows about the way things are, and eventually belief falls away. The child has grown too sophisticated.

So, it seems, with myths generally. The process of abandoning them, at any rate as candidates for the literal truth, may be speeded up by special factors. The ancient Greeks not only had their own myths to reflect upon. Trading from their outposts on the coast of Asia Minor brought them into contact with the myths of other cultures. They were struck by the relativity of myths to cultures. As one of them remarked: 'The Ethiopians say their gods are snub-nosed and black; the Thracians that theirs are blue-eyed and red-haired'. Again: 'But if cattle and horses or lions had hands, or were able to draw with their hands and do the things people can do, horses would draw the shapes of their gods like horses and cattle ones like cattle.'[7] Apart from being forced to notice a whole range of different myths, the Greeks had reasons for seeking good explanations of the sort of phenomena that the myths tended to treat as basic unexplained data. Trading by sea, they had a practical interest in navigation, the weather, astronomy, measurement, chronology. Whatever the exact reasons may have been, they originated ways of describing and explaining reality which differed remarkably from myths.

2 Theories

Before about 500 BC the most important Greek city was Miletus, on what is now the coast of Turkey. Of the three main 'Milesian' thinkers – though we have only traces of their work – the most interesting is Anaximander, who died about 550 BC. The details of his theory of the world are uncertain, but the outlines seem to have been these. The ordered universe, or 'cosmos', with earth, sun, moon, planets, and stars, originated from what he called the 'unbounded'. This was neither earth, air, fire, nor water. Apart from being unbounded in that way, it was unbounded in time, without beginning or end. And it was in 'eternal motion'. At some time the continuous motion resulted in the formation of a kind of seed or nucleus. From this the 'opposites', notably the hot and the cold, were 'separated out'. That process

7 Xenophanes of Colophon (c. 570–475 BC), fragments 16 and 15 (in Barnes, *Early Greek Philosophy*).

resulted in the formation of 'a sort of sphere of flame' surrounding the air which in turn surrounded the earth, 'like bark on a tree'. The process continued with 'the wet' and 'the dry' becoming distinct. The hot outer sphere started to dry the earth. Then the sphere of flame was torn off and three vast rings of fire were formed around the earth. The fire was held within these rings by dense mist. Holes in these mist-rings enabled the fire within to be seen: a single hole in the case of two of the rings, and many holes for the third. The two single large fiery holes formed the sun and the moon; those in the third ring formed the stars. Eclipses occurred when the large holes were blocked; the waxing and waning of the moon were explained similarly. The earth is a cylindrical drum, a third as deep as it is wide. It stays where it is, at the centre, not because it is resting on anything or (as the Milesian Thales had suggested) because it is floating on water, but because there is nothing to make it go anywhere else: 'because of its equal distance from everything'.[8]

You could not have got Anaximander to believe in Father Christmas. There are no mysterious personalities in his story. No gods, no monstrous dragons, no processes unlike those we encounter in ordinary life. No manufacturing of human beings from clay or blood, for instance.[9] True, some things in the story are still mysterious. The nature of 'the unbounded' remains unclear. We have only foggy ideas of how the original kernel of our world was 'separated out'. But the processes involved would not have seemed *more* mysterious to Anaximander than those involved in cooking. We have no reason to suppose he thought he had explained everything. If it is uncertain whether those who devised and passed on the old myths thought they were describing what had really happened, it is certain that Anaximander was at least *aiming* to describe what had really happened, and how things really were in the world. We can say he was aiming at the literal truth about reality, and thought there was something to be right or wrong about.

The same goes for the other main Milesian thinkers and their successors. Their theories of the origin and present structure of the cosmos were all attempts at the literal, non-mythical truth.

Clearly there are many questions about Anaximander's theory to which he could not have provided acceptable answers. He was in no position to

---

8 For more on Anaximander, see, e.g., Jonathan Barnes, *Early Greek Philosophy*. See also Karl R. Popper, 'Back to the Presocratics'. The remarkable view that the earth stays where it is because there is nothing to make it go anywhere else is of course an ancestor of Newton's principle of inertia: any particle remains in a state of rest or of motion with constant magnitude and direction unless compelled to change that state by the impact of a force upon it.

9 He is said to have held that the first animals were produced in the moisture which resulted from the sun's burning off the water on the surface of the earth.

claim, as he did, that the earth is three times wider than it is deep, or that the ring of the moon is eighteen times, and that of the sun twenty-seven times, the size of the earth. If it is unscientific to make claims without being able to substantiate them, Anaximander was in some respects unscientific. But what of it? He and those unrecorded thinkers whose ideas and criticisms contributed to his achievements were pioneers in the attempt to describe the history and nature of the world in terms which, unlike the myths, had some chance of being both true and acceptable to people from different cultures. There were no accurate means for measuring relatively large distances, and no accurate instruments: no telescopes, microscopes, or reliable clocks. Yet evidently these protoscientists were convinced the world *had* a history worth speculating about,[10] that there were truths about reality to be discovered beyond what was immediate and obvious, and that it was possible to devise theories of the world that could be defended against criticisms.

3 The first atomic theory

Those assumptions show up marvellously in the Greeks' original version of the atomic theory. It will be a useful illustration of some of the main issues to be investigated in this book.

As a result of fierce debates on questions raised not only by the Milesians but by other early thinkers, certain issues were acknowledged to be crucial. One of these was the problem of change. When an athlete eats porridge, the porridge is apparently turned into flesh and blood. Something that wasn't there before comes into existence; and something that was there before ceases to exist. How is that possible? If, like Anaximander, you say the cosmos came into existence at some time, why did that happen? More precisely, why did it happen at all? And why did it happen when it did, rather than at some other time? The conclusion seemed to be forced on them: whatever exists must always have existed. Hence an early 'conservation principle': nothing can come out of nothing. Any adequate explanation of change must satisfy that principle. To meet that and other challenges, two thinkers – Leucippus and Democritus – who flourished in the second half of the fifth century BC devised the following theory.

There are infinitely many indivisible things called atoms ('uncuttables'). They have always existed and they will never cease to exist. They have different shapes and sizes; many are too small to be seen. The present cosmos results from the automatic swirling and colliding of atoms, and from processes of sifting out and compacting. Some atoms are relatively smooth,

---

10 Contrast, again, the Siberians imagined by Angela Carter: 'they inhabited a temporal dimension which did not take history into account. They were a-historic. Time meant nothing to them' (op. cit., p.265).

others have sharp angles, some have hooks. As a result of the combinations of atoms that have arisen over time, vast numbers of complex structures have been formed. These include the earth, the sun, the moon, the stars, other animals and ourselves. The different properties of things are explained by the fact that atoms of different shapes and sizes are combined in different arrangements. For example, water and other liquids consist of smooth atoms, which offer little resistance to one another. That explains why water flows and finds its way through cracks. Stones, in contrast, are made from atoms which form relatively strong bonds, and so cannot be readily split apart. But many combinations of atoms can be split apart under the impact of others. That is what happens when wood is burnt, and when an athlete eats porridge. The theory applies to human beings as well as other things. We, too, are made from various different sorts of atoms, combined in various ways. To have a soul, or intelligence, is simply for there to be certain special kinds of atoms present in the body. These small, spherical atoms are more mobile than others, and cause the whole body to move.

We might be inclined to assume that such properties as colours, tastes and so forth must involve something in addition to the combinations and motions of different kinds of atoms. According to the atomists, that is a mistake. In reality, colours, tastes and the rest are just the ways different arrangements of different kinds of atoms affect our sense organs. In the words of Democritus, 'Conventionally (glossed by an ancient commentator as "relative to us") there is colour, conventionally there is sweetness, conventionally there is bitterness; but in truth there are atoms and empty space.'[11] He, for one, thought many of the things we take to be true depend on us. That idea will be a central topic of this book. It paves the way for various kinds of 'relativism'.

Clearly the Greek atomists were attempting to say how things really are. In other words (at least I think this is the same point: see the next chapter) they wanted their story to be true. They offered a theory about reality, they intended it to be seen as such, and, unlike the original myth-makers, they could offer generally acceptable reasons for it. They weren't just telling a story. They thought there was something to be right or wrong about, and they wanted to get it right.

Their theory attempted to explain the observable in terms of the unobservable. We cannot observe the past; but the atomists, like Anaximander, were convinced that the universe had a past in whose terms the observable facts about it could be understood. Their account of the original swirling and colliding of vast masses of atoms claimed to *explain* the present observable state of the universe. We cannot observe the atoms themselves either (or

---

11 The quotation and comments are given by Galen. See Barnes, *Early Greek Philosophy*, pp.254f.

not without instruments that the Greeks didn't have). But they thought they nevertheless had good reasons to suppose that observable changes such as combustion and digestion could be explained in terms of the behaviour of minute invisible particles of different shapes and sizes. It seems they supposed that this 'explanatory power' of their theory itself provided a justi-fication for it in spite of its making claims about features of the world that are beyond the range of our senses, and might remain so forever.

Another striking feature of the atomists' account relates to their treat-ment of the contrast between *appearance* and *reality*. This had received a lot of attention from some earlier thinkers, notably Heraclitus (who died some time after 480 BC) and Parmenides (born about 510 BC).

Heraclitus set out what he called the 'Logos', which explained the true nature of both the cosmos and human beings. (He complained that, not only did other people fail to understand the Logos before he had explained it to them, they failed to understand it even after he had explained it – not an uncommon complaint among philosophers.) Others fail to notice what they are doing when they are awake, he claimed, just as they fail to realize what they do when asleep. 'Nature loves to hide itself.'[12]

Parmenides' ideas powerfully affected the atomists, but he himself was anything but an atomist. For him the contrast between appearance and reality could not have been more dramatic. The true view, according to him, is that what exists is one, homogeneous, unchanging, unmoving, without beginning or end. Not being a fool, he recognized that things seem quite different. It *seems* there are many existing things, of different natures; it seems that things change – for example they change colour – and that things come into existence and perish. According to him that is a mistake. The words used just now are mere words and do not connect with reality: '...all those things must be a name which mortals have laid down, believing them to be true: coming into being and perishing, being and not being, and change of place and alteration of bright colour'.[13]

Evidently, when the atomists later offered their own account of the hidden nature of things, and explained change and what appeared to be 'coming into being and perishing' in terms of interactions among impercep-tible things which were themselves eternal and changeless, they were contributing to an intellectually convulsive debate that had been going on for some time. It was by reflecting on some of the reasons Parmenides had put forward for his own extraordinary position that the atomists arrived at theirs – which to us, at any rate, is much more plausible. The remarkable thing about Parmenides is that he actually presented a chain of reasoning

---

12 This is fragment 123.
13 Fragment 8, lines 38–41.

for his doctrine. It was set out in a poem, 'The Way of Truth'. Reduced to essentials it goes something like this.

1 IT IS OR IT IS NOT. (This is supposed to be indisputable. It is the ancestor of the logical principle of the so-called 'excluded middle': for any proposition p, either p or not p.)

2 Thinking and saying are impossible except when what is thought or said exists. (The interpretation of this step of the argument is disputed, though this reading is natural.)

3 So expressions such as 'it is not' and 'that which is not' cannot be thought or said. (Because they would have to refer to what does not exist.)

4 So 'IT IS NOT' cannot express a truth.

5 So IT IS. (This follows from steps 1 and 4.)

6 That which is cannot be many, since then there would be divisions between the things which are; and the divisions would consist of that which is not, which has been ruled out by step 3.

7 So that which is, is one.

8 It cannot be denser in some places or rarer in others, for that again would require that which is not to be present in the spaces.

9 So that which is, is continuous and homogeneous.

10 That which is cannot have come into existence, nor can it be going to perish, since in that case it would have had to be preceded or succeeded by that which is not, which we have seen to be impossible.

11 Similarly, change is impossible, since that would have involved coming into existence and perishing.

Parmenides' argument is a shining example of a philosopher putting all his trust in what is called 'a priori' reasoning in preference to the evidence of his senses. A priori or 'armchair' reasoning is argumentation that appears to be guaranteed by reason alone, and takes no account of the evidence of the senses. Parmenides actually urges us to *reject* the evidence of the senses. The 'goddess' who presents the argument in his poem urges him to ignore what his senses tell him and to 'judge by reason (logos) the strife-encompassed proof I speak'.

The atomists in effect said 'Yes' to Parmenides' points about becoming and perishing. They accepted that what exists in the most fundamental way cannot have come into existence and cannot cease to exist. But they said 'No' to the crucial step of his argument. Evidently he took steps 3 and 4 to rule out the possibility of empty space. Only if he took it in that way would it serve his purposes. The atomists simply asserted that there *is* empty space. Since the position they stated seemed acceptable to their contemporaries, they thereby undermined Parmenides' rather primitive appeal to the conditions in which thought and talk can be meaningful. It is good to have such a clear illustration of the point that an argument which seems rock-solid to its originator may be defeated by a sufficiently well-thought-out rejection of one of its premisses. What to Parmenides had seemed like a solid foundation in absolute necessity must have appeared mere blinkered prejudice to the atomists.

That conveys some conception of the kind of argument and discussion that provided the fertile ground from which the first atomic theory could grow. It was not purely armchair reasoning. Unlike Parmenides, and like pretty well every subsequent thinker other than, perhaps, Spinoza and Leibniz, the atomists did not suppose that our only route to a grasp of the nature of reality is through a priori reasoning. They accepted that our senses give us some information about the world. But they also noticed that the evidence of the senses cannot take us all the way, because we are interested in causes which may never be available to perception. Sensory evidence has to be backed up with reflection on the constraints on possible theories. For example, they maintained that no theory could be correct if it required things to come into existence from nothing, or to cease to exist completely. Such considerations are very different from whatever influences may have guided the ancient story-tellers who devised the myths. The Greek thinkers brought human thought into the domain of science, where there is a complicated interplay between reason and the senses, and where defensible theories have taken the place of myths.

4 Can we get it right?

All the thinkers I have mentioned thought we could theorize about the nature of reality and *get it right*. That implies that they recognized that it was possible to get it wrong, as they supposed their predecessors had. No doubt the exponents of the ancient myths also thought they were getting things right; but there is a vital difference. Unlike the myth-tellers, the theorists seem to have regarded their theories as proper subjects of critical debate. They could hardly have refused to do so, since they would never have arrived at them except as a result of others putting forward suggestions which were then criticized and revised. But it would be strange if the myths, too, were regarded as subject to revision in the light of further evidence. (We can perhaps imagine exceptional situations. The inspired seer descends from the mountain and reports that the gods have just announced that current stories about the origins of things are wrong: from now on they must believe something different. But if that ever happened, it cannot have been common. Surely the old myths were not thought of as up for criticism and revision).

Is there really such a thing as *getting it right*? Or is the best we can do to tell stories, stories which may give more or less satisfaction, but which cannot be capable of describing how things really are? If so, the contrast between myths and criticizable theories is not genuine after all, and the pursuit of truth a wild goose chase. In that case *there is no such thing as truth independent of point of view*. The best we can hope for is whatever we, or our community, count as true. That is *relativism*.

We have seen how the Greeks became sceptical about the old myths. Once the necessary degree of sophistication had set in, it was easy to be sceptical not only about the myths but about all theories. Obviously our senses can mislead us. Just as obviously, slips can creep into our reasoning. Yet it comes naturally to us to assume there is a true theory to be had even if there are insuperable obstacles in the way of establishing that we have found it. Even if we can never be sure that our theory is right, it is natural to suppose there is something to be right or wrong about.

Those last remarks point to an extremely important distinction. It is one thing to have a theory that is in fact true; something else to be able to *tell* whether or not it is true. Suppose I suggest there may be coal in the ground a mile below this spot. I don't *say* there is coal there; I just suggest there may be, though I have no idea whether there is or not. That means I don't *know* whether the suggestion is true. Most people – at any rate most people uninfluenced by some philosophical doctrine – would agree that it may still *be* true. On that basis what is true is not the same as what is known to be true, and questions about what is true are not the same as questions about whether or how we can come to know what is true. Questions of this second kind belong to *epistemology* (the 'theory of knowledge'). In spite of their great importance, they will not figure centrally in this work. I shall not disregard them altogether, but my chief concern is not with how we can tell whether or not we have hit the truth, but with whether, and how, hitting the truth is possible at all.

5 Plan

Shortly I will set out the plan of this book. But first a word of reassurance. A few technical terms occur in the plan, but I have put them in 'scare-quotes'. I have tried to make the book accessible to beginners and I will explain every technical notion as it comes up. (See also the Glossary.)

All the problems to be discussed arise in one way or another from the project of devising a 'theory of the world'. Such a theory – attempted by several of the ancient Greek philosophers as well as by modern science – is an account of the present nature of the world, together with its past and perhaps also its future. 'World' is to be understood in the most liberal sense possible, to include not only the physical universe but any God or gods there may be, together with the human world – our own lives and natures. The project may be too ambitious for human beings to complete; but every one of us has made a start on it. We all have our own ideas, opinions, prejudices and tentative thoughts about reality. Even as babies we are busy finding out about people and things around us; and as young children we start asking philosophical and scientific questions, such as 'Where is yesterday?' 'Why was that wrong?' 'Where does the sun go at night?' – and finding more or less satisfying answers. Those answers belong to our (inevitably partial) theory of the world.

One problem raised by that project is the nature of truth. What is it for a statement or theory to be true? In the next chapter I will consider some attempts to solve that problem, after sketching the 'Core Scientific Story': the bony central features of the current scientific theory of the world.

As soon as anyone starts talking about truth, someone will say 'truth is relative'. ('We live in a relativist world', a radio presenter remarked on the day I was writing this.) Several different things might be meant by saying that truth is relative; but they all imply that truth in some way *depends on us* – on our point of view, our experiences, our ways of thinking. The idea thrives on reflection about the limited range of human senses and capacities, and the obvious fact that different people see the world differently. It gains extra voltage from the suggestion that, when we think we are describing something 'out there', what we are actually doing is somehow 'projecting' our own idiosyncratic ways of perceiving and thinking. The Greek atomists provide an interesting illustration. As we have seen, they believed certain things are matters of fact while others are matters of 'convention'. On their account there really are atoms and empty space, and there really are vast numbers of structures composed of different kinds of atoms in various arrangements; indeed we ourselves are such structures. On the one hand they had no qualms about the objective existence of such things as sticks and stones. In the philosophical sense of the word they were 'realists' about such things. On the other hand, even Democritus maintained that some kinds of thing we ordinarily take to exist do not exist in reality. He maintained that colours, smells, tastes and so forth exist only 'conventionally' or 'relative to us'. We find it natural to assume that colours and so forth exist 'out there' just as much as atoms and empty space. According to Democritus they are not really there at all. When that idea had been grasped it was easy for some thinkers to suggest that other things, too, do not exist in reality, but only 'relative to us'. Once that thought has taken root, someone is bound to suggest that it applies quite generally.

Today there are many varieties of 'relativism' – alongside views which appear to imply it but actually do not. Richard Rorty has asserted: 'Truth cannot be out there – cannot exist independently of the human mind'.[14] Nelson Goodman has said something apparently even stronger: '...even reality is relative'.[15] A different claim is advanced by Peter L. Berger and Thomas Luckmann: 'Reality is socially constructed'.[16] Bruno Latour and

14 R. Rorty, *Contingency, Irony, and Solidarity*, p.5.
15 Nelson Goodman, *Ways of Worldmaking*, p.20.
16 P. L. Berger and T. Luckmann, *The Social Construction of Reality*, p.13.

Steve Woolgar, having investigated the activities of a scientific laboratory as anthropologists, concluded that 'Scientific activity is not "about nature," it is a fierce fight to *construct* reality'.[17] I will examine all those ideas, and more.

The simpler varieties of 'relativism' will be discussed in Chapter 3. More sophisticated varieties have been based on the very different work of two enormously influential philosophers: Wittgenstein and Quine. Both have made invaluable contributions to the problem of how thought and language relate to the world, hence how there can be a theory of the world, and what it is for it to be true. Chapter 4 will introduce Wittgenstein's work, focusing on his famous idea of 'language-games'. Chapter 5 will expound some of Quine's main ideas, including his 'holistic' conception of our theory of the world. Although these philosophers' ideas appear to drive us towards sophisticated kinds of relativism, I shall try to make clear in the rest of the book that in fact they do not.

Wittgenstein's ideas about 'language-games' have formed the basis for a line of argument, popular today, which appears to support a sophisticated relativism. I will examine that argument in Chapter 6, after explaining various kinds of 'realism' and 'anti-realism'. The 'language-game argument' turns out not to work. However, one of the ideas it exploits, that different cultures have different ways of thinking, raises another important issue, related but distinct, concerning reason and rationality in general. Certain ways of proceeding strike us as rational. Does that mean they are absolutely valid? Why shouldn't there be human beings, or intelligent animals or extra-terrestrial creatures, whose rationality differed sharply from ours, yet was no less valid? We must at least glance at those questions; I shall do so at the end of Chapter 6.

A promising idea for establishing solid knowledge of reality and thereby demolishing relativism is that of basing knowledge on 'foundations'. The search for foundations has inspired many philosophers; the project will be considered in Chapter 7. Unfortunately it seems incapable of fulfilling its promise.

Another line of relativistic thought inspired by Wittgenstein is the type of 'anti-realism' investigated by Michael Dummett. If it is correct, some statements – ones ordinary 'realists' would assume to be either true or false even when we cannot actually tell which – are neither true nor false; which seems to imply that reality itself is to a large extent *indeterminate*. Those ideas will be examined in Chapter 8.

Richard Rorty is a philosopher who has been inspired by both Wittgenstein and Quine among others. His 'postmodern pragmatism' appears to embody a strong kind of relativism. It will be discussed in

17 Op. cit., pp.40, 41, 243.

Chapter 9. I will suggest reasons why it raises no serious problems for realists.

I have mentioned science as at least making a contribution to our theory of the world. But science, especially the core science of physics, is often thought to leave out of account most of what gives our lives their meaning. Is that right – does science really leave meaning out? If scientific theories are true, does it follow that our ordinary ways of talking about ourselves and our interests are inferior or even incorrect? Chapter 10 deals with the question of how the world of everyday life relates to the world described by physics. It includes a discussion of whether 'realism' requires there to be just one true theory of the world.

Finally, Chapter 11 describes a strongly realist approach to theories of the world, inspired by Quine. The main points are illustrated by bringing out contrasts between that kind of realism and Rorty's pragmatism. In these last two chapters I also apply a notion of 'strict implication' to the problem of how different theories may be related.

An introductory work cannot hope to offer anything approaching a satisfying account of our cognitive relations with reality. But it can make a start, point in the directions that deeper investigations might take, notice landmarks, and sketch positions on some of the main issues that will serve as a useful provisional basis for going forward. That is what will be attempted.

To help keep track of these investigations, each chapter ends with a list of the main points considered, and suggestions for further reading. The main bibliographical information is at the end of the book. Two works deserve special mention as valuable, accessible sources of help: the *Oxford Companion to Philosophy*, edited by Ted Honderich (one volume); and the *Routledge Encyclopedia of Philosophy*, edited by Edward Craig (ten volumes).

MAIN POINTS AND QUESTIONS IN CHAPTER 1

1 How far can a 'theory of the world' claim to supply the truth, or even part of the truth, about reality? (This will be discussed throughout, but especially in Chapters 10 and 11.)
2 Can such a theory differ radically from the myths? If not, the pursuit of truth starts to look like a wild goose chase. (Chapter 2, section 3, and Chapters 3, 6, 10 and 11.)
3 How much of reality exists independently, and how much is 'relative to us'? (Chapters 2, 3, 6, 8, 9, 10 and 11.)

4   In choosing between theories, how far should we rely on the evidence of our senses, and how far on reason? Is rationality itself relative? (Chapter 6, section 5; Chapter 7.)

CHAPTER 1: SUGGESTIONS FOR FURTHER READING

On **Philosophy in general**, a clear, very readable, compact introduction is N. Warburton, *Philosophy: the Basics*. A longer introductory work, also reader-friendly and with a great deal of interactive material, is A. Morton, *Philosophy in Practice*.

For more on the most ancient recorded **myths**, see S. Dalley, *Myths from Mesopotamia*. For relations between the early Greek myths and theories of the world, see F. M. Cornford, *Principium Sapientiae*. For other examples and discussions of the theory of myth, see A. Dundes (ed.), *Sacred Narrative*.

An excellent introductory book on **Early Greek Philosophy**, with translations of key texts, is J. Barnes, *Early Greek Philosophy*.

2

TRUTH

Anaximander offered one theory of the world, the Greek atomists another. Both seem hopelessly inadequate today. Anaximander was wrong about the shape of the earth; the atomists were wrong about 'atoms' being solid and indivisible. But what is it for them to be wrong? What would it be to be right, is that the same as the theory being true? What is truth? In this chapter and the next I will introduce some attempts to answer those questions.

1 The sciences

The scientific tradition has generated many theories. A brief mention of some of the main ones impresses us with their power and scope. Physics deals with the fundamental nature of the physical world and includes quantum mechanics, relativity theory, particle physics and thermodynamics. Chemistry deals with the ways in which the materials formed from the fundamental particles of physics behave; like physics it has its own subdivisions. The 'earth sciences', including geology and meteorology, tell us how huge masses of those materials have been built up and behave. Astronomy and cosmology carry those studies into the rest of the universe. The 'life sciences', molecular biology, genetics, microbiology, neurobiology, botany and zoology, deal with those special systems that reproduce themselves, and that we say are 'alive'. There are many further theories which more or less claim to be scientific, including psychology, geography, history and economics. The development of these sciences and near-sciences over the last three centuries has been prodigious. It has involved awe-inspiring manifestations of intelligence, imagination, ingenuity, tenacity and courage, as well as a vast amount of patient teamwork.

Today's sciences got where they are by twisting paths, with failures, exploded theories and disappointments to set against their triumphs. They have not reached a final unrevisable state. What we are inclined to regard as true today may come to be regarded as inadequate or even false, if not tomorrow, then in a few years or centuries, just as we regard the theories of Anaximander and the Greek atomists as false. But my aim is not to pursue the history or philosophy of science, fascinating and rewarding though that is. It is to pursue the question of how, if at all, our beliefs and theories can be true; how, if at all, they are capable of capturing reality, given the relativistic thoughts that surfaced in the last chapter. As a first step in that direction it will be useful to set down here the core of the theory of the world we have acquired as a result of broadly accepting the results of scientific inquiry – a rough and ready skeleton of today's science. It is more or less free from technicalities. Being so free from detail, it may remain acceptable in the teeth of quite radical revisions in physics, cosmology and the rest.

2 The Core Scientific Story

The entire physical universe started thousands of millions of years ago from an incredibly dense, tiny something, which exploded at an astonishing rate, resulting over time in rather unevenly distributed clouds of gas, still continuing to expand from that original Big Bang. As a result of the forces, notably gravity, which then existed, these clouds of gas gradually condensed in many regions, forming galaxies and stars. There are vast numbers, thousands of millions, of stars in the galaxy to which the sun belongs (the Milky Way), and a comparable number of other galaxies in the universe. The distances between them are so huge that they are hard for us to comprehend. Apart from galaxies and stars with their planetary systems, there are all sorts of other remarkable objects, quasars, pulsars and so on, dotted about the universe.

As time passed (the Core Scientific Story continues), our own star, the sun, and the planets orbiting round it were formed. We occupy the third planet from the sun. Originally the earth, relative to our own standards of heat and cold, was extremely hot and incapable of supporting life as we know it. But after many millions of years, as a result of complicated chemical interactions on the earth's surface, the first self-replicating compounds evolved. They 'evolved' in the sense that the first specimens came into existence as a result of the action of blind natural forces; but certain varieties happened to be in environments which supplied them with what was required for the chemical processes of self-replication to continue. Again as a result of the blind forces of nature acting on the environment and randomly producing new variations – 'mutations' – certain more complicated varieties of self-replicators came into existence and, in favourable conditions, multiplied and spread. As a result of this sort of thing happening many times over, living things came into existence. In time, organized structures of several cells developed. First there were plants, composed of many cells combined and blindly cooperating to live off their environment, grow, reproduce and die. Then came animals. First they were very primitive, but by the same processes of evolution more and more complicated species appeared, displaying more and more complicated ways of surviving. One way to improve a species' chances of survival was for its individual members to be capable of learning. The individuals had to be capable of changing in response to what happened to them, so that they were able to *acquire* non-inherited patterns of behaviour which helped them get what contributed to their survival, and avoid what damaged them.

We human beings are the evolutionarily most developed form of life on earth. Our ability to learn has been vastly increased by our ability to store information, not just in our individual brains but collectively in our culture. What above all has made that possible is language. Language marks us off from all other terrestrial animals in a particularly impressive way. It helps to make us seem vastly superior, in intellectual capacities, even to the chimpanzees (to whom we are closely related).

That is what I am calling the Core Scientific Story. As I said, it includes no details and is pretty well non-technical. Understanding it does not call for specialized scientific knowledge.

Here we are, then: evolved from non-language-using hominids but still like them in many ways. Among the many distinctive things we are capable of doing, thanks to language, is to theorize about our history and attempt to place ourselves in the rest of the universe. The Core Scientific Story is a remarkable cultural artefact, the product of sustained, energetic, imaginative, cooperative intellectual labour. Like us, it has evolved over many centuries (even though, as it happens, parts of it are remarkably like parts of Anaximander's theory).

I think the Core Scientific Story is true, or at least very largely true. No doubt the special sciences, physics and chemistry and the rest, are going to be revised, perhaps radically. Yet revisions to the details seem (to me at present) unlikely to require significant revisions to the CSS itself. With the ancient Greek theorists I think there is something to be right or wrong about; and I think the CSS gets things pretty well right, which is not to say I don't think I might be mistaken (see later).

3 Is the Core Scientific Story just another myth?

The theories of Anaximander and the atomists seemed to contrast with myths. If that contrast is genuine, the Core Scientific Story must contrast with the myths even more sharply. Is there a valid distinction here? Or is the CSS just a special kind of myth, tailored to suit the prejudices of industrial societies in the twentieth century? Here are some useful considerations.

The CSS clearly shares some of the motivation of myths. It is an attempt to say how we fit into the world, which includes saying how things are in the world and how they got that way. Both myths and the CSS offer explanations for phenomena. For example, the myth that the sun is pushed across the sky by a god is an explanation of the sun's apparent motion; the CSS provides an explanation of that apparent motion too, though it is very different. But the CSS differs from the myths in at least four significant ways.

First, the CSS invokes no human-type agents in its explanations but relies on a relatively small number of principles, such as gravitational force. The ancient myths treated natural events as the work of agents with thoughts, feelings, purposes and intentions comparable with our own. The CSS treats us ourselves as results of the operations of blind forces on mindlessly churning elementary components. That is a radical difference. Thoughts, feelings and intentions are no longer presupposed as a basic type of explanatory principle with general applicability to natural events. Instead, they have become something whose existence itself seems to stand in need of explanation.

Second, the CSS is systematic in ways the myths are not. It can rely on a small number of principles because it offers explanations of how a vast range of superficially different phenomena are all manifestations of the workings of a few forces on a few elementary kinds of thing. The CSS hangs together as the myths do not.

Third, although the CSS shares some of the motivation of the myths, it is not typically used as myths are used. It results from a long history of theorizing, where each successive attempt to get things right has been challenged and revised. More significantly, the CSS is *required* to stand up to challenge and criticism. Evidence is demanded for each of its component statements and the theory as a whole is required to be consistent. To treat the myths in that way would be to miss the point: they are stories which served to help communities in the ways noted in Chapter 1. It is scarcely even possible to take that critical attitude to them. (To the extent that some people tend to treat scientific theories as beyond criticism and revision, they are abandoning science and embracing 'scientism', on which see Chapter 10.)

Fourth, the CSS is not just required to be open to testing in ways the myths were not; it actually stands up to testing as the myths could not.

All these matters will figure in later discussions. But what has already been said raises a puzzling question.

4 What if there are equally good alternatives to the CSS?

Even if the CSS is not just a myth, why shouldn't there be equally acceptable alternatives to it, just as there were alternative myths in the different cultures encountered by the Greeks? Rightly understood, that is an interesting question; it can also be understood trivially. To make it interesting the alternatives must be genuinely rival theories, not just stylistic variants. (One illustration: you apparently get a rival to the CSS if you swap round the words 'sun' and 'earth' in a statement of the theory. So revised, the theory now includes sentences such as 'The sun is smaller than the earth. It is a planet that goes round the earth.' If we were to do that we should in effect be changing the *meanings* of the words 'sun' and 'earth'. That implies there is no interesting sense in which the resulting theories would be rivals: they could not be understood except as superficially different versions of exactly the same theory, the new version being misleadingly expressed, given how we actually use those words.) The supposedly rival theories must also deal with the same subject-matter: there is no problem if they just cover different aspects of reality, like for example botany and astronomy. Each of the rivals must contradict something in the others, and the contradictions must be genuine, not just apparent.

The question was: why shouldn't there be some equally acceptable rival to the CSS? There is a plausible reply: it has been *tested* and found to work extraordinarily well. Just one example from millions is the accuracy with which the CSS and the special sciences have enabled the Space Shuttle to be launched, circle the earth, and return at the times and places predicted.

Any serious rival to the CSS would have to survive the same sort of testing the CSS itself has survived. Still, why shouldn't that be possible? The old question comes up again even if we insist that any rival theories must stand up to testing as well as the CSS does.

You might now think: even if there are alternatives to the CSS, all equally acceptable to us, all equally capable of withstanding rigorous testing, they can't all be *true*, still assuming the alternatives are genuine rivals to one another, not just verbal variants. Either they are all false or only one of them is true.

It is worth pausing to consider the assumption that such theories could not all be true. Some people might suggest that it is just a prejudice. Is it? Well, if two theories are genuine rivals, one says something that the other contradicts, explicitly or implicitly. One example is the pair of theories (i) that William Shakespeare wrote the plays usually attributed to him, and (ii) that the plays were written by Francis Bacon (assuming, as we know, that these were two different people). To make the argument general: suppose theory A says that *p*, and theory B says that not-*p*. Then if *p* is the case, as A says it is, it follows logically that

(1) *p* is the case or the moon is made of green cheese.

For in order for (1) to be true, it is enough if just *one* of the sentences on each side of 'or' is true; that is how 'or' works. But if not-*p* is also the case, as B says, then, given (1), it follows logically that the moon is made of green cheese! For if not-*p* holds, we can in effect rule out the sentence on the left-hand side in (1). In that way the contradiction we get from supposing that both theory A and theory B are true enables us to derive, by simple logical steps, an arbitrarily chosen and ridiculous conclusion. In a nutshell, any contradiction enables us to prove any proposition whatever. That seems enough reason to reject the suggestion that two genuinely rival theories, theories which contradicted one another, might both be true.

Why should we accept logic, though? I will not pursue that question far; but something quite persuasive can be said about anyone who claims it is acceptable to assert a statement of the form '*p* and not-*p*'. Suppose they say:

(2) It's raining here now and it's not raining here now.

We can point out that they haven't actually managed to convey anything. This is because we normally take the statement (the assertion) that it's raining (here and now) to *exclude* it's *not* raining here and now. By taking away in the second part of the statement what they have apparently asserted in the first, the utterance as a whole is self-defeating: no message has been communicated. They might as well not have spoken. It seems that, unless we make sure our utterances avoid blatant conflict with logical principles, there is no point in saying anything at all. To ensure we can continue to use words to communicate, we have to avoid statements like (2).

5 First thoughts about truth: correspondence

I think the Core Scientific Theory is true. But what is truth (as Pilate asked, confident the question would paralyse his hearers)? Consider this statement about the cat Zoë:

(3) Zoë is sitting on the mat.

It is true, I assure you. The problem is to understand what it means to say it is true. A natural answer is that (3) is true because it *corresponds* to the way things actually are: Zoë is *in fact* sitting on the mat.

That suggestion seems straightforward and attractive. On the one hand there is reality in all its range and complexity. On the other hand there are our beliefs, statements and theories about reality. Beliefs, statements and theories are intended to match or correspond with reality. We recognize that in many respects the correspondence will be inadequate. For some areas of reality we are badly placed to offer more than sketchy theories. We are enormously far away in time from the Big Bang; enormously distant from other galaxies. Even at their best our theories of the world may only be partial; at their worst, so it may seem, there will be no correspondence at all. Still, there are no great problems about cats sitting on mats, and the fundamental thought is

---

1 For reasons that will become clear there is no one reasonably clear theory which may be called '*the* correspondence theory of truth'; but the label is traditional and convenient.

appealing: theories, and individual beliefs or statements, are true as far as they correspond with reality. That is the so-called 'correspondence theory'.[1]

It is less straightforward than at first appears. What is meant by 'correspondence'? Take a very simple example:

(4) John loves Mary.

We find it natural to suggest that 'John' corresponds in the relevant sense to one person, and 'Mary' to another. 'Loves' may perhaps be taken to correspond to a certain emotion. So far, then, so good. Now we hit trouble. Even if we assume those words do indeed correspond with those particular items, those correspondences by themselves fail to distinguish between what is conveyed by (4) and what is conveyed by

(5) Mary loves John.

As we all know, (4) may be true while (5) is false. Clearly, then, the right sort of 'correspondence' cannot just be a matter of the *components* of a statement being matched with items in reality. The way those components are put together is also significant; and it is not at all easy to see how that sort of significance could also be explained in terms of correspondence. In the next section I will look at some suggestions that may help; but first I want to deal with what might for a moment strike you as a quick solution.

It seems that a statement or theory corresponds with reality if and only if it says *what is actually the case*. Does that perhaps explain what 'correspondence' means? Unfortunately, while it is right to say that a statement corresponds to reality if it says what is the case, the expression 'saying what is actually the case' seems no less problematic than 'saying what is true'. The trouble is not that the two expressions are pretty well synonymous. It is that we are equally in the dark about both, so neither will do as an informative explanation of the other. Such 'circular' explanations are useless because they depend on using words or ideas that are essentially the same as the ones they set out to explain. A similar difficulty arises if we try to settle the matter by introducing *facts*, and suggest that a statement is true if and only if it corresponds to the facts. It seems perfectly in order to say that statement (3), for example, is true if and only if it is a fact that Zoë is sitting on the mat. But what is a fact? One suggested definition is that a fact is what makes a statement true. That would be useless for our present purposes, though, because we still want to know what 'true' means. It is reasonable to suggest that facts are whatever it is that true statements correspond to. But the notion of a fact starts to seem no less mysterious than those of truth and correspondence.

There are extra difficulties for truths dealing in abstractions, especially the truths of mathematics. Correspondence theorists may claim that mathematical truths hold because they correspond with mathematical facts. You only have to utter those words to realize the difficulty of explaining what mathematical facts are, given they cannot, on pain of circularity, just be true mathematical statements. However, we are still looking for an account of the more straightforward kinds of truth, exemplified by the statement about the cat.

6 Building up to truth

To say something that might be true or false, to make a *statement* or *assertion*, is just to utter or write a suitable sentence in appropriate circumstances. To state or assert that Zoë is sitting on the mat, for example, I utter sentence (3) in circumstances where 'Zoë' actually is the name of a cat, and there is an appropriate mat in the offing. (More could be said about statements, but that will do for our purposes.) It is worth looking at some of the ways in which sentences suitable for making statements may be constructed and used.

Sentences are typically constructed from smaller components. Very simple examples will help to illustrate some important points.

Socrates is bald

Beth is happy

It is not the case that Socrates is tall

Alf is tall and Beth is happy.

These examples highlight the point that sentences are built up from elementary components such as 'Beth', 'is' and 'happy'. It would be too obvious to mention, except that it is highly important. For one thing, it helps to explain our remarkable abilities both to recognize and to produce indefinitely many different sentences. We build up each sentence from components we have learnt. We have this ability even though most of the sentences we *could* construct are ones nobody will ever actually utter. Knowing the language involves being able to *construct* indefinitely many sentences; equally it involves being able to *understand* indefinitely many sentences. (Life and memory are too short to handle the extremely long ones. If angels live for eternity and have perfect memories, they might use sentences zillions of words long, though it is hard to see why they should bother. Sometimes it is convenient to think of there being infinitely many grammatically correct sentences in an ordinary language such as English.)

Consider some of the ways we construct sentences from smaller components. It seems as if we have mastered rules enabling us to do this. Take the first two sentences. Each is composed of a proper name followed by an expression beginning with 'is'. We say 'Socrates' and 'Beth' are proper names because they pick out or refer to individuals. The words that follow 'is' in those two sentences, 'bald' and 'happy', are not names but adjectives. So a rule enabling us to construct very elementary sentences like the first two might be:

> R1   A sentence may consist of a name followed by 'is' followed by an adjective.

(Other rules are needed to form sentences of the other kinds in the list. One rule could be that we get a sentence by adding 'It is not the case that' to the beginning of any given sentence; another could be that we get a sentence by putting 'and' between two sentences.[2])

Suppose 'Socrates is wise' is true. What makes it true? A correspondence theorist might say this. The idea of such sentences is that the name picks something out and the adjective says something about it. So the general principle, at any rate for the 'elementary' sentences formed by applying rule R1, is:

> P1   An elementary sentence is *true* just in case the name successfully picks out an individual, and the adjective in it applies to that individual.

P1 is an attempt to define truth for all elementary sentences built up in the way covered by R1. (It still leaves all the non-elementary sentences to be dealt with. One further rule could be that a sentence which begins 'It is not the case that' is true just in case the sentence itself is not true; another could be that a sentence consisting of two sentences joined by 'and' is true just in case each of those two sentences is true.)

That gives some idea of how we might start to go about defining truth for the sentences of a language in line with the correspondence theory. However, there is at least one big difficulty with this approach. It uses two key notions: that of a name picking out or *referring to* an individual; and that of an adjective *applying to* an individual. Yet it seems to do nothing to explain those notions themselves. The trouble is that they appear to be just as problematic as the notion of truth! After all, apart from soldiers and people at conferences, individuals don't go around with their names stuck on them. What is it, then, for a name to refer to something? Also, the idea of an adjective 'applying to' an individual seems to be the same as that of its being true of an individual.

To deal with this seemingly devastating objection the logician Alfred Tarski introduced an ingenious and influential idea. Very roughly it is this.

---

2 On the problems involved in the attempt to specify such rules for an actual natural language, see, e.g., J. Lyons, *Chomsky*.

We forget about principles like P1, which just take for granted that the problematic notions of referring and applying are acceptable. Instead, we *define* those notions without actually *using* either them or any other related notions. Tarski's idea was that we can define notions of *refers-in-L* and *applies-in-L*, as follows (where 'L' is the name of the language we are dealing with):

D1(a)   'Alf' refers-in-L to something x just in case x is Alf;

D1(b)   'Beth' refers-in-L to something x just in case x is Beth;

and so on for each in turn of the other names in the language L that we are dealing with. (There is no reason why that should not be done, since there are only finitely many names and adjectives.) Similarly:

D2(a)   'bald' applies-in-L to something x just in case x is bald;

D2(b)   'happy' applies-in-L to something x just in case x is happy

– and so on for each in turn of the other adjectives in the language.

In such definitions the part to the left of 'just in case' is the expression that will be defined by what follows on the right. Since in each of the definitions just listed none of the problematic notions is used on the right-hand side (the 'definiens', the heart of the definition), Tarski claimed to have overcome the difficulty. He claimed to have *defined* reference and application, at any rate for the specified language L, without having *used* any problematic notions in the definitions. So correspondence theorists take some comfort from Tarski's proposals, in spite of numerous difficulties.

Some readers might object that neither the original definition nor Tarski's approach do anything to explain how one could actually *find out* which sentences are true. That would be to misunderstand the point of the definitions. People who accept anything like the correspondence theory of truth insist that it is one thing for a statement to be true, something else to discover just which sentences are true. We shall return to these matters.

7 Is truth redundant?

It is interesting to note what Tarski regarded as a test for a definition of truth for a language. This was that, whatever else the definition did, it must at least ensure that all sentences of a certain special form follow from[3] the definition. A famous example illustrates that special form:

---

3 Here is a rough definition of 'follows from': a statement B follows from another statement A if it is impossible for A to be true and B false. To say B follows 'logically' from A is to emphasize that there is a logical basis for this relation.

(6) 'Snow is white' is true (in English) just in case snow is white.

His reason for insisting on that test is straightforward. Whatever else the notion of truth involves, surely it requires that all sentences of the form exemplified by (6) should be true. Any sentence of that kind must always be accepted. So Tarski's way of defining truth for a language at least conforms to a generally accepted condition.

There is an alternative version of essentially the same thought:

(7) It is true that p just in case p

– where 'p' stands in place of any properly constructed statement-making sentence. (7) would not have done for Tarski's purposes, however, since it does not refer to or pick out any *sentences*, whereas (6) does. The difference is revealed by the use of quotation marks in (6) and their absence in (7). Tarski was specifically concerned to explain what is involved in *sentences* being true. However, (7) is sometimes more convenient for general purposes. Again, we surely have to accept all properly constructed statements of the form represented by (7).

Brooding over these and related considerations has suggested to some thinkers that the notion of truth is dispensable. According to the 'redundancy' theory of truth, saying a statement is true is equivalent to simply asserting that statement: it's just a convenient way of making or endorsing statements. In terms of (7), the idea is that to say it is true that p is just a way of saying that p. Of course, just stating something doesn't *make* what is stated true. But that is no objection to the redundancy theory. The theory concerns what is contributed to a statement by the expression 'is true': it says *nothing* is contributed by it. Redundancy theorists accept that the important questions concern how statements relate to reality, and how they are justified. For them there is no deep question about truth itself.

There are difficulties for the redundancy theory. What about statements like 'Everything the policeman said is true', where the speaker may not even know what the other person actually said? Redundancy theorists have devised ways of dealing with those cases, but we need not pursue the discussion.[4] The point is that, although the redundancy theory has problems, it highlights an important thing about truth: it seems to add nothing to what is stated. In that sense it is transparent.

In its full scope, Tarski's is an impressive approach to providing a grasp of the notion of truth. In spite of its seeming to suggest a redundancy account, it also seems to be at any rate consistent with the general drift of the

---

4 For more discussion, see, for example, Frederick F. Schmitt, *Truth: a primer*, pp.123–44.

correspondence theory. However, that does not mean the correspondence theory has been legitimated: it still faces problems.

8 Conceptual autonomy

One of the deepest of these problems can be appreciated when we reflect that we are just one species of animal among many. If the Core Scientific Theory is right, we have evolved as a result of a particular series of developments on a particular planet. We are a certain size, we need certain kinds of food, we may be advantaged and damaged in certain ways. Our sense organs are not the only possible ones. Unlike bats, we lack the capacity to perceive things by echo location. Unlike snakes, we lack infra-red perception. Unlike bees, we lack ultra-violet vision and the ability to detect patterns of polarized light. So our ways of thinking about things, our classifications, our *concepts*, have likewise evolved to suit us human beings; they are not the sort that would have suited intelligent creature of different kinds, with different kinds of sensory equipment, different needs and interests. Similar considerations apply even if we restrict ourselves to human beings. People suffer from various sorts of sensory deficiency. They may be partially or completely deaf or blind, for example. What fully sighted people take to be obvious and objective features of reality, such as colours, are problematic for blind people; and in a community of blind people would be totally ignored.

The apparent problem for the correspondence theory is this. It appears to presuppose that reality has been classified independently of us: that *what* there is, *the kinds of thing* there are, and *the ways things can be*, have nothing to do with our interests, our perceptual capacities, our intelligence, and our ways of thinking. The picture it suggests is that on one side there is reality, already classified as people, animals, trees, atoms, tables, chairs and the rest, and on the other side there is thought and language, which contribute no more than names and descriptions for those things already classified. But that picture is misleading. It is not as if things had labels on them. Given what has just been noted about our evolution and our distinctive needs, interests and ways of thinking, it seems that our ways of thinking about the world, our ways of classifying things, our 'conceptual schemes' in short, are in an important sense our own work, not fixed independently of our thinking. We have a degree of what I will call 'conceptual autonomy'.

That is not to say external reality has had nothing to do with fixing our concepts. Our environment nudges us in some directions rather than others, and our sensory and intellectual capacities make certain schemes more manageable than others. By suggesting we have 'conceptual autonomy' I do not mean to imply that our remote ancestors consciously decided how they would organize their thoughts before they had had any. ('Well, folks, how are we going to think about things?') The point is that just which conceptual scheme we have results very largely, though presumably not entirely, from

26

the kind of creatures we are. It does not result from a process like the impressing of seals on to soft wax, with our minds the wax, and nature pushing down the seals.

Aristotle was a great thinker who *did* think of the relation between reality and our ways of thinking on that analogy. But even among his predecessors there were some who would have rejected it. Parmenides, as we have seen, regarded the senses as positively misleading: he thought we could come to understand the true nature of reality only by reasoning. Democritus taught that colours and tastes are not out there in the world, but contributed by human 'convention'. A more recent philosopher who insisted that we ourselves contribute much to what we take to be reality was David Hume. Consider causal relations. When the wind blows down a tree, for example, we tend to think that, given all the circumstances, notably the force of the wind, the wind-resistance of the tree, and the weakness of its roots, it was inevitable that the tree would fall: it was a matter of 'natural necessity'. Hume urged to the contrary that this necessity, which we take to be a feature of external reality, is in fact nothing of the sort. We *think* it is out there, but what is really going on is that we are psychologically inclined to move from thoughts of the events we count as causes to thoughts of those we count as effects. Because our thoughts tend to move along those lines, we think the connection is there in external reality: we 'project' the necessity on to the outside world. Hume argued that there is nothing in nature that corresponds to it.

It was Immanuel Kant who first applied that approach to our intellectual powers in general. Most strikingly, he maintained that not even space and time are 'out there'. On the contrary, our intellectual nature is such that the general organizing concepts of time and space form the framework in terms of which we think about the information yielded by our senses. Rather than space and time being objective features of a reality independent of our ways of thinking, there is no more to them than the fact that we perceive and think in spatial and temporal terms. We can't help doing it: we necessarily think of events as occurring in relations of 'earlier' or 'later' than, or as simultaneous; and when it comes to relations between objects, we necessarily think of these relations in terms of relative positions in space. It is an error, on Kant's view, to suppose that these ways of thinking somehow reflect temporal or spatial relations existing independently of us. I am not endorsing these unsettling ideas. I mention them because they illustrate one way in which it is possible to regard ourselves as making a huge contribution to (what we think of as) reality.

If our conceptual scheme owes a lot to our own natures, it seems we have to think of our conception of reality as being, at best, partial. We view things through distorting, narrow-vision spectacles. At worst the picture we create is our own work entirely, or the work of our minds, or perhaps of the mind of God, as in Berkeley's account (see Chapter 6, section 1). Far from our theory being capable of mirroring the world, we paint for ourselves a distorted and selective picture. The question of how far this idea can legitimately be pressed will occupy us throughout. Notice, though, that there is a whole range of views available, from Aristotelian 'wax impression' realism at one end to Berkeleyan idealism at the other.

The straightforward and seemingly commonsense notion of truth as correspondence with reality may therefore need to be superseded. One very different conception is that of truth as coherence.

9 Second thoughts about truth: coherence

In a criminal trial, one side often argues that the other side's case does not hang together: it involves improbabilities or even inconsistencies. For example, it requires the accused to have been in two different places at the same time. If the defence manages to persuade the jury that the prosecution's case is incoherent, or contains too much that is improbable, or implies actual contradictions, the jury is likely to acquit. A story implying a contradiction cannot possibly be true, as we have seen; similarly, one implying something improbable is unlikely to be true.

So we normally regard coherence as a *necessary* condition for truth. If we switch from the special example of a criminal trial to the matter of our total theory of the world, coherence seems not just necessary for truth, but a test of truth. How else could we tell whether a statement is true than by discovering how well it hangs together with everything else we believe (including, of course, our beliefs and memories about our experiences)? What better reason could we have for concluding that our total theory of the world was true than that it hangs together as a whole? At least those seem to be persuasive considerations. Some thinkers who reject the correspondence theory go much further. They argue that coherence is not just a test, but what actually *constitutes* truth. They hold that for a statement to be true just is for it to be coherent with the rest of the current theory of the world.

If we hold the Core Scientific Story, our broad theory of the world hangs together pretty well. The CSS has been tried and tested, and provides a remarkably reliable basis for explaining and predicting a great deal of what happens. It strikes most of us as so compelling that we tend to reject claims which conflict with it (for example, that the earth is not round) and to be favourably disposed to claims which fit in with it. At least, we do so if a statement or assertion is not just consistent with it, but is supported by evidence which also fits, and we have no strong evidence to the contrary. (There may be different kinds of evidence for, or reasons for accepting, a statement. The most obvious is what we can see or hear or otherwise perceive; but we also count the testimony of other people as evidence; and a piece of argumentation may give us reasons to accept the assertion, and count as evidence for that reason.)

So we do actually tend to *count* as true whatever fits in with the rest of our theory of the world, subject to the conditions just sketched. The present suggestion is that there is no more to the truth of a statement than the fact that it fits in with the rest of the theory in this way.

It is not easy to devise an exact definition of 'fitting in', or coherence, for this purpose. Roughly, the idea is that a set of statements is coherent to the extent that the statements are systematically connected in such a way that each contributes to explaining the rest. The point about explanation is included to rule out mere lists of mutually irrelevant statements.[5] The bigger the set of statements, the better.

There is an old objection to the coherence theory: coherence by itself cannot guarantee truth. Compare the Babylonian myths about the creation of human beings noted in Chapter 1. One said that human beings were made from the blood of a certain god; another said they were made from clay mixed with the blood of a different god. Both stories are internally coherent, yet they conflict. It follows that they cannot both be true. Suppose you offer a certain theory of the world A, and claim that truth consists in fitting that theory. Then, given enough time, energy and ingenuity, I could devise a rival theory B, which was just as coherent as A, yet contradicted it. That is, for some statement S belonging to or following from A, my rival theory B implies a statement *not-S*, which contradicts S. But S and not-S cannot both be true. Therefore theory A and theory B cannot both be true. If that is right, truth cannot be mere coherence. For the assumption was that both theories, the one implying S and the other implying not-S, were equally coherent. (It is as if, in a criminal trial, both the prosecution's and the defence's cases were equally strong.) However, a hard-nosed coherence theorist will reply that the objection merely 'begs the question'. It illegitimately presupposes that there is *more* to the truth of a theory than coherence. If truth really is no more than coherence, then the objector has no basis for the assumption that two theories 'cannot both be true' just because they have contradictory implications.

Here is another example: our ideas about the shape and relative size of the earth. The coherence theory seems to provide a way for the shape and size of the earth to depend on what people think about it in a way that utterly conflicts with our ordinary assumptions about such matters. If the coherence theory is right, then it seems that it was true in the tenth century that the earth was more or less flat and a lot bigger than the sun; true now that the earth is round and much smaller than the sun; but also true now that neither the shape of the earth, nor its size compared with the sun, has altered since the tenth century – a contradiction. One possible reply for coherence theorists is that they are not talking about theories of the world

5 Jonathan Dancy, *An Introduction to Contemporary Epistemology*, pp.110–36.

which float free of the data of experience. Theories have to fit the same vast mass of experiential data. Mere internal coherence is not enough. Since the objection ignores the requirement that theories of the world must be coherent with the data of experience, it fails. (Just what the data of experience are is not altogether clear. We can think of them as the perceptual experiences, or observations, of the intelligent creatures whose theories we are considering.) Although our medieval ancestors did not realize it, arguably they had in their possession enough perceptual data to rule out the flat earth theory: for example, observations of the way distant ships disappear beyond the horizon, and of eclipses of the moon.

That reply depends on a vital assumption. It will meet the objection only if no more than one internally coherent theory could fit the data of experience. Is that assumption correct? The question is not simple; I will merely note some relevant points. First, suppose the 'data of experience' were restricted to whatever experiences are *actually* had. In that case the assumption is false. The experiences people actually have cannot determine what experiences they *would* have had if things or people had behaved differently. My actual experiences of seeing the movements of the clouds through my window just now couldn't determine what experiences I would have had if I had looked out five seconds ago rather than just now. So two conflicting stories could be told about the earlier movements of the clouds, both coherent with my actual experiences. Therefore the coherence theorist cannot maintain that the truth of a statement consists in its coherence with an internally coherent theory of the world, even if that theory also coheres with all actual experiences or observations. That would imply that statements contradicting one another were true.

You might suggest that coherent theories need only be required to cohere with all *possible* experiences. But that would undermine the whole basis of the coherence theory. What are to be counted as possible experiences for this purpose? Not all the ones we can imagine or conceive of, since we can conceive of experiences contrary to the laws of nature, such as seeing pigs flying or boulders floating on still water. They would have to be defined as all possible experiences *consistent with the laws of nature*, or in some similar way. But that implies that the laws of nature hold in a way which does not depend on their own coherence with anything. Statements of those laws would be exceptions to the coherence theory, which would therefore be mistaken.

Even if some satisfactory way of defining the data of experience were available, it is still not obvious that two conflicting theories could not both fit that mass of data. If that is possible, the original objection still applies. If a true statement is one which fits a coherent theory of the world which itself fits all the possible data of experience, then if two contradictory theories may both be in that position, a statement and its contradiction may both be true. That cannot be right.

30

Those reflections may drive us back to some version of the correspondence theory, in spite of its difficulties. Correspondence theorists will say that only one theory can fit the data of experience because only one theory will provide a correct statement of the way things really are. There is something outside both theory and experiences which determines whether or not a theory is true, and that is *reality*. Even if two theories were tied for first place by all the tests of scientific virtue, so that we ourselves had no basis for deciding in favour of one rather than the other, reality itself would ensure that no more than one of them was actually true.

Coherence theorists will say that that is just whistling in the dark. They will maintain that the idea that reality can determine which of two conflicting theories is true is a mistake. It is not as if we could compare a theory with the world. On the contrary, we cannot think or speak at all except from within some conceptual scheme in terms of which we organize our thoughts: we cannot think or speak except from within some language or theory (Chapter 7, section 6). The objections we have been considering spring (so coherence theorists urge) from a failure to grasp those vital points. Once they have been recognized, it becomes clear that there is something wrong with the idea of a genuine rival to the theory of the world we actually have. That is a thought we shall return to. Regardless of whether or not it is correct, we need to take note of a third broad approach to truth.[6]

10 Third thoughts about truth: pragmatism

In *Pragmatism: a New Name for Some Old Ways of Thinking* (1907) the American philosopher and psychologist William James emphasized the importance of the practical consequences of our ideas and theories. ' "Grant an idea or belief to be true," it [pragmatism] says, "what concrete difference will its being true make in anyone's actual life? How will the truth be realized? What experiences will be different from those which would obtain if the belief were false? What, in short, is the truth's cash-value in experiential terms?" '[7]

At first those remarks seem to suggest no more than a test for truth. Regarded in that way his suggestions are appealing. James goes well beyond that idea. He states pragmatism's view of truth as follows: '*True ideas are*

---

6 To reinforce the point that what may appear to be solid conclusions are likely to be challenged, it is worth noting that the distinguished American philosopher Donald Davidson has remarked: 'Truth is beautifully transparent compared to belief and coherence, and I take it as primitive' ('A Coherence Theory of Truth and Knowledge', in Ernest LePore, ed., *Truth and Interpretation*, p.308). Incidentally, although Davidson appears to endorse a coherence theory, he also asserts that 'truth is correspondence with the way things are' (op. cit., p.309).

7 William James, *Pragmatism*, p.97.

those we can assimilate, validate, corroborate and verify. False ideas are those that we cannot. That is the practical difference it makes to us to have true ideas; that, therefore, is the meaning of truth...'[8] In connection with theories, he remarks, 'Theories thus become instruments, not answers to enigmas...'[9] Again, 'Truth for us is simply a collective name for verification-processes....Truth is *made*, just as health, wealth and strength are made, in the course of experience.'[10]

Some of those remarks are confusing. James was more concerned to convey his general approach than to worry over the details of how he put it across. Apart from that, the implications of his ideas take time and careful consideration to appreciate. I will note below three of the main suggestions in the quoted remarks, and postpone further discussion of pragmatism until later in the book.

(1) For an idea to be true is for it to be (among other things) *verifiable*.

(2) Truth is *made* analogously to the ways health, wealth and strength are made.

(3) Theories are *instruments*.

Each suggestion is interesting and each has been influential. But there are obvious difficulties. For example, if being true is being verifi*able*, *capable* of being verified, as (1) has it, then there may be countless undiscovered truths that are never *actually* verified. We tend to suppose there are discoverable answers to questions such as 'How much does that pebble weigh?', even though there is no prospect of weighing all the pebbles in the universe and actually verifying their weights. In contrast to (1), (2) seems to imply that truth requires *actual* verification, not just the possibility. Further, in suggesting that truth is made, (3) seems to suggest that it is *up to us* what is true; which is puzzling if you think truths are capable of being discovered.

Rather than pursuing the question of just what William James was getting at, in later chapters I will examine the work of two contemporary American philosophers, W. V. Quine and Richard Rorty, who have been influenced by James and other pragmatists. Their approaches to the problems outlined in Chapter 1 are in some ways similar, but there are significant differences; indeed their ideas about reality and truth are in sharp conflict.

None of the accounts of truth sketched so far seems entirely satisfactory. Things have turned out to be more complicated, or at any rate more diffi-

8 Loc. cit. Italics in the original.
9 Op. cit., p.32.
10 Op. cit., p.104.

cult, than may at first have appeared. I will begin deeper investigations in the next chapter, with an examination of some of the simpler varieties of relativism.

MAIN POINTS IN CHAPTER 2

1   The Core Scientific Story differs from the myths in at least four significant respects (sections 1–4. That is a partial answer to question 2 at the end of Chapter 1).
2   The correspondence theory of truth is threatened with emptiness or circularity. But perhaps Tarski's approach can save it (sections 5–7).
3   The availability of 'redundancy' accounts of truth suggests that it may not be such a basic notion as at first appears (section 7).
4   The coherence theory of truth faces serious problems (section 9).
5   Samples of William James's pragmatism have been noted (section 10).

CHAPTER 2: SUGGESTIONS FOR FURTHER READING

On the **history of science** A. R. Hall, *The Scientific Revolution 1300–1800*, and A. Koestler, *The Sleepwalkers*; both offer engaging accounts.

On theories of **truth**, F. Schmitt, *Truth: a primer*, gives a good introduction and many useful references. For a slightly more advanced treatment see A. C. Grayling, *An Introduction to Philosophical Logic*, chs. 5 and 6. S. Haack, *Philosophy of Logics*, sets theories of truth in a wider context. On coherence theories see also chs. 8 and 9 of J. Dancy, *Introduction to Contemporary Epistemology*.

The main ideas of **Tarski's** approach to truth are clearly outlined in W. V. Quine, *Philosophy of Logic* and in A. Miller, *Philosophy of Language*. For a wider discussion see, for example, ch. 7 of S. Haack, *Philosophy of Logics*.

Hume is one of the most readable of philosophers, although expert commentaries are needed for interpretation. His main work is *A Treatise of Human Nature*, though his *An Enquiry into Human Understanding*, sections III, V and VII, is most relevant here. J. Broackes, 'David Hume', in *The Oxford Companion to Philosophy*, ed. T. Honderich, pp.377–81, is helpful; see especially p.379. J. Bennett, *Locke, Berkeley, Hume: Central Themes*, goes into more detail.

Kant, in contrast, is hard to read and to understand. For a brief, readable introductory work see R. Scruton, *Kant*, which offers helpful suggestions for further study.

William James writes engagingly – though not particularly clearly – on **pragmatism**. See, for example, his *Pragmatism: a New Name for Some Old Ways of Thinking*. For a brief, highly individual and readable treatment of pragmatism together with the other themes of the present book, try Hilary Putnam, *Pragmatism*, in which he offers many useful references. Ch. 3 of F. Schmitt, *Truth: a primer*, is a brief and sober discussion.

3

RELATIVE TO US?

Suppose you and I both accept the Core Scientific Story. When people contradict it, for example by saying the sun is smaller than the earth, we judge them to be mistaken. We do so from our own point of view, which means we do it on the basis of our own theory. (We could hardly do it on the basis of someone else's.) That doesn't mean we regard our theory as beyond correction. We are open to reason. We have to admit the likelihood that some of our beliefs, though we don't know which, are false. But at any particular time we assume our theory is true – that is why it is ours – and there are parts of it which at present we cannot imagine could be seriously mistaken. For example, I cannot imagine how we could be mistaken in the belief that the sun is bigger than the earth.

Judged on the basis of our own theory, then, the theory of someone who thinks the sun is smaller than the earth is false and ours is true. But the situation is symmetrical. Judged on the basis of *their* theory, their beliefs are true and ours, when they contradict theirs, are false. There is no way out of this situation. We *can* only judge from our own point of view, and on the basis of whatever theory we may happen to have at the time we judge.

Certainly I can do my best to understand your point of view and your theory. If you believe the earth is bigger than the sun I can come to grasp, for example, how powerfully you are impressed by the vast size and solidity of the earth under your feet and the fact that the sun appears to be quite small in comparison, and how sceptical you are about the reliability of telescopes and other instruments. Perhaps I can even learn enough about your way of seeing things to enable me to predict accurately how you will reply to questioning on these matters. But the views I attribute to you will not be *my* judgements, but my idea of what *yours* would be. I cannot make my own judgements about things except on the basis of my own theory.

Still less can I do anything like stand outside all theories and judge on the basis of none. To use a current phrase, there is no God's Eye View – an idea to be examined in Chapter 7 (section 6).

1 Relativism

Those points are hard to deny; but some people go on to make what at least seem much stronger claims, to the effect that truth and reality *depend* on our point of view, or our theory. We noticed examples in Chapter 1 (section 5). In this chapter I will examine some relatively simple varieties of relativism. They can fairly easily be seen to be unsatisfactory. In later chapters we shall consider more sophisticated doctrines.

Relativism is a heady but unsettling idea. Could it be right? Let us agree that we cannot think or state truths except in terms of a theory. It is one thing to admit as much, something very different to say that *which* statements are true itself depends on our point of view or theory. We certainly need a theory on the basis of which to hold the belief that the sun is bigger than the earth. There has to be a network of beliefs which help to explain our ideas of what sort of things the sun and the earth are, and how they relate to the rest of the world. Aristotle and his medieval followers, for example, held that the sun and other heavenly bodies were set in vast transparent concentric spheres, turning around the unmoving earth at the centre; modern astronomy sees the sun as one star among many billions scattered around the universe, and the earth as one of the sun's planets, circling around it. There cannot be such a thing as having beliefs about the relative sizes of sun and earth without their being supported in some such network of beliefs. Accepting such a network of beliefs goes with certain ways of thinking, certain concepts.

However, holding a particular belief, or thinking in terms of a particular theory or system of concepts, does not make that belief or theory actually true, does it? For us to have that system of beliefs is one thing; whether or not the system is true is something else – so most of us tend to assume. Suppose we believe the sun is bigger than the earth. What makes it true (if it is true)? Surely it is the sun and the earth themselves – the relevant parts of reality – not our beliefs about them. If we are wrong to make that assumption, a powerful argument is needed to counter it.

The problem does not seem so great if relativism is limited to certain special areas, such as moral or aesthetic values. It is easy to suppose that they depend on one's point of view. But I am concerned with 'global' relativism, which is supposed to apply to all kinds of discourse without exception. And for some central types of discourse it is hard to avoid thinking that the way things are is completely independent of our points of view, beliefs or theories. It seems just impossible to be a global relativist in practice, however strongly one may be inclined to accept it in theory. To mention just a tiny sample, the following statements seem to be true or false regardless of anyone's thoughts or point of view – regardless of whether there are any thoughts or points of view at all. 'It's snowing here now', 'There's a robin in that tree', 'It snowed here yesterday', 'The sun is very much larger than the earth', 'There was a battle at Hastings in 1066', 'London is a city', 'Rabbits have fur'. When you consider wars, diseases and natural catastrophes, which cause so much suffering, the very suggestion that in some way they are not objectively real matters of fact, regardless of how or what people may think, seems not just untrue but outrageous. Still, raised eyebrows are no substitute for argument. Let us look at some simple varieties of relativism.

2 'Truth for me'

Protagoras famously asserted that 'Man is the measure of all things: of what is, that it is, and of what is not, that it is not'. What did he mean? Plato took him to mean: 'Everything is for me as it appears to me, and is for you as it appears to you'.[1] That may seem an appealing idea at first glance. But it is not much clearer than Protagoras' original statement; it too needs interpretation. One suggestion might be:

(1) Whatever seems to me to be true is true for me, and whatever seems to you to be true is true for you.

That still leaves room for different interpretations, depending on how we understand the phrase 'true for'. Suppose we take it to mean 'seems true to'. Then statement (1) means that whatever seems true to me seems true to me, and whatever seems true to you seems true to you. That makes Protagoras' position clear – but deprives it of all interest. A more interesting interpretation is:

(2) Whatever seems to me to be true is true, and whatever seems to you to be true is true.

That is *subjectivism*, and quite exciting. Consider its implications. If we assume (2), then if it seems to you (or to anyone) that the earth is flat, it is true that the earth is flat. Equally, if it seems to me that the earth is not flat, it is true that the earth is not flat. As we noticed in the last chapter, we have to accept that if it is true that S, then S (where 'S' stands in place of any statement). Hence, given our contradictory views about the shape of the earth, (2) has the surprising consequence that *the earth is flat and the earth is not flat*. But we also saw in the last chapter that such contradictions cannot possibly hold. So, given that at least two people hold contradictory beliefs on some matter, (2) cannot possibly hold. Which shows that subjectivism, exciting though it may be, is a completely untenable variety of relativism.

---

1 Plato, *Theaetetus*, 152a.

However, neither (1) nor (2) is a fair reading of Protagoras' position. (1) makes it trivially true, (2) makes it plainly false. A third interpretation is much more interesting.[2] The central thought is that *there is no such thing as truth full-stop; there is only truth for people at times*. The nearest we can come to truth is that kind of *relative* truth. All truth is truth for me, or truth for you, or truth for....On this view, strictly speaking, it is neither true nor false that the earth is bigger than the sun. Instead, it is just true (or false) for you, or for both of us, or at any rate for some people. (For the moment we can take it that a statement is true for a given person just in case that person believes it; but see section 9 below.) In brief:

(3)   All truth is relative.

(3), understood on the lines just explained, is not obviously correct – but perhaps not obviously incorrect. Notice how very different it is from subjectivism (2). One thing wrong with subjectivism was that it produced *too much truth*. According to it, everything anyone believes is true, so that when people contradict one another their contradictory beliefs are all true; which we have seen to be impossible. In contrast, if (3) holds, disagreements do not produce contradictory truths. Suppose you believe the earth is round and I believe it is not round. (3) provides no direct path to the conclusion that it is both true that the earth is round and true that the earth is not round. The point of (3) is that we are never entitled to say things like 'It is true that the earth is round'; for that would be a case of non-relative truth – truth full-stop. The nearest (3) permits us to get to truth is to say something is true *for me*, or *for most educated people*, or something of the sort. (We ordinarily use the words 'true' and 'false' without any explicit additional phrase relativizing them to some individual or group. Relativists can claim that, when we do, the relativization is implicit: we mean something like 'true for most people in my community now'.)

Relativism of this sort, which from now on I will call Protagorean or 'true-for-me' relativism, can be appealing. Certainly it is more sophisticated than the subjectivism of (2). How much it appeals in advance of detailed discussion may depend largely on temperament. Some of us think of ourselves as no-nonsense realists, feet squarely on the ground. We smile at the idea that truths about matters of fact depend on what people think. Others are sure these no-nonsense types are fooling themselves, ignoring subtle considerations which undermine their innocent crudities. But although temperament may influence us, we are in the business of considering reasons. What good reasons are there for or against true-for-me relativism?

2 Whether it is true to Protagoras' own intention I do not know.

3 False beliefs and undiscovered truths

One main objection to true-for-me relativism is that, when we form our beliefs and theories, we are aiming to represent things as they really are. That means we think it is possible not only to succeed, but to fail. We succeed when our beliefs and theories represent things as they are (when our beliefs and theories are true) and we fail when they do not (when they are false). Aristotle and our medieval ancestors failed – so we think – in their attempts to represent the relative sizes of the sun and the earth. In the twelfth century people believed the earth was bigger than the sun. Nevertheless, in the twelfth century the earth was *not* bigger than the sun; and from the discussion in the last chapter we have 'if p, then it is true that p'. It follows that in the twelfth century it was *true* that the earth was not bigger than the sun full-stop – and that their beliefs were false full-stop. It may have been true-for-people-living-in-the-twelfth-century that the earth was not bigger than the sun; but the example shows there is *more* to truth than truth-for-people. It thereby highlights the strangeness of true-for-me relativism: it cannot allow that any beliefs are false!

A related objection is that we assume there are *undiscovered* truths, which no one has any beliefs about at all. There seem to be excellent reasons to suppose that what is actually known or believed is only a tiny subset of truths. Truths about the numbers and exact details of remote galaxies, stars and planetary systems are one obvious example. Closer to home there are truths about the location of minerals underground and about the distribution of viruses in the bodies of individuals and populations. What ensures there are all those undiscovered truths – so we tend to assume – is that if the world *is* thus and so, then it is *true* that the world is thus and so. If there is coal three thousand feet beneath this spot, then it is true there is coal three thousand feet beneath this spot. Quite generally, if p, then it is true that p. (Not all undiscovered truths are worth bothering about, by the way. What is the exact weight of that pebble? How many grains of sand are there in this part of the carpet?) True-for-me relativists seem compelled to claim that such truths are not true *for* anyone, hence that there are no such truths in any sense. (Whereas subjectivism implies there is too much truth, true-for-me relativism implies there is too little.) By doing so, they also seem compelled to claim that *there are no facts about the world* other than whatever people happen actually to believe. That is very hard to accept. How could there possibly fail to be any unbelieved facts about the world?

There seems to be an *essential* difference between what is true and what is known or believed to be true. To repeat, the point of our beliefs and theories seems to be that they should somehow capture how things are. If they succeed, they are true; but we realize they may fall short, in which case they are false. If on the other hand true-for-me relativism is the correct view, we need an explanation of why the assumption that there is this essential difference is so widespread and compelling, and why we should take seriously a position according to which none of our beliefs can be false.

One possible reply would be that false beliefs and unknown truths only appear to be counter-examples if you start with the assumption that relativism is mistaken. True-for-me relativists who take this line will maintain that, although it may be natural to resist relativism, deeper consideration of our situation forces us to accept it. They will insist that what is mistaken is the common presupposition to the effect that there are truths which are not *for* anyone.

4 Is relativism inconsistent?

Opponents may think they sniff inconsistency there. That reply seems incompatible with relativism itself. How can relativists consistently maintain that their opponents are *mistaken*? Doesn't that imply there is after all something to be non-relatively right or wrong about, something about which some of us actually have false beliefs? The attack can be broadened a little. Doesn't the actual statement of true-for-me relativism itself amount to a claim which is intended to be true full-stop, independently of what people may think? To put it another way: when relativists assert 'All truth is relative', they must surely think their claim holds good universally, and would hold good even if nobody actually maintained it. If so, they inconsistently maintain that something is non-relatively correct – that is, true.

They may feel they can afford to take a relaxed attitude to that objection. Can't they simply reply that their opponents are mistaken *according to them, the relativists*? Relative to their opponents' own position, the latter are not mistaken; but relative to the relativists' position they are. So when relativists describe their opponents as mistaken they are not after all being inconsistent. All they have to do is insist that, just as there is no such thing as truth full-stop, so there is no such thing as falsity, or being mistaken, full-stop. Instead, there is only being mistaken relative to what a given person holds true.

That may seem to allow them to breathe freely. Unfortunately for them it allows the same objection to pop up again. When the relativists say 'There is no such thing as being mistaken full-stop', they once more appear to intend that assertion to hold good independently of what people may think. It is hard to see how they can get out of this difficulty. We shall return to it in section 9.

5 Coherence again

Shortly we shall notice further difficulties for true-for-me relativism. Now let us consider another possible reply to the objection about undiscovered truths. Instead of just denying the seemingly obvious claim that there are plenty of truths that no one knows or even believes, they might fall back on the coherence theory of truth. Why not explain unbelieved truths simply as statements that cohere with systems of statements which *are* held true? Take the statement 'There is coal three thousand feet beneath this spot'. I have no idea whether it is true or false; and quite likely no one else has either. But it coheres with the rest of my beliefs. Why not count it as true for me? The answer has probably struck you: the contradictory of that statement, 'There is *no* coal three thousand feet beneath this spot', *also* coheres with the rest of my beliefs. If all statements that would cohere with the rest of my beliefs were to be counted as true for me, then contradictory statements would have to be counted as true for me as well. Even relativists could not claim to have explained the possibility of undiscovered truths by maintaining that two inconsistent statements were *both* true for me. It is not as if I should accept them both as true if I were to consider them. I should either accept one and reject the other, or suspend judgement. The suggestion was supposed to explain undiscovered truths in terms of statements true for me. It turns out to make nonsense of the claim that the statements in question are true for me in any way. The original difficulty remains: true-for-me relativism seems incapable of accounting for unbelieved truths.

Here is a popular response. 'All that matters is what's actually believed. There's no point bothering about truths that no one believes. If no one believes them, they don't matter.' The appeal of that suggestion evaporates after a few milliseconds of reflection. The question is: what is it for beliefs, statements and theories to be *true*? Whether the only truths that *matter* also happen to be believed has nothing to do with it; so the present suggestion misses the point. Even if it were relevant it would be mistaken. Many things matter to us enormously even when we have no beliefs about them. To take one obvious class: it matters to us whether or not we are suffering from fatal diseases.

6 How is disagreement possible?

If you say the earth is round and I say it's not round but flat, the relativist says it's true for you that the earth is round, true for me that it's flat; but that there is no contradiction there. The statements 'It's true for x that the earth is round' and 'It's true for y that the earth is not round' are not contradictory. However, if there is such a thing as *disagreement* over facts at all, you and I are plainly in disagreement. That is shown by our making contradictory statements. Nor is it hard to explain what makes them so. They are contradictory because, while both pick out the same object (the earth), what one of them says about it the other denies.

That seems unproblematic. But consider what it implies. One thing it implies is that we both agree there is such a thing as the earth. We also both agree that its existence and shape do not depend on what either of us believes. In the special philosophical sense of the word, we take a *realist* attitude to the existence and shape of the earth. (More on realism in Chapter 6.) If we genuinely disagree, it seems we are forced to take a realist attitude to the matters we disagree about. If we thought the shape of the earth involved nothing more than someone's having beliefs about it, the idea of disagreement would not apply – any more than it applies to expressions of different tastes in food. Suppose I say I like Stilton cheese and you say you don't, we are not expressing disagreement, just different tastes. That may still be a matter of passionate interest; but it is very different from disagreement about the shape of the earth. Such disagreement commits us to the 'realist' view that what is actually the case (or, equivalently, what is true) is independent of our beliefs. If that is right, true-for-me relativism cannot be reconciled with the existence of genuine disagreement over factual matters.

It seems that true-for-me relativists must either abandon their position or grit their teeth and maintain that, contrary to the general assumption, *genuine disagreement over matters of fact is impossible*. That is another route to our earlier conclusion that they must reject the assumption that there can be false beliefs.

7 How can our statements mean what they do?

Things are even worse for relativism than we have seen so far. Recall that in the last chapter, in explaining what it was for sentences to be true, we exploited the thought that proper names such as 'Beth' and 'Socrates' pick things out. For this purpose we can count the expression 'the earth' as a proper name. Like those others, it is used to pick something out, something about which it is possible to agree or disagree. If relativism is correct, however, the idea of 'picking something out' is problematic because it implies the existence of something independent of our beliefs. If the earth can be picked out, its existence and shape (for example) do not depend on what anyone thinks; contrary to what we have seen is implied by relativism.

How, then, can true-for-me relativists explain the fact that our words and sentences mean what they do? They may still perhaps hope to use sentences like ' "The earth" picks out the earth'. But such sentences will have to be understood not to commit them to the existence of anything independent of people's beliefs. That immediately raises a question which is – for them – extremely hard. If 'picks out' does not imply that what is referred to exists independently of what people may think, how is it to be understood? We normally assume the phrase 'the earth' picks out something independent of our beliefs and theories. If that assumption is mistaken and it doesn't pick out anything independent, how can sentences including that expression still have the meanings they do have? I *think* I can think about an independently existing earth. If that is a mistake, how could I have got that mistaken idea and still understand the expression 'the earth'?

The only explanations of it that we ever come across involve a theory of the world – a theory explicitly intended to describe features of an independently existing reality! For example: 'The earth is a very large object; most of its surface consists of huge masses of water; on the dry parts there are mountains, valleys, rivers, forests and deserts; the earth is (or appears to be) surrounded by other large bodies: the sun, the moon and so on. All these objects are at certain distances from one another. We think the earth goes round the sun...' If we are not always offered precisely that explanation of what 'the earth' means, still we are offered explanations of that general kind. Crucially, they require the earth, the sun and the rest, to be things whose existence does not depend on whether or not we happen to hold certain beliefs about them. Relativism is forced to rule out such explanations; but what can it possibly put in their place? It seems to have no alternative story at all.

Relativists face a dilemma. Do *they* accept the idea that the earth, sun, moon and the rest exist independently of what people may think, or not? If they accept it, then they are being inconsistent, since it implies there are facts about the universe which do not depend on what is true for someone. If they reject it, what can they put in its place? They might perhaps suggest something like Berkeley's brand of 'idealism'; but that is a strange doctrine indeed (see Chapter 6, section 1).

8 The existence of relativists undermines relativism

Truth *for persons* presupposes the existence of persons who believe certain things rather than others. But consider what persons are: they are individuals whose existence is independent of what other people may think. You very likely had no idea I existed until you came across this book. Similarly I have very little idea of who, if anyone, is reading it. But you, the reader, exist regardless of whether I know you are there – don't you? (Chuang Tzu dreamt of a butterfly. 'Is it I who have just dreamt of a butterfly, or a butterfly which has dreamt of Chuang Tzu?' Presumably, though, Chuang Tzu was not so intoxicated by relativism that he overlooked the point that only someone who really exists can ask a question, and that one's dreams cannot bring persons into existence, however appealing that thought may be.)

Does the relativist accept those points about persons? If so, the doctrine collapses for that reason alone. For in that case the following statement is true non-relatively:

(4) Persons exist independently of what anyone may think

– and the relativist cannot deny it. True-for-me relativism has it that *all* truth is relative. So a single non-relative truth, such as (4), is enough to refute it. If however the relativist rejects the above points about persons, then they are committed to *solipsism*: the view that oneself is the only intelligent being there is. Although a refutation of solipsism is not straightforward, no sane person could actually be a solipsist. It isn't psychologically possible. Quite generally, if your philosophical position implies solipsism, it is untenable. At this point the determined relativist might decide to endorse solipsism anyway, in spite of not really being able to believe it. But even that desperate move would not help. The solipsist still accepts the existence of *one* person. And the existence of that person (the solipsist) doesn't depend on what the solipsist thinks. The solipsist is wild enough, it may seem, to adopt any crazy idea whatever, so perhaps might start to believe that he or she doesn't exist. But believing you don't exist doesn't make you not exist. On the contrary, as Descartes pointed out, if you have any thoughts at all, even the thought that you don't exist, that very fact guarantees you do exist. So, even for the solipsist, there is a matter of fact which is independent of what the solipsist may happen to believe. The solipsist must concede that the solipsist exists (and thinks) regardless of what that same solipsist's beliefs may be.

In the end, then, solipsism provides no comfort for true-for-me relativists. They are compelled to accept that the existence of persons doesn't depend on what anyone thinks. If other people exist regardless of what we may think, then, for example, it is true that you exist regardless of whether I believe you exist, even if I believe you do not exist. So there is a vast sea of truths which are not just truths-for-someone, but truths full-stop: truths about the existence of actual persons. Since true-for-me relativism maintains there are no such truths, it is false (full-stop) for that reason alone. No one, relativist or not, can consistently accept that truths about the existence of people – even truths about the existence of the sole intelligent being in the universe – are relative.

Relativists can hardly stop there. They can hardly maintain, for example, that it's absolutely true that RK exists, but only relatively true that RK is now in his room in his house, breathing, using his word-processor, sipping coffee, and so on. So 'true-for-me' relativism collapses completely.

9 Another awkward question

Recall the statement of true-for-me relativism:

(3) All truth is relative.

It looks as if it is intended to be true full-stop or 'absolutely', not just true-for-the-relativist. However, relativists clearly cannot accept it is true in that way: that would be inconsistent with relativism itself. They are forced to say it is true only relatively, true for them. But here is another awkward question.

What is 'true for them' supposed to mean? Earlier I provisionally suggested it meant simply that they *believed* it. The trouble is that we normally believe only what we take to be true – what we take to be the case regardless of whether we happen to believe it – which we have seen to be inconsistent for them. It seems, then, that relativists do *not* believe (3), or not in the usual sense of 'believe'. Whatever their attitude to (3) may be, it is not one of accepting it as true. (Nor, for the same reason, can it be an attitude of accepting (3) as accepted-as-true-by-them, since that expression would have to give way in turn to 'accepted-as-accepted-as-true-by-them', then to 'accepted-as-accepted-as-accepted-as-true-by-them', and so on to infinity, without ever managing to give a complete explanation of what their attitude was.)

The temptation now is for us to say: 'If not even the relativists believe their own doctrine, why should anyone else take it seriously?' But that might be too quick. Relativists could complain that the objection presupposes a framework of ideas that they reject wholesale. (See Chapter 9 for further discussion of related ideas.)

10 The fundamental trouble with relativism

The true-for-me relativist appears to have lost sight of the point of the notion of truth, and associatedly of the point of assertion or statement-making. Uninfluenced by philosophy, we assume that if it is true that p, then p – whatever statement is substituted for 'p'. If it is true that the earth is round, then the earth is round, and similarly for all other statements. That was a vital lesson of Chapter 2. That is why, if, for example, we want to discover whether it is true that smoking causes cancer, we try to find out whether smoking causes cancer. What we do *not* investigate, in that situation, is whether people *believe* smoking causes cancer. Why not? Because we think there is something to be right or wrong about, something that does not depend on what people happen to believe. Indeed, when you think about it, it seems impossible to avoid that conclusion. How could there fail to be a reality independent of what people happen to believe? In a nutshell: p is true if and only if p; but p is *not* the same as *thinking* that p.

Of course, we disagree over what reality is actually like. Some of us say it is at bottom purely physical (whatever that may mean); others insist there are also spirits or immaterial minds; still others that there are nothing *but* spirits. But we all agree there is something or other which does not depend for its existence on what anyone may think or experience. In that sense everyone has to be a 'realist' – of the philosophical variety – about something. When you start to take relativism seriously, you end up realizing it is impossible to take it seriously.

The same vital considerations can be put in other words, and reinforced. We can start from the fact that we have theories (at any rate beliefs, or information) about how things are. That is indisputable even by true-for-me relativists. After all, they assert there is no more to truth than the fact that these theories or beliefs are held. We may say these theories and beliefs are about 'the world', since that leaves it open what sort of world we are in. And we accept that any of our beliefs has to be given up if we find reasons to conclude it is false: if we think it is inconsistent with what we count as 'the way the world is'. That explains how our beliefs, theories and assertions may be said to aim to capture the way the world is. But the very fact of having beliefs that we may have reasons to give up commits us to accepting that there is a difference between the way things are and what we believe. It commits us to there being something to be right or wrong about: being right full-stop and being wrong full-stop, not just relatively so. The fundamental trouble with true-for-me relativism is that it attempts to deny that there is this difference between the way things are and the way we suppose things to be.

There are still many considerations which, although they don't force us into that sort of relativism, seem to lead us close to it in one way or another. Much of this book will be devoted to examining them. To conclude this chapter I will look briefly at some related ideas.

11 All our own work?

We have just seen that true-for-me relativists cannot avoid supposing that persons exist absolutely – regardless of what beliefs may be held about their existence – and that such relativism is untenable for that reason alone. But you may think there is still room for a view which, if it is not strictly a variety of relativism, has a large relativizing component. This is the view that in a sense we *construct* reality (apart from persons) for ourselves.

In the last chapter we noticed a worry in connection with the correspondence theory of truth. The idea of correspondence appears to presuppose that reality comes already classified – as if things had labels attached to them by nature. It suggests that perception, thought and language merely register those naturally classified things and kinds, without themselves making any contribution. Reflection on the varieties of perceptual capacities, needs, interests and ways of thinking which exist among ourselves and other animals appears to undermine that simple conception. According to the simple conception, our theory of the world is a mirror of what is 'out there'. According to the rival conception encouraged by those considerations, there is a sense in which we construct the world. Another metaphor: we paint for ourselves a picture that is both highly selective and distorted. A brief consideration of colours will illustrate the main issues.

12 Are colours real?

Democritus said, 'Relative to us there is colour, relative to us there is sweetness, relative to us there is bitterness; but in truth there are atoms and empty space.'[3] You may object that the colours of things are just as real as their other properties, such as their shapes or sizes. Surely red things, for example, are so because they reflect or transmit light with predominantly long wavelengths (around 620 nanometres)? Surely it is a matter of objective fact whether something reflects or transmits light of that sort? How can that be only 'relative to us'? How can it depend on us at all?

Colours may be thought to depend on us in two distinct ways. One is that our natural *abilities* to discriminate things by colour depends on the nature of our visual system. The other is that, given we have this particular kind of visual system rather than another, our colour *concepts* seem to depend on cultural factors, at least to some extent. We need to consider both these aspects.

Colour blindness, and the fact that other animals have different colour-sensitivities from us, help to bring out relevant considerations. Some people cannot tell red from green, and the vision of achromats is something like the night vision of those with normal vision. Human colour vision depends on three systems of receptors in the retina, the 'cones', each system being sensitive to light from a different part of the spectrum. But the grey squirrel has only two cone systems, and so is colour blind compared with us. Some birds and reptiles have four types of colour receptors, and so can make colour discriminations which humans cannot. (I am no zoologist: I picked up these facts from reading.[4]) One consequence of these natural-scientific facts is that it is wrong to say, as was assumed in the retort to Democritus just imagined, that for something to be a certain colour is just for it to reflect or transmit light of a certain wavelength. No simple correlation of colours with wavelengths is possible. For some colours, widely different mixes of wavelengths will produce effects indistinguishable by the human viewer – the same green, the same brown, or whatever. Our classifications of colours depend essentially on specific features of human vision, not purely on patterns of light reflected or transmitted. That is one way in which colour essentially involves human beings, and may also be thought to depend on them. A Martian might have colour vision of *some* kind; but it might easily be different from ours. If we asked it to classify a collection of, say, woollen threads 'by colour', the Martian would in a way understand the request. But its classifications might be different from ours. In that sense colours cannot properly be regarded as provided by nature independently of us. There is no such thing as 'the colours things are' without implicit or explicit relativization to the sort of creature the classification is to be based on.

The point, however, is that colours depend on how things *can* be

---

3 See Chapter 1, section 3, substituting the ancient commentator's 'relative to us' for Democritus' word 'conventionally' (or perhaps 'by convention').

4 See, e.g., the *Oxford Companion to Animal Behaviour*, ed. D. McFarland.

classified by us, not just on how they actually *are* classified. We can still say that things would have had this or that colour even if there had been no human beings. Compare the question whether certain particles would pass through a sieve with a certain mesh. The question whether they *would* pass through the sieve has an answer even if no such sieve actually exists. Similarly we can say that what colour something is depends on how it would be classified by us, and so is independent of our actual existence. So far, then, colours may well be perfectly objective features of things.

Our powers to discriminate colours are given by nature. But how we exploit them depends on our culture, since different cultures emphasize different aspects of the world. It is well known that societies differ in the richness of their colour vocabularies (presumably because of differences in the importance of colour in their lives). Having a comparatively poor colour vocabulary may make it hard to describe colours with the ease and accuracy that a richer vocabulary would have facilitated. But such differences of vocabulary do not prevent people from being able to detect subtle differences between different shades. People from different societies group otherwise similar samples by colour equally well.

The situation appears to be this. Human beings have evolved in ways that have left us with visual capacities of certain particular sorts, and, in particular, we are able to discriminate things by what we call 'colour'. Our ability to make these discriminations depends partly on the different powers of the surfaces of things to reflect light with various wavelengths, partly on the structure of our visual systems. From the fact that we cannot tell two coloured pieces of plastic apart in normal daylight – they look the same – it doesn't follow that their surfaces have the same composition, or even that they reflect the same patterns of light.

However, our ability to make colour discriminations, and to use our inherited colour vocabularies, does not require us to have any conception of the mechanisms of colour vision. So far as we are concerned, while we are innocent of philosophy, a thing's colour strikes us as an objective fact about it. We realize that special lighting conditions can affect the way things look. Normal daylight is best for judging colours. But we tend not to doubt that the colours are out there, and that we can be right or wrong about them. So when Democritus said it is only 'relative to us' that there are colours, it was a strongly 'counter-intuitive' remark: it conflicted with what people unacquainted with his or other theories would be inclined to say. Was he wrong?

John Locke's solution continues to be influential. He suggested that colours (together with the other so-called 'secondary qualities') 'are nothing in the objects themselves, but powers to produce various sensations in us...'.[5] For the ripe tomato to be red is for it to have a power to produce an

5 Locke, *Essay*, Bk. II, ch. viii, sec. 10.

experience of one sort, for the unripe one to be green is for it to have the power to produce an experience of a different sort. The tomato's shape, on the other hand, doesn't depend on any such power: it is a quality of the fruit itself. Shape, motion or rest, quantity and extension, were for Locke 'primary' qualities, which things possessed quite independently of their powers to produce effects on us. Colours, sounds, tastes, smells, in contrast, are 'secondary' qualities: powers in things to produce certain distinctive effects on our experiences. From the point of view of our interest in reality and truth, Locke's was a 'realist' solution. On his account, in contrast to that of Democritus, things really do have colours. It's just that having colours or being sweet involves things being related to human capacities, while having shape, extension and the other primary qualities does not. Clearly that sort of relatedness doesn't detract from the reality or objectivity of colour and sweetness – any more than having the power to promote the growth of plants detracts from the reality of a fertilizer. It is still a matter of objective fact whether a given surface has the power to produce a particular sort of experience in us: whether or not it has that power is independent of what people may believe. Locke's position goes no way towards supporting true-for-me relativism.

Locke's solution is not the end of the story. But the example of colour illustrates one way in which the conception of things and their properties as quite independent of human beings and their capacities, interests and intelligence is too simple. At the same time, Locke's suggestion shows that there may be a certain kind of relatedness to human sensory capacities without loss of objectivity. That sort of relatedness need not imply true-for-me relativism. Still, the example of colour does show that much of what we tend to assume is 'out there' would never have come into our minds if our minds themselves had not had certain special features.

13 More on 'constructing reality'

The notion that we construct reality is exciting, and some of the considerations we have noticed may seem to justify it. But it remains obscure. I will comment on what seem to be the most natural ways to understand it.

'Reality is socially constructed', according to Peter L. Berger and Thomas Luckmann in their book *The Social Construction of Reality*.[6] Do they really think human societies made the sun and the earth? No; that question springs from a misunderstanding. They immediately go on to explain that what interests them is human *conceptions* of reality: it is those which are socially constructed, and whose construction, as sociologists of knowledge, they aim to understand and explain. When they say, for example, 'What is "real" to a

6 Peter L. Berger and Thomas Luckmann, *The Social Construction of Reality*, p.13.

Tibetan monk may not be "real" to an American businessman',[7] they make it clear that they mean the sort of thing that struck the ancient Greeks: different societies and individuals differ in what they take to be real. Berger and Luckmann 'disclaim any pretension to the effect that sociology has an answer' to questions such as 'What is real?'[8] Still, it is striking how easily some of their remarks later in the book can be misconstrued. For example, they say:

> The world of everyday life is not only taken for granted as reality by the ordinary members of society in the subjectively meaningful conduct of their lives. *It is a world that originates in their thoughts and actions, and is maintained as real by these.*[9]

Surely the sun and the moon belong to 'the world of everyday life'. In that case the sentence I have italicized in the passage from Berger and Luckmann implies that the sun and the moon, together with people, animals, plants, rivers, mountains and other familiar things, 'originate in', and are 'maintained as real' by, human thoughts and actions – a truly radical idea. In spite of their highly misleading words, it is nevertheless clear to the careful reader that Berger and Luckmann mean no such thing. What they mean is that how the world of everyday life is *conceived of* in a given society depends on the thoughts and actions of its members – something the strongest realist could not seriously dispute. If that is how the expression 'constructing reality' is to be understood, it does not support any problematic variety of relativism.

Bruno Latour and Steve Woolgar investigated the activities of a scientific laboratory as anthropologists. In their book *Laboratory Life: the Social Construction of Scientific Facts*, they say their 'very specific interest in laboratory life concerns the way in which the daily activities of working scientists lead to the construction of facts'. They describe the laboratory as 'a system of fact construction', and say that 'Scientific activity is not "about nature," it is a fierce fight to *construct* reality'.[10] Such remarks are aggressively relativistic. Even so, the most natural way to interpret them is not that these authors believe scientists working in laboratories actually fix what the scientific facts are, but only that they fix what will be *regarded* as the scientific facts. If that is what they mean, they are not relativists in any interesting sense. However, in this particular case there is evidence that a tame interpretation would be wrong. The authors recognize that readers, 'especially practising scientists, are unlikely to adopt this perspective [that facts are constructed] for very long before returning to the notion that facts exist, and

7 Op. cit., p.15.
8 Op. cit., p.13.
9 Op. cit., p.33. Italics mine.
10 Op. cit., pp.40, 41, 243.

that it is their existence that requires skillful revelation'. They deprecate such 'resistance to sociological explanation'.[11] In the end, although their intention is still not as clear as it might be, they do seem to favour a kind of true-for-me relativism.[12]

This is a good place to recall the familiar point, so provocatively elaborated by Michel Foucault, that conceptions of reality, access to knowledge, and opportunities to think independently, are to a greater or lesser extent influenced by the way power is exercised in society. But having attended to it, we can see that it does not touch the main concerns of this book. It is clearly consistent with a strong realism, according to which *what there really is*, and *the truth about what there really is*, are independent of whether or not any society or any individual exploits them or has any idea of them at all.

Let us return to the idea of constructing reality. Although few would claim that we have anything to do with the existence of the sun and the moon, some realities are certainly the results of our efforts. Social institutions are our own work and 'maintained as real' by our thoughts and actions. One example is money. These pieces of metal and printed paper perform their functions because of our habits, conventions and laws. In that clear sense the existence of money depends on us. Even the metal coins and the paper notes exist only as a result of human activity. But those examples bring out how much of reality cannot easily be regarded as our own work. Metallic ores, and the plants from which paper is made, are independent of us. Once the coins and notes have been manufactured, their places in time and space are matters of fact independently of what people may think – otherwise why bother to hide or steal them?[13]

A different approach may be suggested by reflection on the fact that our information about the world comes via the senses. We are bombarded by sensory stimulation, we detect patterns, and we treat certain patterns in similar ways. Do we detect patterns that are objectively there – that is, independently of what we think – or do we impose them on an otherwise meaningless torrent of stimulation? Is that perhaps how we may be said to 'construct reality'?

Whatever else it involves, that suggestion implies that we, and the stimulation of our senses, exist regardless of what we may think. It is thereby committed to there being at least some realities not 'constructed' by us: it is committed to 'realism' with respect to ourselves and our senses. Still, it

---

11 Op. cit., p.175.
12 Latour and Woolgar may be obscurely advocating what Michael Devitt calls 'constructivism' and criticizes in ch. 13 of his *Realism and Truth* (2nd edn). According to constructivism: (a) 'The only independent reality is beyond the reach of our knowledge and language' (this is what Kant called the world of 'noumena'); (b) 'A known world is partly constructed by the imposition of concepts' (op. cit., p.235).
13 See John Searle, *The Construction of Social Reality*.

leaves quite a lot of construction work for us to do; though how much is not clear. Does it hold that we fix the *ways* our senses are stimulated, or more generally the ways in which sensory input is organized into the experiences we have? The answer must be 'No'. No sane person can maintain that it is always up to us what impinges on our sense organs. That would not just undermine the whole conception of 'sense organs': organs by which things independent of ourselves affect us. It would make nonsense of our experience. We cannot but conceive of ourselves as interacting with a world many of whose features are independent of us. That being so, the suggestion must be merely that we *organize* the torrent of sensory stimulation which is largely independent of us. That is hard to dispute, but a long way from saying we construct reality.

14 'Cosmic porridge'

A more radical version of the idea of constructing reality would involve a sort of 'cosmic porridge'. On this view, all that really exists (apart from ourselves) is an indeterminate something, and – the key component of the idea – this something *has no features of its own*: the porridge is undifferentiated. Instead, we somehow impose features on it – features which depend on which concepts we happen to have. On the one hand, *something* really exists 'out there', but on the other hand nothing else can be said about it which is objectively true, hence nothing else exists which is real. Sticks and stones, atoms and electrons, stars and clouds are our constructions in the strong sense that there is no more to their existence than the fact that we have imposed those particular concepts on the otherwise indeterminate stuff, the cosmic porridge itself.

The idea is not that *we* are our own work. (It had better not be. It makes no sense to say something depends for its existence on itself. To be depended on, it must not at the same time be dependent; but it is also supposed to be dependent – a contradiction.) Nor can the cosmic porridge be our own work. In order for the rest of reality to be our own work, though, the cosmic porridge would have to impose no constraints on how we brought it under our concepts. The trouble is that, as we just noted, we are not free to construct whatever world we choose. It is not in our power to 'think away' floods, hurricanes, earthquakes or injuries. Anyone who believed that would be, if not crazy, then sadly mistaken. (If you disagree, just provide a demonstration of such things being thought away.) What is 'out there' has enough features and properties to impose severe restrictions on our ideas of reality. Since the doctrine is that all such features are our own work, it is untenable for that reason.

A closer look reveals difficulties of interpretation. What would it be to 'impose' features on the undifferentiated stuff? Two contrasted suggestions come to mind. According to one, we bring it about that the stuff which at first lacks features comes to acquire them. No mountains or valleys, no galaxies, no stars, no sticks and stones, no rain, to start with; then, by the mysterious action of our minds, they really come to exist 'out there'. However, if all those things now exist, they are not the kinds of things that could be altered just because people started thinking differently – assuming they could agree on which alterations they wanted. (If they were that kind of thing, praying for rain would work better.) So the other interpretation seems more likely, according to which, 'it's all in the mind'. The cosmic porridge itself is unaffected; all that changes is our experiences, which are, of course, exactly what they would have been if we had been in a world of real galaxies, stars, mountains, valleys and rain. On this second interpretation, the cosmic porridge itself plays no part in explaining our experiences: it might as well not exist. It is hard to see why anyone should believe that (but see the discussion of Berkeley in Chapter 6, section 1).

I am not sure anyone has ever seriously accepted the cosmic porridge doctrine. According to Richard Rorty, both Kant and Frege 'thought of our concepts as carving up an undifferentiated manifold in accordance with our interests'.[14] That would have both philosophers wallowing helplessly in the cosmic porridge – but his interpretation is open to question. (Did they really conceive of the 'manifold' as undifferentiated?) Nietzsche sometimes seems to come close to it, for example when he writes of the 'invention of thinghood and [our] interpreting it into the confusion of sensation'. Like James, he also writes of truth as something which is 'made'.[15] Ernst Mach wrote of the construction of objects from sensations in terms suggestive of the cosmic porridge doctrine; but for him the sensations have properties fixed independently of us. Finally, Hilary Putnam sometimes seems to teeter on the edge of the doctrine, as when he says ' "objects" themselves are...as much products of our conceptual invention as of the "objective" factor in experience, the factor independent of our will...'[16] Those last words appear to save him from toppling in. Even if no one has actually held the full cosmic porridge doctrine, it is worth mentioning as something we can see to be untenable when we confront it squarely, though it can seem attractive to a superficial glance. Any view which has it as a consequence must be rejected for that reason.

What I am calling the cosmic porridge doctrine must be carefully distinguished from the view that it is up to us which words or concepts we use to classify things in the world. It *is* up to us whether and how we use words like 'flood' or 'earthquake'. But that by no means implies that the existence of floods or earthquakes is also up to us: they are there regardless of how we

---

14 R. Rorty, *Consequences of Pragmatism*, p.xxiii.
15 Nietzsche, *The Will to Power*, §552. See also §§500, 501, 511, 521. The quotation from William James is in §101 of the preceding chapter.
16 H. Putnam, *Reason, Truth and History*, p.54

think, classifi*able* by us in those ways if we choose. According to the cosmic porridge doctrine, in contrast, their very existence depends on our classificatory drawing of lines.

Other philosophical approaches may also seem to imply that, in some sense, we 'construct reality'. Some of them will be examined later. But so far it seems that the expression is at best misleading. It is curious how often people writing on these matters say things that more or less deliberately invite misunderstanding. When Jean Baudrillard famously declared that 'the Gulf War did not take place', he was not suggesting that no warlike events of any kind occurred at the times and places in question: he was making political claims about the nature of what happened: points entirely consistent with strong realism.[17] Some of Richard Rorty's claims are similarly misleading, as I will try to make clear in Chapter 9.

MAIN POINTS IN CHAPTER 3

1   When we judge truth we can do so only from within our theory. There can be no 'God's Eye View' (section 1. See also Chapter 9, section 3).

2   'Subjectivism', according to which whatever anyone believes is true, is quickly ruled out. Protagorean or 'true-for-me' relativism is more sophisticated. It is the suggestion that *all there is*, by way of truth, is what is judged true by someone in terms of some theory of the world (section 2).

3   'True-for-me' relativism faces several difficulties: over false beliefs and undiscovered truths (section 3); over the possibility of genuine disagreement and the facts about meaning (sections 6 and 7); over their own existence (section 8); over the fact that we actually do theorize, and the further fact that we do so on the basis that there is a difference between getting things right (full-stop) and wrong (full-stop) (sections 9 and 10).

4   Everyone has to be a realist about something (section 10).

5   The case of colour illustrates different ways in which truths may involve relations to ourselves without losing their claim to absolute validity or objectivity (section 12).

6   The idea that we 'construct reality' is untenable when construed in any interesting way, but has unproblematic interpretations (section 13); unlike the 'cosmic porridge' idea, which is problematic in all ways (section 14).

---

17 See J. Baudrillard, *The Gulf War Did Not Take Place*.

CHAPTER 3: SUGGESTIONS FOR FURTHER READING

For more on **Protagoras**, G. B. Kerferd, *The Sophistic Movement*, gives a scholarly account of the background to Protagoras' thought. M. Burnyeat, *The Theaetetus of Plato*, provides more detailed philosophical discussion of the issues raised in Plato's famous dialogue.

There is a brief discussion of **relativism** on pp.59–75f. of Schmitt, *Truth: a primer*. For a defence of a kind of relativism from an important contemporary philosopher, see Nelson Goodman's *Ways of Worldmaking*. For a number of useful discussions, see Hollis and Lukes (eds) *Rationality and Relativism*. For discussion, see A. C. Grayling, *An Introduction to Philosophical Logic*, ch. 9, and Michael Devitt, *Realism and Truth* (a rather advanced work).

On **colour, etc.**, much has been written about John Locke's distinction between 'primary and secondary qualities'. For his own thoughts, see his *An Essay Concerning Human Understanding*, book II, ch. viii. For an introduction to Locke, see E. J. Lowe, *Locke on Human Understanding*, especially ch. 3. C. L. Hardin, *Color for Philosophers*, offers relevant scientific information. For thought-provoking emphasis on the evolutionary value of colour, see D. C. Dennett, *Consciousness Explained*, pp.370–82.

The idea that **reality is 'socially constructed'** is the theme of Peter L. Berger and Thomas Luckmann's *The Social Construction of Reality*. See also Bruno Latour and Steve Woolgar, *Laboratory Life: the Social Construction of Scientific Facts*; and John Searle, *The Construction of Social Reality*. Michael Devitt devotes ch. 13 of his (advanced) *Realism and Truth* (2nd edition) to 'constructivism'.

Friedrich Nietzsche's views are difficult to extract from his writings. Consult Robert Schacht, *Nietzsche*.

4

WORDS AND WORLD: WITTGENSTEIN

True-for-me relativism doesn't work. It is too crude. But the ideas which seemed to nudge us towards it have not gone away: it is just that true-for-me relativism was the wrong conclusion to draw from them. Nothing said so far threatens, for example, the insight that we cannot judge reality except from within some theory or system of beliefs. What we need is ways to reconcile that insight with the possibility of being objectively right or wrong. We need more sophisticated approaches to the question of how our thoughts relate to reality. Two twentieth-century thinkers have made highly influential contributions to this project: Wittgenstein and Quine. In this chapter I will examine some of Wittgenstein's main ideas.

1 Wittgenstein

The only philosophical book Wittgenstein published in his lifetime is *Tractatus Logico-Philosophicus* (1921).[1] Later he came to think he had made some fundamental mistakes in that work. He died in 1951; *Philosophical Investigations*, which is the chief published source for his later views, did not appear until 1953. The originality, depth and intellectual stringency of Wittgenstein's thought on fundamental topics are enough to explain his enormous influence in philosophy since the 1920s, and to justify the effort of trying to understand him. For unfortunately neither the *Tractatus* nor the *Philosophical Investigations* is easily accessible, even to philosophers, let alone to non-specialists. Both are remarkable pieces of writing; but they don't readily give up their meaning.

The style of the *Tractatus* is compressed and highly polished, with a strong tendency to the gnomic. Its propositions are numbered in a fussy

---

1 Though ready in 1918, this work was not published until 1921, in an ill-corrected German version. For details of the whole saga of the composition and publication of it and of *Philosophical Investigations*, and for a superbly written and insightful account of Wittgenstein's life and work, see Ray Monk, *Ludwig Wittgenstein: the Duty of Genius*.

decimal notation borrowed from engineering textbooks. Here is a sample from the beginning:

1   The world is everything that is the case.

1.1   The world is the totality of facts, not of things.

1.11 The world is determined by the facts, and by their being all the facts.

1.12 For the totality of facts determines both what is the case and whatever is not the case.

1.13 The facts in logical space are the world.

1.2   The world can be decomposed into facts.

The sentences sound tremendously significant, even if you don't get the point of what's being said – and you can't hope to discover that until you've read the whole thing through more than once, preferably with a commentary to hand (which may help to explain why parts of the *Tractatus* have been set to music[2]). Wittgenstein acknowledged in his Preface that his book would perhaps be understood only by those who had already had similar thoughts to those expressed in it.

Its topics are at the heart of philosophy: the relations between thought, language and reality, the nature of logic, the nature of ethics. What must reality be like for us to be able to think and speak about it? What must language be like for it to be capable of describing reality? What is it for sentences to express truths? How can sentences be meaningful? What is it for them to have the meanings they do? What is the nature of logic and mathematics? In the *Tractatus*, Wittgenstein offered definite answers to these and related questions.

For example he maintained that statements are in a certain sense pictures of reality. Each element of a statement corresponds to an element of reality, and:

2.15 That the elements of a picture [statement] are related to one another in a certain way represents the [corresponding] things being related to one another in that way.

How exactly that could be so is not clear, though evidently the account is a very literal version of the correspondence theory of truth.

Wittgenstein was so confident of his solutions to these fundamental

---

2 By Elizabeth Lutyens.

problems that he actually said, again in the Preface: 'The truth of the thoughts communicated here seems to me unassailable and definitive'. However, his doctrine also entailed that many apparently meaningful propositions were strictly meaningless. Near the end of the book we read:

> 6.53 The correct method in philosophy would be this: To say nothing but what can be said, viz. statements of natural science – something which has nothing to do with philosophy – and then, whenever someone else wished to say something metaphysical, to point out to him that he had given no meaning to certain signs in his sentences.

Aware that these remarks imply that most of his own book was unintelligible, he added (proposition 6.54) 'My propositions are explanatory in that someone who understands me eventually recognizes that they are meaningless, when he has climbed out through them, on them, over them. (He must, so to speak, throw away the ladder after he has climbed up it.)'

Philosophical Investigations is unlike the *Tractatus* in several ways. The whole structure is much looser, the individual sentences are fluent and less gnomic; there is less technical jargon – indeed none at all in the ordinary sense, although there are certain special phrases. These differences reflect significant differences in philosophical content and outlook, even though the two works largely share their subject-matter. The tight analytical structure and lapidary style of the *Tractatus* were appropriate for a philosopher setting out 'unassailable and definitive' truths. In the *Investigations* Wittgenstein not only spends a lot of time criticizing his earlier doctrines: he has a different conception of the philosopher's role. Not that he has become less confident of the truth of what he has to say: the point is that now the truths he sets out are, at least when he is following his own advice, commonplaces. According to his new conception of philosophy, 'Philosophy only states what everyone admits' (§599). The main reason for this otherwise puzzling remark is his special, and original, conception of philosophy.

In the past, philosophy has sometimes been conceived of as a sort of superscience, capable of establishing fundamental truths to which all the special sciences have to defer. Both Plato and Aristotle held something like that conception. A very different conception is of philosophy as part of science, as a contributor to the same project as the special sciences, and in no way prior to them. That is in particular the pragmatists' attitude to philosophy, and strongly urged by Quine. Wittgenstein's conception is quite different from both of these. It is encapsulated in the following famous remark:

309 What is your aim in philosophy? – To show the fly the way out of the fly-bottle.[3]

He thinks most philosophy is symptomatic of confusions resulting from the theorist's failure to grasp how words actually work. We 'do not command a clear view of the use of our words',[4] so we find ourselves wrestling with questions that we would never have taken seriously if we had not allowed ourselves to be bamboozled by overhasty, superficial assumptions about how words work. So:

119 The results of philosophy are the uncovering of one or another piece of plain nonsense and of bumps that the understanding has got by running its head up against the limits of language...

Uncovering these 'pieces of nonsense' and exposing these 'bumps' is to be achieved by patiently bringing the philosophical 'fly' to *see* how language actually works and thus escape the trap of tempting but mistaken assumptions. It will not be achieved by further theorizing or arguments. Somehow or other the Wittgensteinian philosophical therapist must ensure that victims are released from the influence of the distorting pictures which almost force themselves on us when we think about thought and language. This is to be done by careful presentation of matters that, once stated, everyone will immediately agree upon:

109 ...we may not advance any kind of theory....We must do away with all explanation, and description alone must take its place. And this description gets its power of illumination – i.e. its purpose – from the philosophical problems. These are, of course, not empirical problems; they are solved, rather, by looking into the workings of our language, and that in such a way as to make us recognise those workings: in despite of an urge to misunderstand them. The problems are solved, not by giving new information, but by arranging what we have always known. Philosophy is a battle against the bewitchment of our intelligence by means of language.

---

3 Numbers heading quotations in this format give the sections of *Philosophical Investigations* from which the quotations are taken. A fly-bottle, by the way, looks like a fat broad-based bottle on small legs. There is a large opening in its base, whose inner wall, with the bottle's outer wall, forms a circular channel containing a fluid attractive to flies. The insects are lured in through the central opening, whose incurving walls frustrate their attempts to escape.
4 *Philosophical Investigations*, §122.

You might have expected that, if *Philosophical Investigations* has the features I have mentioned, it cannot be too hard to understand. Unfortunately that is not so. The point of Wittgenstein's remarks is often hard to discover. Part of the reason is the form of the work. The very nature of the investigation, he says in the Preface, 'compels us to travel over a wide field of thought criss-cross in every direction. – The philosophical remarks in this book are, as it were, a number of sketches of landscapes which were made in the course of these long and involved journeyings'. The result is, in his words, that 'this book is really only an album'. In what follows I will concentrate on one enormously valuable and influential idea: that of language-games.

2 Undermining an ancient assumption

At the start of *Philosophical Investigations* Wittgenstein invites us to consider an imaginary use of language:

> 1 ...I send someone shopping. I give him a slip marked 'five red apples'. He takes the slip to the shopkeeper, who opens the drawer marked 'apples'; then he looks up the word 'red' in a table and finds a colour sample opposite it; then he says the series of cardinal numbers – I assume that he knows them by heart – up to the word 'five' and for each number he takes an apple of the same colour as the sample out of the drawer. – It is in this and similar ways that one operates with words.

Wittgenstein was an unworldly man, but there is no reason to think he imagined this is what actually happens when people go shopping. The example is intended to help break the grip of some of the assumptions we find it so difficult to resist when we think about language. One of those assumptions is that words are meaningful because they name or stand for objects: that 'rabbit' is meaningful because it stands for those furry creatures with long ears and short fluffy white tails; 'green' because it names that colour; 'four' because it names a certain number. (When Parmenides argued that it is impossible to have the thought 'it is not', it looks as if it was this assumption which influenced him most powerfully. The phrase 'that which is not' could not possibly stand for anything, hence on that assumption could not mean anything either, hence could not express a thought.) Wittgenstein's little invented language, or 'language-game', helps us to see how wrong that tempting assumption is.

Consider that string of words 'five red apples' as it is used in the shoppers' language-game. If 'five' names some object, what object is that? You may suggest *the number five*. But how could that supposed object find a place in this particular language-game? If you happen to be Plato, you may argue that numbers are examples of a very special class of objects beyond the reach of our senses, whose relationships explain, among much else, the truths of arithmetic. For example you might maintain that it is true that *two plus two equals four* precisely because of relationships between four of these special objects, addition, equality, and the numbers two and four. You might go on to maintain that we can know that two plus two equals four because we can acquire a special kind of intellectual grasp of these special objects and their relationships. Wittgenstein will invite you to step down from the heights of your theory and look at the language-game he is talking about. He will challenge you to provide a good reason to introduce your special realm of numbers – conceived as a special class of entities in order to account for what happens there. Do you really have to bring them in to explain how that simple language-game works?

Consider what sort of *training* is needed to enable the shopper and the shopkeeper to work the system successfully. Evidently both need to know how to count. (They don't need to be able to count very large numbers, by the way, only the numbers that actually get used in this particular situation.) So they will need plenty of practice, not only in counting but in related activities; for example, the shopkeeper's practice will include the activity of taking pieces of similarly coloured fruit from drawers. Compared with many things we are able to learn, it is not a particularly difficult task. One thing emerges clearly when we contemplate this process. Neither shopper nor shopkeeper need know anything about numbers (as contrasted with number-*words*); nor do we need to introduce numbers into our explanation of what is going on. All we need is the ability to produce the sequence 'one, two, three,…', in accordance with rules we can be trained to follow, plus the physical surroundings of the shop and the ability of shopper and shopkeeper to go through the routines described. None of this calls for any reference to a special realm of entities called 'numbers'. Those remarks can be strengthened. Not only would reference to numbers add nothing to our grasp of what is going on. It would tend to introduce confusion, by making us wonder where these special entities are. So the number-words in the shoppers' language should not be supposed to have their meanings in accordance with the ancient assumption that words have meanings because they name objects.

What about colour-words in this little language? Doesn't 'red' name the *colour* red, 'green' green, and so on? Surely colour-words, at least, are meaningful because they name objects – objects of some special kind? Here again, if we actually look at what goes on, rather than staying frozen in the grip of a theory, we find no support for that assumption. The nearest things to objects that would qualify as 'the colour red' would seem to be either the red apples, or the colour sample on the shopkeeper's list, where colour-words are correlated with colour samples. But no single red apple or collection of red apples can do the job assigned to the colour red in the hallowed name-and-object theory. The colour red may be supposed to ensure that the word keeps its meaning even when there are no examples of it, in which case it cannot be the same as any particular object. But even if examples have to exist in order for the colour to exist (which was Aristotle's view, incidentally, in contrast to Plato's), there are plenty of examples of red things other than the apples in the grocer's drawer – where anyway there might be no red apples. Nor can the colour sample do the job. The way the word 'red' is actually used in this language-game does not justify the suggestion that it names that or any sample. The word performs a certain role in the language-game as a whole; and the shop-keeper matches apples to the colour sample; but the word doesn't *name* that sample. (If you are still doubtful, notice two things. First, the shopper need know nothing about the sample: the shopper's routine will work provided the shopkeeper has *some* way of picking out the red apples. Second, the shopkeeper could perfectly well have been trained to pick out red apples in some different way. Using the sample was just one way of doing it.)

Finally, does the word 'apples' itself work according to the ancient assumption? Does it name an object? You might think so: doesn't it name apples? Even here the situation is nothing like as simple as that model suggests. The shopkeeper has a drawer marked 'apples'. What if the drawer is empty? Does it follow that the word 'apples' in this language-game no longer has any meaning? Clearly not: there may be no apples in the drawer just now, but there may be some in boxes, waiting to be transferred. Even if there are none in the shop, there still could be. An apple shortage would not prevent the word retaining its meaning in the language-game. It follows that the word's having its meaning does not consist in its naming any red apples that may happen to be in the drawer. Even if, for whatever bizarre reason, there were at present no apples in the whole world, that would still not prevent the word retaining its meaning (would it?). So in this case, as in the very different cases of the other two words in the shopper's sentence, the meaningfulness of these words cannot consist in their naming objects. The whole ancient assumption – which Wittgenstein himself had expressed in such confident crystalline fashion in the *Tractatus* – seems not only unjusti-fied if we look at how language actually works, but actively misleading. As he puts it, 'That philosophical concept of meaning has its place in a primi-tive idea of the way language functions.'[5]

5   Op. cit., §2.

3 Language-games

Wittgenstein remarks: 'For a *large* class of cases – though not for all – in which we employ the word "meaning" it can be defined thus: the meaning of a word is its use in the language'.[6] We have seen that the meanings of words cannot in general be things such as rabbits or colours; nor, contrary to the suggestions of Plato and many others, can meanings be a special class of entities quite different from things such as rabbits, occupying a realm of existence beyond the reach of our senses and accessible only to the intellect. Those philosophical theories spring from mistaken assumptions. One thing Wittgenstein's imagined 'language-games' do is to help us see for ourselves how mistaken those assumptions are, and to reduce the appeal of a mistaken picture of how language works. In addition to that negative purpose they also have the positive purpose of helping us see what is actually involved in the meaningfulness of linguistic expressions, and more generally what is involved in relations between words and the world.

Wittgenstein's discussions of language-games illustrate clearly how our use of language is one kind of behaviour among others, in particular how it is a special kind of rule- or norm-governed behaviour, serving a whole range of needs and purposes, and involving many kinds of interaction among people, and between people and the world. Contrary to what earlier theorists (including himself in the *Tractatus*) had supposed, there is no single answer to such questions as 'What is the meaning of a word?' or 'What is language?' or 'How do words relate to the world?' Instead there is a whole range of different sorts of linguistic behaviour, interwoven with activities involving other people and the rest of the world, which can be illuminated by considering a range of different language-games, and by noting similarities and dissimilarities between the rule-governed activity of linguistic behaviour and other sorts of rule- or norm-governed behaviour, such as games.

Immediately after the shoppers' language-game Wittgenstein describes another:

> 2 ...The language is meant to serve for communication between a builder A and an assistant B. A is constructing a building from components. There are blocks, pillars, slabs and beams available. B has to pass the components to A in the order in which he needs them. For that purpose they use a language consisting of the words 'block', 'pillar', 'slab', 'beam'. A calls them out; B brings the component he has learnt to bring at such-and-such a call. – Conceive of this as a complete primitive language.

---

6 Op. cit., §43.

In contrast to the shoppers' language-game, this provides some basis for thinking of its words as names for objects. When people are learning it they will in a way 'name' objects. The trainee may repeat the words after the trainer, who will no doubt point to the different kinds of components. Something like this 'naming' goes on when infants are learning to talk – a fact which no doubt has made it natural to assume that for words to be meaningful is for them to name objects. But this language-game, like the first, also helps to bring out the point that there are many ways for words to be meaningful without being describable as names. Although he introduces the builders' language by saying it is one for which the 'name-object' description is right, he makes clear that even there the description is at best misleading. The way the words 'block', 'slab' and the rest function involves a great deal that is both more than, and different from, what might be called mere naming. By uttering one of these expressions the builder *gives an instruction* to the assistant: gets the latter to pass the appropriate item. In different language-games, exactly the same utterance could have resulted in the assistant just looking at the item, or sitting on it, or breaking it up with a hammer – all different from what happens in the language-game described, and different again from merely naming the item.

Wittgenstein describes some ways in which the builders' language might be extended. It could include a series of numerals used similarly to the shopkeeper's use of them; it could include some colour samples; and it could include the words 'there' and 'this'. A could then give an order like 'Four–slab–there', at the same time showing the assistant a colour sample and pointing to a place on the site. B complies by taking one slab for each numeral up to 'four', of the same colour as the sample, to the place indicated. Or A might simply order 'This–there', pointing first to a building component, then to where to put it.

He is not saying that 'natural' languages, such as English, German or Chinese, have actually developed from such language-games, nor that these are in any straightforward way components of ordinary languages. He is drawing attention to various features of language-games in order to bring us to acknowledge some of the facts about language in general that philosophical theories have tended to ignore – such as the fact that words are meaningful in many different ways, not just because they 'name' things.

Two further points about this brilliant device need emphasis. One is that the workings of these imaginary language-games are so easy to grasp that we can see there is no mystery involved – at any rate nothing more mysterious than the fact that we are creatures capable of being trained, or at any rate habituated, to pick up patterns of behaviour like those described. The other point is that these patterns of behaviour are of kinds which don't belong uniquely to language. They are, for example, in some ways like the patterns we find in children's games.

4 Building up to meaning, truth and knowledge

One thing Wittgenstein's examples help us to understand is how some words can intelligibly be said to pick out, or *refer* to, things in the world, and how other words may *apply to* things. Recall the remarks about elementary sentences in Chapter 2. 'Alf' was assumed to pick out Alf, 'Beth' Beth, and so on. 'Bald' was supposed to apply to an individual just in case that individual was bald, 'happy' if and only if the individual was happy, and so on. When we first considered those ideas they seemed mysterious. What is it for words to pick out or apply to things? But with Wittgenstein's examples to brood over, further reflection suggests there is no intractable mystery here. His discussions free us from the assumption that there has to be a single answer to the question of what it is for a word to pick out or apply to something. Instead, expressions can be put to work in a whole variety of ways. He compares the variety of word-uses with that of the tools in a tool-box.[7]

There is a clear and unproblematic way in which, in the builders' language, the words 'slab', 'pillar' and the rest 'pick out' kinds of building components. By choosing the right word the builder can get the assistant to bring a particular sort of component – for the assistant has been trained to do just that. No doubt the assistant was rewarded for bringing a slab when, and only when, the builder called 'slab', and punished for doing anything different. Once that utterance reliably ensures that slabs, and only slabs, are picked out and passed along, we can say that 'slab' picks out or refers to those components. It is a fact about human beings that they *can* be trained to do such things. So the business of 'picking out' or 'referring' to things has become unmysterious. In Wittgenstein's words, 'everything lies open to view'.[8]

When the builders' language has been extended to include 'this', it has the resources to enable the builder to ensure that the assistant moves a particular individual block, beam, or whatever. Notice, though, that the builders' language, even in its extended version, illustrates only some aspects of the multiplicity of ways in which words can be said to pick out or refer to things. Other aspects are illustrated by the shopping language, but others are different again. I will not pursue the matter: it seems to me that although there are all sorts of technical problems surrounding the idea of reference, the philosophical ones are no longer serious. (However, that remark is contentious: there is today a lot of detailed philosophical argument about reference.)

The other notion was that of adjectives 'applying to' things. In the sentence 'Socrates is wise', for example, once the individual Socrates has been picked out by means of his name, the adjective 'wise' is applied to him. That particular sentence can be used to make a *statement*: to say something

---

7   See *Philosophical Investigations*, §§ 11, 14.
8   Op. cit., §126.

that might be true or false. Neither the shoppers' nor the builders' language provides for statements. But by following Wittgenstein's hints we can expand the builders' language so that it includes statement-making sentences. There are various ways to do this, but for a bit of fun let us imagine a rather extravagant possibility: the builders use personal names for individual blocks, slabs, and so on; they call one slab 'Bill', another 'Fred', and so on. Suppose too that they have a number of colour words. With that equipment they can use utterances of the two forms 'This grey', 'Fred brown', in ways it is easy to imagine (following the example of the Russian language in leaving out 'is').

We know the existence of a language-game depends on the possibility of training. Its players have to be capable of learning to behave in certain ways in certain kinds of situation. In the present case, if there is a brown slab, say, appropriately linked by the rules with the expression 'Fred', and someone says 'Fred brown', they are rewarded with approval (they use 'black', 'brown', 'grey' and the rest more or less as we would). If on the other hand they say 'Fred black' in the same situation, they are not rewarded but corrected. That is how they are trained to behave in accordance with the rules or norms of this particular language-game. Following the rules involves, for example, saying 'This grey' only when faced with a building component that is in fact grey. We can now note some extremely important points.

5 Meaning, truth and knowledge

First, the very existence of the language-game depends on its players following the rules, at least most of the time. It is not a matter of politeness or consideration for others – as promoted by signs like 'Keep off the grass'; nor of mere rules of linguistic style, like avoiding split infinitives. The point is that there just wouldn't be a language at all unless the people who spoke it generally kept to the rules. It is *only* because they do so that they can use certain patterns of sound as words and sentences; only because the noise we represent by 'grass', for example, is regularly used in the way that it is that it *means* grass in the first place. Not only would widespread persistent breaking of such linguistic rules be counter-productive: it just could not be done. Without general conformity there would be no rules there to be broken. Utterances become useless if not reliably linked with conditions for their use.

Second, when the players do behave according to the rules, most of the time they will produce an utterance such as 'Fred grey' only when the slab or whatever it is that they pick out by means of 'Fred' is in fact grey. And that seems to amount to the same thing as saying that *most of the time utterances of that sort will be true*. It is not necessary for the players themselves to use a word like 'true'. They need only be capable of expressing approval – or disapproval, for example when someone says 'Fred grey' when the component in question is brown. So, for this particular little language-game at least, the possibility of its assertions or statements being true or false seems not to be mysterious. Indeed the fact that its assertions are typically true is so far from being mysterious that it is clear there could not be such assertions at all unless that were so. The point becomes even clearer when we consider that, in order for our language to be capable of being learned or taught, we must be capable of *telling* when infants or foreigners are using its expressions correctly. If an infant says 'Raining' when it's not raining, for example, we tend to put them right – which means we can often tell whether or not they are speaking the truth. (Not on every occasion; but often enough to be able to ensure they are following the rules.)

Although the remarks in the last paragraph are brief, they are extraordinarily important. By themselves they amount to an explanation of how at any rate some kinds of truth are possible: how we can capture reality in words. Provided we do not later find reasons to reject this conclusion, it now at last begins to look as if the pursuit of truth is not a wild goose chase.

The third point I want to make concerns knowledge. What is knowledge? I will not go deeply into that ancient question. But one thing has generally been accepted from the time of Plato: knowledge is not just a matter of true belief. In a law court, for example, merely believing the prisoner in the dock is innocent is not enough to ensure you know it, even if the prisoner really is innocent. As Plato himself pointed out, you might have been induced to believe the prisoner was innocent by the thoroughly misleading arguments of a clever lawyer – who could as easily have persuaded you that the prisoner was guilty.[9] So it is widely held that if your true belief is to count as knowledge, you must have some kind of respectable justification or warrant for it. The point is that in our little language-game there is already provision for such justification.

If a speaker of this language-game utters, for example, 'This black' in appropriate circumstances, not only will that utterance be acceptable and true; it will also be warranted and justified: as justified or 'epistemically virtuous' as it is possible to be. It is not as if there could be some circumstances in which the speaker could have been significantly better justified in producing it. So on most accounts of knowledge the speaker will count as *knowing* what is asserted by means of that utterance. Nor is that just a happy coincidence. The circumstances in which such utterances are in accordance with the rules or norms of the language-game have to be, in general, ones in which such utterances are justified. (Or could there possibly be other considerations, outside that language-game's rules or norms, which could provide independent justification? It seems not. Certainly the language-game is not

9 See Plato, *Theaetetus*, 201a–d (using the standard page-numbering for Plato's works).

cut off from other activities. It may or may not suit the players' purposes well. But it is hard to see how an utterance made inside that language-game could be justified from outside it.)

Fourth, since there is nothing outside the language-game that could give meaning to its expressions, there is no higher authority to appeal to in judging whether speakers are using a given expression correctly, hence in judging what it means. If the speakers of our little language-game agree in using the utterance 'This brown' in circumstances where *we*, as speakers of English, would classify the object picked out as black, we should be in no position to tell them they had got it wrong. That little language-game is after all *their* language; we shall conclude that their 'brown' means the same as our 'black'. (There is an important qualification to be noted in this connection: see the remarks about theoretical language, on the next page.)

6 The state of play

To summarize the points made so far:

(a) The device of language-games helped Wittgenstein with what he believed was philosophy's main task: to reveal ways out of the confusions we tend to get into when we lose sight of how words actually work.

(b) One long-standing confusion has been our tendency to assume that words are meaningful purely because they stand for things. The shoppers' language-game illustrates how wrong that assumption is. Words are generally meaningful not because they stand for things, but because they have some *use* in our lives; and their uses are very various.

(c) At the same time the idea of language-games helps us to see that the meaningfulness of words is not mysterious – no more than the fact that we can be trained to play games according to rules. Using words is one kind of rule-governed behaviour; playing football and chess are others.

(d) The existence of a language-game is totally dependent on its players following the rules.

(e) Most of the time, when the players of a language-game make assertions in accordance with the rules, their assertions will be *true*. It is only because we can usually tell whether or not they are following the rules that the language can be learned and taught.

(f) Most of the time, when the players of a language-game make assertions in accordance with the rules, those assertions will be not only true but *justified*.

(g) If the speakers of a given language-game agree in their use of a given word or other expression, for example a colour-word like 'red', their judgement is final. There is no higher authority.

Those ideas provide a solid basis for improving our understanding of how it is possible to capture reality in our thoughts and words. At the same time, as we shall see, they suggest some interesting relativistic theories.

7 Some difficulties

Does the last section settle the main questions about meaning and truth? Can we breathe again, and turn to something else? Unfortunately things are not so simple – at any rate not for all types of statements. I will mention three areas where difficulties lurk.

One concerns the meaning and truth of statements incorporating highly theoretical words, such as those of particle physics. All the language-games so far considered are restricted to expressions whose use is rather directly related to readily identifiable items in everyday life: fruit, building components, and their colours and quantities. But theoretical statements, for example those about 'vector bosons' or the 'colours' of 'quarks', are only indirectly related to everyday life. We can't see or touch the entities those expressions apparently refer to. Such expressions are only intelligible to people who have received a training in theoretical physics – a special sort of language-game. So it is correspondingly more difficult to tell whether or not what is said is actually the case. The use of these theoretical language-games is less perspicuous, less easily 'surveyable', to use Wittgenstein's word. That doesn't mean the idea of language-games is of no help in connection with theories. It can be applied to them as well as to everyday components of language. Just as we can be trained to engage in the kind of behaviour we describe as 'talking about fruit and vegetables', so we can be trained to engage in the rather more complicated behaviour described as 'talking about quarks and vector bosons'. The point is that not everything said in the last sections can be assumed to carry over automatically to theoretical language. Since a great deal of our language is tied up with some sort of theory, that is important.

A second area of difficulty shows up when we think of the different attitudes our statements may express. We are often interested in facts; but we are also interested in matters of taste and feeling. Without benefit of philosophy we tend to distinguish questions of fact from questions of taste or 'subjective opinion'. Is the sun larger than the earth? – surely a question of fact, with an answer that doesn't depend on tastes or values or preferences. Is treacle tart nice? – a question of taste. But what about these questions: Is there a God? Is killing ever justified? Do animals have rights? Is Picasso's 'Guernica' a good picture? – are these questions of fact or just questions of taste or opinion? Are they statements which may be true or false, or do such notions not apply to them?

The third area of difficulty is raised by the fact that we can be *trained* to follow the rules of a language-game, and of our native language. Involved in the fact that we can be trained to follow rules or conform to norms are facts about our abilities to recognize likenesses, to find certain kinds of things salient, and to agree with one another in what we count as 'behaving acceptably' and 'not behaving acceptably', 'following the rules' and 'not following the rules'. Wittgenstein had penetrating things to say about these matters.

8 More on rule-following

A foreigner looks admiringly at a horse and remarks, 'A fine cow'. Suppose this person actually trains horses, so there is no possibility that they don't realize what sort of animal stands neighing in front of them. It's just that they mistakenly assume the word 'cow' applies to such animals. Wittgenstein would say they don't know the rules for using the English word 'cow'. He would also say it is only because there are such rules that we are in a position to put the foreigner right.

As our consideration of language-games has shown, he also thinks the very existence of a language depends on there being such rules. The rules that matter are not minor rules of spelling or grammar, but ones that enable us to do useful things with our words – which in some sense connect our use of words with the things the words are about. If you are still in doubt about this view, try to imagine a language without any rules at all. For example, try to imagine a word that could be used in any situation whatever, whenever you liked. Could there be such a word? If so, would it be of the slightest use to us? Some swear-words may seem to fill the bill; yet even they tend to be used only when there is some strong feeling to be expressed. (That isn't always so, but if so, surely, the words really have become meaningless.[10]) Certainly a word usable on any occasion whatever could not be used to convey information, or perform any other act, except by accident. Like coughing, making that particular noise might have the useful effect of drawing attention to the fact that you were among those present. But in such cases any noise would do: the effect doesn't depend on which noise it is.

Consider the situation from a different angle. If linguistic expressions do not owe their significance to rules or conventions, what on earth makes them significant at all? Bear in mind that there is no limit to the number of different patterns of sound or shape that could have served to represent words. Whether or not a given pattern is meaningful does not depend on the nature of the pattern itself. It would be ridiculous to suggest that the pattern represented by 'by', for example, is *intrinsically* meaningful. That pattern is

---

10 As in these remarks fictionally attributed to the Teamster union boss Jimmy Hoffa in James Ellroy's *American Tabloid*: 'I've spent six hundred grand on the primaries and bought every fucking cop and alderman and councilman and mayor and fucking grand juror and senator and judge and DA and fucking prosecutorial investigator who'd let me. I'm like Jesus trying to part the Red Fucking Sea and not getting no further than some motel on the beach' (p.293).

meaningful only because of how it is used. But how it is used is bound up with the rules or conventions for using it. Again, the conclusion seems inevitable: the existence of meaningful language depends on rules (or conventions or norms). (We can bend or break the rules on occasions, for some special effect, of course, as with metaphors and jokes.)

There is no implication that the rules or norms we follow when we use our native language in the ordinary way are ones we could easily formulate, much less that following them requires us to be able to formulate them. We just pick them up by living among speakers of the language when we are infants. There are plenty of children's games whose rules (or norms or conventions, if you prefer) are similarly inexplicit yet usable, as Wittgenstein pointed out. One point he insists on is that conceivably someone, in other respects like one of us, should have lacked the same innate tendencies that all human beings seem to share, notably our tendencies to react to similar training in similar ways. The point is glaringly obvious for the case of our sensitivities to colours, as we noticed in the last chapter. We have evolved so that certain wavelength-distributions are particularly salient, while those above and below the 'visible spectrum' are not, though they are noticeable to other creatures such as snakes or bees. But those tendencies and capacities are not the ones Wittgenstein is most concerned with. More important are our tendencies to agree among ourselves when it is a question of whether or not someone is following the rules.

9 The Odd Adder

To illustrate this point Wittgenstein invites us to consider a strange imaginary case. One kind of language-game involves training someone to write down a series of signs, say those for numbers, according to a certain rule. The first is the rule for writing down the natural numbers (1, 2, 3, 4,...) in ordinary notation. Getting the pupil to do that will involve a lot of practice, copying, trial and error – and may fail altogether if the pupil lacks the usual capacities or tendencies. But suppose that phase of the training is successful. Next we teach our pupil, in Wittgenstein's own words:

> 185 ...to write down other series of cardinal numbers and get him to the point of writing down series of the form
>
> $$0, n, 2n, 3n, \text{etc.}$$
>
> at an order of the form '+n'; so at the order '+1' he writes down the series of natural numbers. – Let us suppose we have done exercises and given him tests up to 1000.
>
> Now we get the pupil to continue a series (say +2) beyond 1000 – and he writes 1000, 1004, 1008, 1012.

We say to him: 'Look what you've done!' – He doesn't understand. We say: 'You were meant to add *two*: look how you
began the series!' – He answers: 'Yes, isn't it right? I thought
that was how I was *meant* to do it.' – Or suppose he pointed to
the series and said: 'But I went on in the same way.' – It would
now be no use to say: 'But can't you see…?' – and repeat the old
examples and explanations. – In such a case we might say,
perhaps: It comes natural to this person to understand our
order with our explanations as *we* should understand the order:
'Add 2 up to 1000, 4 up to 2000, 6 up to 3000 and so on.'

It is important that the Odd Adder has *not* just made an ordinary mistake,
not just failed to add 2. The point is that, although he is like us in many
ways, he is different from us internally: presumably his brain works differently from ours in some subtle respects. He has received exactly the same
training in counting and adding as the rest of us have; and to start with he
seems to have come away from it with the same results. But then, when he is
required to apply that training to a case he has not so far come across, he
goes completely haywire – or so it strikes us.

The case brings home to us how the mere *statement* of a rule cannot by
itself completely determine what counts as following it. Not even the statement of the rule in the context of a certain type of training can determine
what counts as following it. What counts as following the rule depends
partly on the inbuilt tendencies of members of the community whose rule it
is, on how their brains work. Conceivably there might have been a community who all shared the same inbuilt tendencies as the Odd Adder, where the
Odd Adder would have been entirely at home and we should have been the
weird aliens. In one main sense of an expression used by Wittgenstein, they
would have shared the Odd Adder's 'form of life'. They might have been
perfectly capable of agreeing among themselves on what counted as
following *their* rules; and they might even have been able to operate rules for
their ways of doing arithmetic. But we should not be able to follow their
rules. They would regard us as bizarrely stupid or crazy – just as at first we
are inclined to regard the Odd Adder. The difference, however, is in form of
life.

The point of this example is by no means limited to arithmetic. Similar
considerations apply to all kinds of rule-following, including, of course,
ordinary linguistic rule-following. The fact that we agree in what we count as
using words and constructions according to the rules depends partly on our
innate dispositions and tendencies, not on what we might think of as statements of those rules.

All of which may seem to feed relativizing tendencies. I will return to the
example later in the book.

MAIN POINTS IN CHAPTER 4

1 Wittgenstein's idea of 'language-games' is a valuable aid to deepening our understanding of the ideas of meaning and truth, and their relations to reality (sections 2–6).
2 One main implication is that there is no uniquely correct or simple answer to questions such as 'What is the meaning of a word?' or 'How do words relate to things?' (sections 2–5).
3 Reflection on some kinds of language-games helps us to understand how the meaningful use of language can provide for truth, justification and knowledge. That gives at least part of the answer to the question of how we can capture reality in thoughts and words, and thereby seems to justify the view that the pursuit of truth is not a wild goose chase (sections 5 and 6).
4 That there can be rules or norms governing our uses of expressions depends on facts about our inbuilt dispositions and tendencies which might have been different. If we ignore this we cannot properly understand how meaningful discourse is possible (sections 8 and 9).

CHAPTER 4: SUGGESTIONS FOR FURTHER READING

Though ready in 1918, Wittgenstein's *Tractatus Logico-Philosophicus* was not published until 1921, in an ill-corrected German version. A version with parallel English translation appeared in 1922. See also the translation by D. F. Pears and B. F. McGuinness. For details of the whole saga of the composition and publication of it and of *Philosophical Investigations*, and for a superbly written and insightful account of Wittgenstein's life and work, see Ray Monk, *Ludwig Wittgenstein: the Duty of Genius*.

It is extremely hard to grasp the point of Wittgenstein's key text, *Philosophical Investigations*, without guidance. Anthony Kenny, *Wittgenstein*, remains a good general introduction. See also Marie McGinn, *Wittgenstein and the* Philosophical Investigations. An advanced book, David Pears, *The False Prison*, has illuminating discussions of both the early and the later work. For an exhilarating controversial development of Wittgenstein's ideas in this area, though it too is not elementary, see Saul Kripke, *Wittgenstein on Rules and Private Language*.

5

WORDS AND WORLD: QUINE

W. V. Quine (born 1908) is in many philosophers' opinion one of the greatest philosophers of this century. Unlike Russell and Wittgenstein, his name is scarcely known outside the narrow circle of professional philosophers and their students. He has made important contributions to discussion of most of the main problems tackled by Wittgenstein, but usually in very different ways. Like Wittgenstein, he offers his own promising approach to the central questions of how it is possible for thoughts and theories to latch on to reality, and how far, if at all, reality and truth depend on us. Also like Wittgenstein, his suggestions lend themselves to relativizing interpretations. In this chapter I shall be concerned to set out Quine's main ideas in the areas that interest us. How far they really support relativism, and, if so, what kind of relativism, are questions for later chapters.

1 Quine's naturalism

Influenced by James and other pragmatists, Quine has developed a view that is in some respects similar to theirs. He is a 'naturalist'. That is, he regards the task of discovering the nature of reality as part of science. To the extent that philosophy is concerned with that task, it, too, is part of science and cannot be an independent basis for contributing to our theory of the world:

> What reality is like is the business of scientists, in the broadest sense, painstakingly to surmise; and what there is, what is real, is part of that question. The question how we know what there is is simply part of the question...of the evidence for truth about the world.[1]

Quine sees us as organisms that have arrived at our present stage of development as a result of evolution. Our use of language to construct theories is

---

1 W. V. Quine, *Word and Object*, pp.22f.

74

itself an evolved pattern of behaviour, kept going by social factors: 'Language is a social art'.[2] A truly scientific account of our ability to use language would have to specify the neurological patterns underlying linguistic behaviour. In the absence of such an account, we should focus on the behaviour. Talking and writing are, after all, things we *do*. Since our ability to use language is not fully accounted for by a mere description of our actual utterances – as we noticed earlier, there are countless sentences that will never actually have been constructed – we had better think in terms of behavioural 'dispositions': not what we actually do, but what we would do if certain conditions were satisfied. This idea calls for some explanation.

2 Dispositions

I may never actually say that human beings don't sprout leaves like trees; but I *would* say it if it ever seemed appropriate. That means I am disposed to accept that statement if asked. Two comparisons may help to make this idea clearer. One is with a lump of sugar. Thanks to features of its microscopic structure, it dissolves in water; yet a particular lump of sugar may never come into contact with any water: it might be crushed by a hammer or burnt up. Even so, it is solu*ble*, it has a *disposition* to dissolve in water, which means it *would* dissolve if it *were* left in water. Another useful comparison (though it is not one Quine tends to use) is with a programmed computer. A complicated program endows the machine with a hugely complex system of interlocking behavioural dispositions. The computer's memory makes it a significantly different sort of thing from a sugar lump, which has, in effect, just one internal state. The computer's memory enables it to be in any of a vast number of different internal states. The program currently running determines what happens when a given sequence of keystrokes is typed in, given the machine's current internal state. Typically, different internal states will yield different outputs even if the same input is typed in. (The same is true even for a simple pocket calculator: if you key in '=' when it's in the state resulting from your just having keyed in '2 + 2', it will put out '4'; if you key in '=' when you have keyed in '3 + 3' it will put out something else.) There is no simple 'stimulus–response' relation between inputs and outputs.

The idea of dispositions takes care of a lot of facts about a system that may never show up in its actual behaviour. Consider for example a computer programmed to play chess. It may have been given to a spoilt child who plays only one game on it then throws it away. If so, it will never have displayed its chess-playing abilities. All the same, *if* it had been faced with such-and-such a position, it *would* have moved its Queen to *a*5; if it had been faced with that other position, it would have castled; and so on. If the

2 Op. cit., p.ix.

program is very complicated, as it may be, specifying the machine's chess-playing dispositions would be extremely difficult, especially if those dispositions included ones to change other dispositions – that is, to learn. Yet, because the machine's behaviour is controlled by a certain definite program, a specification of its dispositions could be provided, and would be correct if it accurately reflected the behaviour laid down by the program.

Quine thinks our ability to speak a language similarly constitutes a vast and hugely complex system of dispositions, built up and modified in the course of our lives as a result of interacting with other people and the things around us.

3 Quine on language, knowledge and belief

For Quine's purposes it is convenient to think of our knowledge of the world, and our beliefs in general, as represented by a huge system of sentences. At any instant there is a set of sentences that we hold true at that instant, in the sense that we are disposed to accept or 'assent to' any one of those sentences. At the moment, for example, if anyone asks, I am disposed to assent to 'Summer has come at last', 'There goes a rabbit', 'The battle of Hastings was in 1066', 'There have been black dogs', '2 + 2 = 4', and a vast number of others. If we conceive of *all* the sentences I am disposed to assent to at a given moment, they embrace my entire 'theory of the world', together with all my transient beliefs about how things are in the particular tiny portion of space and time I happen to occupy. Speak any of these sentences with a querying intonation, and I will say 'Yes', or nod, or otherwise assent.

This complex system of interconnected behavioural dispositions, represented by the sentences to which I am disposed to assent, is a vital device for dealing with the world. It is *practically* useful. (Compare William James's remark about theories as 'instruments' in Chapter 2, section 10.) The fact that each of us has such a sentence-system is partly a result of the sort of creatures we have become by evolution, partly a result of having been brought up in our own particular environment. Now for a crucial feature: these dispositions are constantly being revised. I shall cease to have the disposition to assent to 'The weather's fine' if I notice spots of water on the window and rain-clouds covering the sky, for example. In that way the network of sentences that represents my beliefs is constantly changing as my experience changes. But many of my beliefs represent much more central aspects of my total 'theory of the world' than transitory experiences can affect in any direct way. They include the theoretical framework in terms of which I think about my experience and deliberate about things. So they are rather well insulated from the flow of experience. However, reflection on that theoretical framework itself may lead me to change some of my more central beliefs. Such reflection may be spontaneous, or it may be prompted by experience. New historical research might even prompt me to reconsider my belief about the date of the Battle of Hastings. Experience is one main factor influencing revisions to my total system of beliefs; another is the need to keep the whole system manageable, which tends to make us avoid change as far as possible – to be 'conservative' – but also to keep things simple. It was the need for the system to be manageable that eventually induced astronomers to abandon their long-held view that the planets move round the earth, and to adopt instead the theory that on the contrary the planets, the earth among them, orbit the sun.

4 Revising beliefs

If an experience drives me to revise some of the sentences that I currently hold true, it is 'recalcitrant' to my system. Here we encounter an important Quinean idea. We might have assumed that a particular recalcitrant experience would force me to revise some *particular* sentence or sentences and no others. Quine denies this. *A recalcitrant experience doesn't determine just which revisions have to be made.* In the case of 'The weather's fine', for example, I might on reflection decide that it wasn't rain that was falling on the windows after all, but just someone on the roof using a pump to water the flower-pots there. In that case I would not give up that particular sentence. I would just bring into my web of beliefs the belief that someone upstairs was doing some watering. Which revisions we make depends on a number of factors, including the nature of the actual experiences; but the practical needs to avoid unnecessary change and to keep things simple are always among them. They ensure the system functions as a whole, not just as a collection of individual atoms. This idea – that we have to consider a system of beliefs as a whole – is Quine's 'holism', to which I will return in section 7.

He makes two remarkable claims in connection with revisions to our system. One is that 'no statement is immune to revision'. Contrary to a strong tradition in philosophy, according to which certain statements, called 'analytic', are necessarily true and cannot possibly be revised, he denies there is any such distinction. 'All bachelors are unmarried' is a simple example of an analytic statement; and you might well wonder how on earth anyone could consider it somehow subject to revision; but Quine insists that it is. The other remarkable claim, linked to the first, is that 'any statement can be held true come what may' provided we are willing to make sufficiently drastic revisions in the remainder of the system, including, perhaps, revisions of 'statements of the kind called logical laws'. I will discuss these claims later (section 7). Just now I am focusing on the implications of this approach for questions about existence, reality, and truth.

5 Wittgenstein and Quine on science, language and philosophy

Earlier, I said 'everyone must surely agree' with the points Wittgenstein makes with the aid of his examples of language-games. But in philosophy you never get everyone agreeing. Among philosophers hostile to much of Wittgenstein's approach are those who regard our ordinary ways of talking about mental states such as belief, desire, intention and relatedly meaning, as deeply flawed or even false. The most distinguished representative of that approach is Quine.

As we noticed just now, he holds that a truly scientific account of our behaviour, in particular our verbal behaviour, would have to specify the neural patterns underlying it. Since at present we lack such specifications, the next best thing, in Quine's view, is talking in terms of behavioural dispositions. He thinks such talk is more hygienic than talking about meaning, sameness of meaning, intentions, beliefs, desires, or other mental states. He admits we have no serious alternative to using these intellectually unhygienic notions at present. But he argues that they tend to reflect no more than rough ways of interpreting what goes on, rather than describing what is really the case. (More on this shortly.)

As we also noted, he thinks it is up to scientists to decide 'what there is, what is real'. Scientists 'in the broadest sense' include philosophers of Quinean stripe. For him, philosophy cannot claim to occupy some independent position from which it can judge science. On the contrary, philosophy is a contribution to the seamless web of science. And 'The last arbiter', when it comes to judging what there is, and how we know what there is, 'is scientific method, however amorphous'.[3]

That view is starkly opposed to the conception of philosophy as a kind of superscience with the means to judge science, religion, and all other human claims about knowledge – a conception Wittgenstein also rejected. However, Quine is at odds with Wittgenstein's conception too. For Wittgenstein, science is one kind of 'language-game' or cluster of interrelated language-games (in a broad sense of that expression). Philosophy, in contrast, though perhaps a language-game in some sense, is different in many ways. It is not at all concerned with discovering 'what there is'. It does not build up theories. It is not a kind of inquiry, but more like a skill, a method of therapy, aimed at freeing us from confusion.

Quine is obviously in favour of battling against the 'bewitchment of our intelligence' too. But he sees more in philosophy than that battle alone, valuable though it is. Theorizing about the nature of theories, and about their relation to reality, is very much part of his scientific–philosophical project.

3 Op. cit., p.23.

6 'Posits'

An intriguing notion Quine uses when talking about our theories of the world is that of 'positing' things. What he means is that, in our theorizing, we find it necessary to say 'there are' certain kinds of things, or that they 'exist'. For example, readers of this book are likely to agree with me that *there are rabbits*; which in Quinese means that we 'posit' rabbits. (The animals, the things we thereby posit, are themselves 'posits'.) Equivalently we posit things by saying for example 'Some rabbits have white fur'; 'Some black holes are bigger than the sun'; for by talking in terms of *some* things of a kind we are committing ourselves to the existence of such things. The ancient Greeks posited Zeus, Athene and other gods. We don't posit the gods, but we do posit atoms, electrons and other subatomic particles. Both the ancient Greeks and ourselves posit ordinary middle-sized physical objects: sticks and stones, shoes, ships, sealing-wax, cabbages, rabbits, and lots of other ordinary things. Quine insists that these positings of these physical objects and of the ancient Greek gods are the same sort of thing. As organisms active in the world, we are on the one hand bombarded by a constant stream of sensory experience, or in Quinese 'the triggering of our sensory receptors'.[4] On the other hand we are constantly working on that complex system of dispositions which constitutes our total theory of the world. Positing things helps us to give our theory a manageable structure.

Positing is definitely something we do, as indeed is theory-construction in general. So we ourselves, and the biological facts about us, play an enormous part in our theorizing according to Quine. Does that mean he is committed to relativism? I will return to that question in the final chapter, at which point we shall have become better equipped to answer it.

7 Quine's holism

A centrally important feature of Quine's views on these matters is his 'holism' (which just means 'whole-ism'). Recall his conception of theorizing as an instrument for helping us to get on in the world. We have evolved to be creatures who – subject to the influences of the culture we are brought up in – acquire a huge complex system of dispositions to verbal behaviour, notably a system of dispositions roughly capturable in terms of dispositions to assent (say 'Yes', nod, and so on) to sentences when they are spoken to us questioningly. The exact contents of this system, for each of us, are constantly changing, especially at the edges, where the sentences to which we are disposed to assent can be thought of as descriptions of our immediate experience, such as 'It's snowing here', 'There goes a rabbit'. In its more central regions the system includes the whole of our 'theory of the world', which of course is largely shared among members of our culture.

---

4 Quine, *Theories and Things*, p.1.

Quine insists that this system of dispositions must be regarded as a whole. Traditional philosophy distinguished between 'necessary' and 'contingent' truths. Examples of necessary truths are '2 + 2 = 4' and 'Cats are animals'. Such statements are supposedly true in any possible circumstances. Contingent truths are all the rest, such as 'It's raining in London now', which could have been false. Hume used the expressions 'truths of reason' and 'truths of fact'; Kant wrote of 'analytic' and 'synthetic' truths. (There are distinctions to be drawn among these distinctions, but Quine ignores them.) Because Quine thinks the system of all those sentences that we count as true should be thought of as working as a whole, he thinks no such distinctions can be drawn in an intellectually respectable way. He also argues that no satisfactory definition of 'analytic' or 'necessary' has ever actually been produced, except in terms that are equally problematic (see the next section). So the traditionally necessary truths, including the truths of mathematics and logic, are not, according to Quine, set apart from the rest. As already noted, he thinks we might even decide to give up believing some of them if we were prepared to make drastic enough changes in the rest of the system. It will be useful to pause over the analytic–synthetic distinction.

One traditional explanation of the existence of necessary truths was that they depended purely on the meanings of words, while contingent truths depended both on the meanings of words and on non-linguistic facts about the world. For example, a statement such as 'It's snowing' depended for its truth partly on the meanings of the words in it, but also – of course – partly on how things are in the world. On the other hand, 'analytic' statements such as '2 + 2 = 4' and 'Cats are animals' depended for their truth on nothing but the meanings of the words in them. That particular truth of arithmetic provides a specially clear-cut illustration. It seems the meaning of '2' may be given by '1 + 1', so the meaning of '2 + 2' may be given by, first '(1 + 1) + (1 + 1)' and then, removing the brackets, by '1 + 1 + 1 + 1'. Similarly the meaning of '4' may be given first by '3 + 1', then by '(2 + 1) + 1' (since '3' is taken to mean '2 + 1'), then by '((1 + 1) + 1) + 1', and finally by '1 + 1 + 1 + 1'. In this way we get exactly the same expression on each side of the equals sign. The successive steps in this argument are exceedingly hard to challenge. So it looks like a prime illustration of the idea that analytic truths hold on account of the meanings of the expressions which make them up. 'Cats are animals' is not quite so straightforward, since there is a problem over just how to define 'cat'. Yet the basic idea is quite compelling. It seems somehow *part* of the meaning of 'cat' that it applies only to animals. If that is so, that statement too is analytic, and cannot possibly be false.[5]

Quine denies all that. 'The truth of statements does obviously depend

---

5 Arguably this particular statement can be construed in such a way that it doesn't count as analytic, or not in the usual sense, on the ground that 'cat' names a 'natural kind'; but it is certainly the sort of statement that was earlier counted as analytic.

both upon language and upon extralinguistic fact', he concedes. But 'it is nonsense, and the root of much nonsense, to speak of a linguistic component and a factual component in the truth of any individual statement'. And then: 'Our statements about the external world face the tribunal of sense experience not individually but only as a corporate body'. (Both those remarks are from the famous article in which he attacked the analytic–synthetic distinction, 'Two Dogmas of Empiricism'.) That is his 'holism'. Note that, with the remark just quoted, he is going beyond the point noted in section 4 above, that a 'recalcitrant experience' doesn't determine just which statements must be revised. He is saying there are *no* restrictions on which aspects of the total theory must be revised. The theory faces experience as a whole, so in principle we could adapt it in any way we choose.

You may find Quine's claim that not even statements such as '2 + 2 = 4' are 'immune to revision' hard to swallow, especially in view of the seemingly unstoppable way that particular equation can be transformed into '1 + 1 + 1 + 1 = 1 + 1 + 1 + 1'. However, that claim does not commit him to the extremely dubious view that *as things are* we could conceive how to make such revisions. His point is rather that, contrary to the traditional doctrine, there is no sharp line to be drawn between such statements and ones more obviously dependent on how things are in the world. It is vital to keep in mind that, for him, the whole system of interconnected sentences that represents our knowledge or beliefs is there for us to use: it is conceived of pragmatically, as an instrument. Who can say, in advance, what changes may eventually help to make the system more useful to us? The following dialogue may help to bring out some of the main ideas.

A   It's easy to imagine revising '2 + 2 = 4'. Simply imagine the symbols acquire different meanings. For example '2' and '1' have their meanings swapped round.
B   That's trivial – it has no philosophical significance at all. If Quine means no more than that, we can forget about his famous doctrine of revisability. He isn't making a serious point.
A   You're forgetting he rejects the notions of meaning and sameness of meaning. You have no basis for what you have just said unless you beg the question against him. He will deny there is any intellectually respectable way to distinguish trivial from non-trivial changes of meaning.
B   That sounds as if he can't tell the difference between an interesting claim and a boring one. I'm not impressed.
A   Perhaps Quine would paraphrase his claim as: 'There is an interesting way in which no statement is immune to revision'.
B   I'm still baffled. How *could* we give up '2 + 2 = 4' except in the trivial way I mentioned at the start?

A Why does he have to concede we could understand that possibility now? His point seems to be that there might conceivably be circumstances in which we'd find it on balance less disruptive to give up that statement than to hold on to it. He is not suggesting that such circumstances are at all likely to come up, nor that at present we have the slightest conception of what they might be like.

So matters are not straightforward.[6] But notice how the tricky question of relations between truth and what we believe surfaces again here. Suppose Quine is right about the revisability-in-principle even of logical and mathematical statements. What has that to do with their truth? There still seems to be a difference between what *is* true and what we *hold* to be true. We can revise what we hold true, and that goes for mathematical and logical beliefs as well as for factual ones. Does he think there is no real difference between what is true and what is held true? Again we may be inclined to suspect that he is committed to a variety of relativism. That is one of several philosophical hot potatoes we shall pick up in later chapters.

But now I will say something about his views on meaning, concluding with a brief account of his famous (or infamous) doctrine of the indeterminacy of translation. This adds a startling new dimension to the varieties of relativism. So far we have discussed ways in which it may seem that the 'external' world, the world of stars and planets, sticks and stones, somehow depends on us, on our point of view, on what we think. However, in discussing relativism we have tended to assume that *what* we think about the world is itself a perfectly objective matter of fact. We have assumed there is no problem about just what our thoughts and theories themselves are – what we mean by them. If Quine is right about meaning and translation, that assumption is wrong. Even the contents of our thoughts may have to be considered in a relativistic way!

8 Quine on meaning

Quine has strong doubts about the soundness of common assumptions about meaning. Those doubts showed up in his attack in 'Two Dogmas of Empiricism' on traditional ideas about the analytic–synthetic distinction. As we saw, he thinks there is no way to make that distinction reasonably clear, let alone scientifically respectable. He points out that that distinction is inti-

---

6 Especially because since 'Two Dogmas' he has conceded that acceptance of the law of non-contradiction is a result of learning logical words: '…to affirm a compound of the form "*p* and not *p*" is just to have mislearned one or both particles', *From Stimulus to Science*, p.23. But there is no point in attempting here to track modifications to Quine's position over the years.

mately linked with the idea of sameness of meaning or synonymy. Take for example the sentence:

(1) All and only vixens are female foxes.

That is a typical example of an 'analytic' statement. What makes it so? We could say it is analytic because 'vixen' and 'female fox' are synonyms. Equally, if asked what makes those two expressions synonyms, we could say it is because sentence (1) is analytic. Analyticity is definable in terms of sameness of meaning, or synonymy; and synonymy is definable in terms of analyticity. But according to Quine both notions are highly problematic, as are others by means of which we might have hoped to define them, such as those of *proposition* and *necessity*. (Two sentences might be defined as synonymous if they convey the same proposition; and a statement might be defined as necessary if it is analytic.)

He will not concede that the problem is just that these notions are *hard* to define. He maintains there is no respectable way to define them at all because they lack objective validity. His reason, broadly, is that there is no way to link them to objective matters of fact. They depend too much on how we interpret one another's behaviour.

As far as inanimate nature is concerned, sciences such as physics, chemistry and astronomy offer much objectively reliable information about what exists and how things happen. When we turn to consider mental states and the meanings of linguistic expressions, science is a long way from objectively reliable accounts – and there are serious doubts as to whether such accounts are possible at all. For Quine, everyday psychological language is a feeble instrument even though, having no practicable alternative, we are forced to use it. Its explanations are a sham. Question: Why did the French physicist say 'Les photons n'ont pas de masse'? Answer: 'Because she believes that photons have no mass, and her sentence *means the same* as "Photons have no mass"'. That kind of thing, Quine thinks, is 'spurious explanation, mentalistic explanation at its worst'.[7] Of three levels of explanation of behaviour the mental is 'the most superficial', 'scarcely deserving the name of explanation'; the physiological is 'deepest and most ambitious'; but for practical purposes we must rest content with the third variety: explanations in terms of behavioural dispositions. That is 'what we must settle for in our descriptions of language, in our formulations of language rules, and in our explications of semantical terms'.[8] Unfortunately, although the dispositions are reasonably well-behaved, there seems no satisfactory way to connect them to statements about mental states and meanings.

In the recent past a number of philosophers favoured the idea that the

7 'Mind and Verbal Dispositions', p.87.
8 'Mind and Verbal Dispositions', p.87.

meaning of a sentence was associated or even identical with a set of experiences: the experiences that would assure us of its truth, or 'verify' it. Take the statement 'It's raining', for example, and consider all the types of experience that would lead you to accept it: seeing spots of water on the windows, hearing a pattering sound on the roof, and so on. It once seemed reasonable to suggest that the set of all such experiences could be taken to be the meaning of that statement, or at any rate to be a theoretically useful substitute for the meaning. That suggestion seemed capable of being applied to the whole range of factual statements, even historical ones such as 'The Battle of Hastings was in 1066'. Same verifying experiences, same meaning. On Quine's holistic approach the grounds for accepting or rejecting individual statements can never be so simple. Which beliefs we admit to our total web of beliefs has to be assessed in relation to the system of beliefs as a whole. An experience may suggest that the total theory needs revision – it may be 'recalcitrant '– but which revisions to make is not determined by whichever components of the system are most directly associated with the experiences, but by consideration of the system as a whole, as we have seen. (Newton's theory of light, according to which light *always* travels in straight lines, predicts that light passing close to the sun will not bend. Observation suggests it does. Do we stick with Newton and discount the observation, or do we revise his theory?) Holism rules out any neat linkages between individual statements and experiences, hence between them and our behavioural dispositions. And if there are no reasonably clear-cut links between meanings and dispositions, the notion of meaning seems to float out of control. The whole idea starts to seem much less firm and objective than we tend to assume.

Quine associates rejection of the objectivity of meaning with rejection of the ancient idea, traceable to Plato, of meanings as a kind of entities – the myth of the mind as a museum where 'the exhibits are meanings and the words are labels'.[9] As we have seen, Wittgenstein also rejects that primitive conception. However, it seems quite possible to join both philosophers in rejecting it while insisting that it is a matter of fact whether two sentences mean the same. Indeed, it seems that Wittgenstein would have rejected Quine's view on this. Just maintaining that relations of synonymy are matters of fact by no means implies commitment to the museum myth.

Quine's radical views on meaning and mental concepts are dramatized in his doctrine of the indeterminacy of translation, which has been described as 'the most fascinating and the most discussed philosophical argument since Kant's Transcendental Deduction of the Categories'.[10]

---

9 *Ontological Relativity*, p.27.
10 H. Putnam, 'The Refutation of Conventionalism', p.159.

9 Quine's doctrine of the indeterminacy of translation

Suppose a German physicist remarks, 'Das Photon hat keine Masse'. We tend to assume it is a question of objective fact what this German sentence means. Any linguist acquainted with physics would accept 'Photons have no mass' as a translation, and indeed there seems no room for serious disagreement. Quine challenges that assumption. He maintains that we could construct an alternative to the generally accepted scheme for translating sentences between German and English (similarly for any other pair of languages). The rival scheme's rendering of the German sentence would be quite different from 'Photons have no mass', so different that we should not accept it as even loosely equivalent. The same would go for the rival scheme's translations of countless other sentences. Yet, by means of cunning compensatory adjustments, the rival scheme would fit all the facts as well as the usual scheme does.

The most relevant 'facts' for this purpose, by the way, are those about the behaviour and dispositions of speakers of the languages in question. We can also take them to include all facts about the world (past, present and future) that could be stated in terms of physics – including facts about people's nervous systems. For, according to Quine, the indeterminacy thesis 'withstands even…the whole truth about nature'.[11]

You will have noticed that I didn't actually mention an alternative translation of the German physicist's sentence. Quine himself provides no serious examples of the alleged indeterminacy. That, he thinks, would require a hugely laborious reworking of our schemes for translating between the languages involved, all to illustrate a philosophical point. (Others have tried to fill the gap, but without much success, or so I would argue.)

The indeterminacy doctrine is easily mistaken for others. It seems so peculiar when you first learn about it – and even on deeper acquaintance – that you wonder if you have understood it properly. (If you don't find it puzzling, you haven't grasped it.) It is not, for example, the truism that, for any partial data, there will be conflicting ways to extrapolate beyond the data. If we had only the inscriptions on the Rosetta stone to go on, for example, we could devise infinitely many incompatible schemes for translating between the three languages represented on it (hieroglyphic, demotic Egyptian, Greek). But Quine is saying it would be possible to devise a rival to the usual scheme for translating between, say, German and English, which would fit not just the data we happen to have about the actual behaviour of German and English speakers, but *all* relevant objective facts about those two languages.

Another mistake is to assume that he is just making a fuss over the commonplace point that translation requires the exercise of judgement. Of

---

11 *Words and Objections*, ed. D. Davidson and J. Hintikka, p.303.

course it does: because of the range of alternative but conflicting versions in one language of sentences in a different sort of language. No one expects a poem, for example, to have a uniquely correct translation. But Quine is not making a point about subtle nuances, but about major conflicts between translations. That may make you suppose he is just stressing another familiar thought: that in translating between remote languages and cultures, sentences of one language that are acceptable as *rough* translations of a single sentence of the other may not themselves be equivalent. Colour words are a familiar example. Look up 'purpureus' in a Latin dictionary and you may find the following offered as English equivalents: 'purple-coloured, purple; red; reddish; violet; brownish; blackish; etc.'. That suggests we could translate a single Latin sentence in two alternative ways: by 'His face was purple' and 'His face was red' – two English sentences that do not mean the same. But that does not illustrate Quine's point, for two important reasons. The first is that one of his main purposes in pressing the indeterminacy doctrine is to undermine the assumption that it is a *question of fact* what we mean by what we say. He appeals to the alleged indeterminacy to back up his claim (to be discussed shortly) that the whole idea of meaning and sameness of meaning is no more than a convenient way of talking, without solid empirical foundation. Obviously the fact that there may be inequivalent rough English translations of a single Latin sentence has little tendency to support that claim. Even exponents of the myth of the meaning-museum are not troubled by such cases, which they can explain by saying English has selected a slightly different set of exhibits to label. The second reason is conclusive: Quine maintains the doctrine holds *even within a single language*, where it would be nonsense to say there was conceptual incongruity. I will return to this special 'domestic' case.

You might protest that bilinguals could settle any potential disagreements. But according to Quine they are no better placed than anyone else. Their schemes of translation are as underdetermined as other people's. If bilinguals agree, that is not surprising, since they probably acquired their languages in the context of a generally accepted system for translating between them.

One last possible misconception is to suppose that Quine has merely chosen a picturesque way of restating ordinary scepticism about other minds. The other-minds sceptic says: 'We can never know what other people are thinking' – yet still assumes there is a matter of fact to be right or wrong about; it's just that the sceptic thinks we can never know whether we have got it right. Quine's point is radical. According to him 'there is not even…a matter of fact to be right or wrong about'.[12] So he is not so much a sceptic about meaning as a nihilist. The *objective* facts leave translation and interpretation underdetermined; and nothing that requires translation or

---

12 Quine, *Word and Object*, p.73.

interpretation is objective fact. The best we can do is provide translations and interpretations *relative to a given scheme of translation*.

The truly radical nature of Quine's claim emerges when he points out that, if he is right, relations of synonymy are not matters of fact even when they are supposed to hold between sentences of one and the same language. I tend to assume that, for each sentence of our shared language, what you mean by it is also what I mean by it. In Quinean jargon, I use the 'homophonic' translation manual. But he thinks an alternative scheme could be devised that would attribute to you 'unimagined views', while still fitting all the facts about your verbal and other behaviour. (The alternative scheme would of course have to be very complicated.)

You might now protest that a whole range of absolutely crucial facts is being overlooked: facts about people's beliefs, desires, intentions and so on. Surely they would enable us to obtain such firm indications of what people mean that there would be no room for significant conflict – no interesting indeterminacy. Quine agrees the implication holds. If such attitudes are counted as objective, they do fix meanings and block the indeterminacy. As he remarks in *Word and Object*, '...using the...words "believe" and "ascribe", one could say that a speaker's term is to be construed as "rabbit" if and only if the speaker is disposed to ascribe it to all and only the objects that he believes to be rabbits'.[13] But instead of caving in, he rejects the assumption that the contents of our beliefs, desires and the rest are matters of fact. If his indeterminacy doctrine is right, such 'intentional' notions do not identify matters of fact at all! So the doctrine cannot be bracketed off inside the relatively narrow confines of the philosophy of language. It threatens the whole of everyday psychology, at least to the extent that everyday psychology appears to presuppose that it is a matter of fact what our beliefs, desires and the rest are. (The words 'intentional' and 'intentionality', by the way, apply in this context to something very ordinary, though puzzling: the seeming fact that beliefs, desires, intentions and so on are 'about' things, or have 'objects' or 'content'. Intentionality is typically conveyed by means of a sentence introduced by 'that' – for example: 'I believe that there are tigers in India', 'She hopes that it will rain soon'; but the 'object' may be mentioned instead, as in 'We want some coffee'. Today there is much interesting discussion about what intentionality involves: what it takes for there to be such a thing. Note that intentionality is not confined to what someone intends to do.)

Now you have some conception of what Quine's indeterminacy doctrine is, you may be impatient to know what are his arguments for it. One famous line of argument starts from considering the enterprise of 'radical translation'. Linguists encounter a population whose language and beliefs are

---

13 *Word and Object*, pp.220f.

completely unknown to them, and have to work out both a scheme of translation and a way of ascribing beliefs and desires to the foreigners. He argues that the objective facts about the two languages involved – the foreigners' and the linguists' – will always leave room for rival schemes of translation: schemes which conflict with one another yet fit all the objective facts. No one scheme will be uniquely correct.

The argument goes as follows. Imagine the foreigners use the one-word sentence 'Gavagai' in situations where English speakers would use 'Rabbit' or 'There's a rabbit'. That certainly justifies using 'Rabbit' as one possible translation of 'Gavagai'. But the linguists cannot stop there. They have to provide ways of breaking up sentences into parts, and on that basis devise a scheme by which any given foreign sentence is rendered by a sentence in the linguists' own language. For that purpose they will have to match sentence-parts with sentence-parts. In particular they will have to deal with (what we can suppose) is the foreign sentence-part 'gavagai' – not in this case a sentence standing on its own, but a component of any number of different sentences. The overwhelmingly natural and practical thing would be to pair 'gavagai' with 'rabbit'. Quine does not dispute that. But he is making a theoretical point, and practical considerations are not dominant. He claims that, if the linguists disregard what they find most natural and practical, then there is no limit to the number of different ways of pairing-off 'gavagai'. It might be taken to refer not to rabbits but to such radically different items as 'mere stages, or brief temporal segments, of rabbits'.[14] That would be consistent, he maintains, with 'Rabbit' and 'Gavagai' being intertranslatable as whole sentences; for we are never stimulated by a rabbit without at the same time being stimulated by a rabbit-phase, and vice versa. Alternatively 'gavagai' might be matched up with 'undetached rabbit part'. Or yet again, it might be equated with the 'fusion' of all rabbits, 'that single though discontinuous portion of the spatiotemporal world that consists of rabbits'. Finally, it might be taken to be 'a singular term naming a recurring universal, rabbithood'. Nor could we rule out any of these alternatives by pointing, or by staging experiments, since those operations would depend on untestable assumptions. Such 'inscrutability of reference' appears to entail indeterminacy of sentence translation. If he is right, our *own* word 'rabbit' could be interpreted as referring not to rabbits, but to any of these other things.

That is just a sample of a complicated web of reasoning. You may suspect there is something wrong with it; and indeed it is fiercely contested at every point. Quinean indeterminacy of translation implies a kind of relativity we should not otherwise have envisaged, according to which the very contents of our minds are not objective matters of fact, but relative to some assumed scheme of interpretation. I will leave that particular loose thread hanging.

14 *Word and Object*, p.51.

MAIN POINTS IN CHAPTER 5

1   Quine is a 'naturalist': the task of discovering the nature of reality is part of natural science. Philosophy, too, is part of science, not an independent basis for contributing to our theory of the world (section 1).

2   He suggests our knowledge and beliefs can be represented by a complex system of sentences – which is just a way of talking about a system of behavioural dispositions (sections 2 and 3).

3   This system is an instrument for handling sensory stimulation and enabling us to get on in the world. It faces sense experience as a whole. Which parts of it we revise when faced by a 'recalcitrant experience' does not depend purely on what the experience is, but on how to keep the whole system manageable: considerations which balance conservatism and simplicity (sections 3, 4 and 7).

4   He suggests that even the 'truths' of logic and mathematics may be 'revisable' and are not 'necessary' in any respectable sense (section 7).

5   'Positing' things helps to give our theory a manageable structure (section 6).

6   The indeterminacy of translation is supposed to support his view that the notions of meaning, synonymy and analyticity, and by implication those of belief, desire, intention and related notions, are not objectively sound (sections 8 and 9). If he is right, he has identified a further dimension where relativism reigns.

CHAPTER 5: SUGGESTIONS FOR FURTHER READING

The classic text for Quine's **holism** and his attack on the **analytic–synthetic distinction** is 'Two Dogmas of Empiricism'. Section 6 is the most relevant to our interests. For an influential (advanced) discussion of his views on the analytic–synthetic distinction see Grice and Strawson, 'In Defense of a Dogma'. Ch. 2 of Christopher Hookway's *Quine* provides useful background and discussion. Alex Miller's *Philosophy of Language* provides good discussions.

For Quine's **indeterminacy** doctrine the classic text is ch. 2 of *Word and Object*. See Miller for exposition. Many discussions of the doctrine are considered in R. Kirk, *Translation Determined*.

Quine's *Pursuit of Truth* (rev. ed. 1992) gives a useful introduction to his overall philosophical position and motivation, with the emphases subtly different from what appeared in his main earlier works.

6

LANGUAGE-GAMES V. REALISM

It looked earlier as if everyone had to be a realist about something (Chapter 3, section 10). At that point I was using the word 'realism' for any view opposed to true-for-me relativism. Normally it is applied to more interesting views. In this chapter, having noted some of the main positions typically describable as 'realist' and 'anti-realist', I will examine an argument for a variety of anti-realism which exploits Wittgenstein's idea of language-games – though not, I think, in a way he would have endorsed. The argument is seductive, and seems actually to have convinced a lot of people. However, it is not compelling.

1 Realism, instrumentalism, anti-realism

I expect almost every sane person who has ever lived would accept this variety of realism:

> Most of the things we ordinarily and confidently suppose to exist do exist, independently of what we may think or experience.

Let us call that normally unstated assumption *commonsense realism*. The phrase 'and confidently' helps to ensure that ghosts, thought-rays, and so on are not included among the things whose existence is implied by common-sense realism. With that proviso, 'we' can be taken to be the majority of people, who confidently suppose that shoes, ships, sealing-wax, cabbages and kings exist, independently of what we may think or feel.[1] The few who reject commonsense realism tend to be philosophers, or are influenced by philoso-phers. However, those who think common sense gets too much wrong for

---

1 Even kings exist independently of what we may think or feel, although of course their exis-tence does depend on social institutions, as also do money, sports and crime. See Chapter 3, section 13 and, again, Searle's readable discussion of such matters in *The Construction of Social Reality*.

commonsense realism to be plausible may reject commonsense realism – in reflective moments if not in practical life – and adopt *scientific realism*:

> Most of the things said to exist by accepted scientific theories do exist, independently of what we may think or experience.[2]

You can be in favour of science without being a scientific realist. To illustrate that point, and to plunge immediately into some of the philosophical questions surrounding realism, I will briefly consider a view directly opposed to scientific realism.

Scientific realism maintains that atoms, for example, are made up of protons, neutrons, electrons and so on, which really exist and have the properties ascribed to them by accepted science. In the sharpest possible contrast, *instrumentalism* about the theoretical entities of science tells us that a scientific theory is just a convenient way of talking about observations. According to this view, the theory is no more than an instrument (just as James said all theories were) which enables us to predict one lot of observations on the basis of another lot of observations. In spite of the fact that scientific theory makes free use of what look like names for classes of things that are not observable – names such as 'atom', 'electron', 'proton' – those are just fictions. In reality there are no such things. All we really have is observations and a more or less complicated scheme for calculating what observations we can expect to make, given observations already made. The theory is a calculus: put observables in and it puts out further observables.

That is one *anti-realist* way of regarding the theoretical entities of science. Its appeal comes from its extremely cautious approach to what we claim to *know* and what we claim to *exist* (so it has both 'epistemological' and 'ontological' aspects). If you are reluctant to make claims going beyond actual experience, or if you want to cut down the number of different kinds of things you say exist, then instrumentalism may strike you as a good idea. If you are willing to stick at the existence of observations and theories (whatever they may be), it seems to allow you to do without other kinds of entities. It doesn't actually compel you to go to that extreme: it is compatible with commonsense realism. However, it does leave you with two problems.

First, you must say something about what is involved in the existence

---

2 Of course there are more sophisticated statements. See for example the discussions in Van Fraassen's *The Scientific Image* and the collection of critical essays on his views, *Images of Science*. In both statements of realism I say 'most of the things' to avoid committing realism to the unacceptable position that, respectively, common sense and science include no errors. The phrase 'independently of what we may think or experience' does not apply, of course, in the special case where our thoughts or feelings are the things supposed to exist.

of the observations and theories themselves. Observations require on the one hand observers, and on the other hand whatever is observed; theories require theorists. What does instrumentalism say about observers and theorists? Are they just disembodied minds? Does that even make sense? If they have bodies, what do their bodies consist of – they must consist of *something*? In any case, what are the observers supposed to observe: things 'out there' in the world? Pure 'sense data' (whatever they may be)? Or what? How can there be minds *or* observables unless they are somehow composed of things not themselves directly observable? Those are troublesome questions for any instrumentalism about the theoretical entities of science.

Second, it is strange if we are *completely* mistaken in our common assumption that what is observable can be explained in terms of what constitutes or underlies it, even if the underlying things and events are not themselves observable. That is what Democritus was trying to do with the first atomic theory; and it is what most of today's physicists take themselves to be doing.[3] For them, the theory that instrumentalists regard as a mere calculus is an attempt to describe and explain what really exists. Instrumentalists are not completely at a loss when faced with these objections. One reply might be that, although what is observable has unobservable causes, we cannot know anything about those causes. That seems to amount to saying that in fact there *is* a truth about the hidden nature of reality, but that we cannot discover it. But that amounts to changing the doctrine. If you try to defend your instrumentalism in that way, it is no more than the sceptical view that, roughly, we cannot know more than we can observe. It would no longer be an anti-realist view according to which nothing actually *exists* apart from what we can observe. That full anti-realist view is hard to maintain. Though interesting for purposes of illustration, it is not widely held today.[4] (Instrumentalist interpretations not of the theoretical statements of physics but of psychological statements, in contrast, have distinguished adherents.)

Now let us consider, again briefly, a different sort of anti-realist view, an extreme position which has seemed tenable to some. It is the most radical and dramatic contradiction of commonsense realism in Western philosophy: George Berkeley's kind of *idealism*. Berkeley did not deny that ordinary

---

3 See, for example, Richard Feynman, *QED: the Strange Theory of Light and Matter*.

4 Instrumentalism has charms for those who are in any case inclined to some version of anti-realism, for example phenomenalism (the view that statements about physical objects are equivalent to statements about possible experiences). Note that, although Van Fraassen describes his position in the philosophy of science as 'anti-realist', he explicitly rules out instrumentalism (*The Scientific Image*, pp.10f.) and states 'I wish merely to be agnostic about the existence of the unobservable aspects of the world described by science' (op. cit., p.72).

objects such as sticks and stones exist – which is why Dr Johnson's attempt to refute him just by kicking a large stone seems misconceived.[5] His doctrine concerned what is *involved* in their existence: the underlying 'metaphysics'. On his account, the existence of ordinary objects consists in our having experiences, brought about by the activity of God. The tomato I now see, for example, exists only so long as certain characteristic 'ideas' occur in my mind, or in someone else's: ideas of a certain shape, a certain colour, and so on. With respect to 'all those bodies which compose the mighty frame of the world', he says that they

> have not any subsistence without a mind, that their being is to be perceived or known; that consequently so long as they are not actu-ally perceived by me, or do not exist in my mind or that of any other created spirit, they must either have no existence at all, or else subsist in the mind of some eternal spirit.[6]

Recall the statement of commonsense realism:

> Most of the things we ordinarily and confidently suppose to exist do exist, independently of what we may think or experience.

It is the second part of this statement that Berkeley disputes, not the first. He is happy to agree that sticks and stones exist. What he denies is that they exist independently of minds, or of thoughts and experiences. 'To be', as he notoriously puts it, 'is to be perceived.' (He allows things to exist when not perceived by *us*: God perceives even when we do not.)

Both Berkeley's idealism and scientific instrumentalism claim to be consistent with what might be called (very vaguely) the immediate evidence of the senses. That claim seems plausible as far as instrumentalism is concerned. Our experiences do seem to leave plenty of scope for a whole range of different theories about what causes them. Certainly our actual experiences fall far short of determining any particular physical theory. Nor does instrumentalism have to deny that *something* causes our experiences: it denies only that any particular physical theory succeeds in naming any real entities. So there seems no conflict between instrumentalism and the evidence of the senses.

---

5 '...we stood talking for some time together of Bishop Berkeley's ingenious sophistry to prove the non-existence of matter, and that every thing in the universe is merely ideal. I observed, that though we are satisfied his doctrine is not true, it is impossible to refute it. I never shall forget the alacrity with which Johnson answered, striking his foot with mighty force against a large stone, till he rebounded from it, "I refute it *thus*".' J. Boswell, *Life of Johnson*, p. 333.

6 G. Berkeley, *Principles of Human Knowledge*, I, vi.

Berkeley's doctrine is very different, although its justification is similar. He claims his views are consistent with our actual experience; and he also avoids what seems to him to be the unnecessary burden of postulating the existence of mind-independent entities dotted about in space. But the claim that his idealism is consistent with the evidence of our senses has to be interpreted in a special way. When Dr Johnson kicked the stone, he might be interpreted as making that very point. We normally suppose our senses provide evidence of things which exist independently of what we perceive, think or feel. What, after all, is a stone, as ordinarily understood? Surely it is not something whose existence depends on being perceived! Stones are just the sort of thing that we expect to exist unperceived by anyone. We seem to have a primitive *theory* about what stones are; and an important component of that theory is precisely this: that their existence does not depend on what anyone perceives or thinks. (I have asked a lot of people about this. Those I have managed to persuade I am not crazy have agreed they subscribe to that theory.)

It seems that the evidence of our senses gives us plenty of reasons to accept that there are such things as stones. Berkeley will object that here we are simply ignoring his actual doctrine. Certainly we talk about stones. But, he maintains, we are mistaken about what is involved in the existence of such things. In reality they consist of nothing but 'ideas' – mental events. There are two popular responses. One is more or less the same as Dr Johnson's: we just know we are in the middle of a world that includes sticks and stones, other people, rivers and hills, stars and planets; and we cannot make sense of Berkeley except on the basis of that knowledge.[7] The other is this: the best *explanation* of our 'ideas' – what we tend to think of as our perceptual experiences of the things around us – is that there is an independently existing world which causes them. The experiences we have when we see the sun are caused by that very large, very hot object millions of miles away; the experiences we have when we hear someone speaking are caused by that person's actually talking and causing the surrounding air to vibrate in ways we have learned to recognize; and so on. Perhaps that 'argument to the best explanation' does not absolutely settle the matter; but it cannot be ignored.

2 Other varieties

If someone maintains that *all killing is wrong*, and someone else objects that there are special circumstances where it is not wrong, they appear to be in disagreement. One seems to be denying what the other asserts. In this respect

---

7 Heidegger and the later Wittgenstein, in their different ways, offered sophisticated versions of this approach. On Heidegger see H. Dreyfus, *Being-in-the-World: a Commentary on Heidegger's Being and Time, division I*. On Wittgenstein see A. Kenny, *Wittgenstein*, ch. 11.

their disagreement resembles disagreement about matters of fact. But is it? If so, there must be moral facts to be right or wrong about. What is the nature of those facts? According to Plato, moral facts are entirely objective, and consist in relations that hold among the 'Forms', such as those of the Good, the Right, and Killing. That variety of moral realism has proved hard to defend. One difficulty is to understand the nature of the Forms whose relations are supposed to constitute moral facts. Another is to explain how we can get in touch with the Forms. How can we tell we have correctly apprehended the real relationships between them? It seems we could get along perfectly well in practical life if there were no Forms at all. So most moral realists are likely to reject Plato's account of the realities. If you still want to be a realist about the subject-matter of moral statements, the problem remains: what is the nature of moral facts? There are several doctrines on offer, though it would take us out of our way to discuss them. There is obviously scope for commonsense realists to reject moral realism.

One alternative closely parallels the view I ascribed to Protagoras. As we saw in Chapter 3, he seems to have maintained that there is no such thing as truth full-stop; all we have, when it comes to truth, is beliefs or statements being held true by persons (at times). Analogously, one form of moral anti-realism consists in maintaining that all we have, when it comes to right and wrong, is people *valuing* or *approving* or *commending* certain types of actions and states of affairs, and disvaluing, disapproving or deprecating others.

Religious language is another area where realist and anti-realist interpretations abound. If a religious believer says 'God exists', is that to be regarded as a statement of fact, capable of being true or false just as, for example, 'Ben Nevis exists' is capable of being true or false? In other words, does its truth value (that is, whether it is true or false) depend on whether or not there really exists, independently of what people may think, a being who created the universe, is perfectly good, all-powerful, and so on, as has typically been said by believers in the past? Or is that straightforwardly 'realist' way of taking the statement a mistake? Is religious discourse instead to be understood non-realistically, as some theologians now maintain – as encapsulating a certain attitude to life and the world, or a commitment to a certain sort of life, without implying the existence of any kind of supreme being who is independent of what people may think or do?

One more example of opposition between a variety of realism and anti-realism: mathematical statements. What makes them true or false? As we saw, Plato tells us they are true if they reflect relations among the mathematical Forms. $2 + 2 = 4$, for example, because of relations between the Forms of Two, Plus, Equality, and Four. But again we encounter the difficulties of explaining both the nature of the Forms and the possibility of knowing when you have managed to track down these relations correctly. As Michael Dummett comments, not only in connection with Plato's own position but in connection with any variety of mathematical realism (platonism):

The platonist metaphor assimilates mathematical enquiry to the investigations of the astronomer: mathematical structures, like galaxies, exist, independently of us, in a realm of reality which we do not inhabit but which those of us who have the skill are capable of observing and reporting on.[8]

You might suggest that in mathematics we have rather good indications of whether statements are true: we have *proofs*. However, if a proof of a mathematical statement is what guarantees that we have correctly apprehended the relations between the relevant Forms, the proof itself seems to make it superfluous to appeal to the Forms. Why not say that for a mathematical statement to be true *is* for it to be provable?[9] That is an appealing suggestion. Notice, by the way, that this example illustrates how difficult it can be sometimes to distinguish between realism and anti-realism. Is the suggestion that mathematical truth is the same as provability a realist or an anti-realist idea? You could say it was realist because it makes the question whether or not a given statement is true a matter of fact: either there is a proof or there isn't, independently of what we may think. On the other hand, you could say it was anti-realist because it avoids appealing to a realm of special mathematical entities or states of affairs. We have to look carefully at what 'realist' means here. We can understand perfectly well what is being said; but in this particular case the labels 'realist' and 'anti-realist' are even less helpful than usual.

If it is sometimes unhelpful to talk in terms of things being real or not, matters of fact or not, is it equally unhelpful to talk in terms of objectivity? In the case of mathematical statements, at any rate, we might maintain that provability is an objective matter, given that trained mathematicians can recognize a proof when they see one. Certainly it is helpful to avoid the assumption that objectivity requires the existence of independent *objects*, such as Plato supposed the Forms to be. To say that '2 + 2 = 4' has a proof need not be taken to imply that there are mathematical objects existing independently of what we may think. It need imply only that anyone who follows certain procedures – anyone who acts in certain ways – will be able to establish the proposition in question. Unfortunately the distinction between the objective and the subjective is not always clearcut. Even in the mathematical case, the procedures that count as giving proofs are, after all, agreed to be so by human beings. Is it conceivable that creatures with different 'forms of life'

8 M. Dummett, *Truth and Other Enigmas*, p.229.
9 A major setback for the proposal to equate mathematical truth with provability was Kurt Gödel's famous 'incompleteness theorem'. Gödel showed that, for any system of axioms and logical rules capable of yielding the truths of ordinary arithmetic, if the system was consistent (i.e. involved no contradiction), then it was incomplete (i.e. could not prove some mathematical truths).

should have arrived at different procedures and a different mathematics? That appeared to be the moral of Wittgenstein's 'Odd Adder' story. If all there is to objectivity is the agreement of human beings, it is open to someone like Protagoras to claim there is no genuine objectivity. All we have, by way of objectivity, he might say, is general agreement in what is counted as being correct. To concede that point would seem to be to concede that subjectivity rules – or at least some kind of anti-realism.

The various paired anti-realisms and realisms mentioned so far, especially those of instrumentalism about the theoretical entities of science contrasted with scientific realism, Berkeleyan idealism contrasted with commonsense realism, and anti-realism about the existence of God contrasted with traditional theism, help to show how we can regard some area of discourse as not doing what at first we might have supposed it did – that is, pick out real facts or things whose existence in no way depends on what we think, or on our point of view. It is important to notice, though, that an anti-realist position about some limited area of discourse may well be consistent with a strongly realist position about others. We noticed just now that instrumentalism about the theoretical entities of science is compatible with commonsense realism. Equally, any anti-realist or 'subjectivist' position on moral discourse can be combined with either commonsense or scientific realism. Indeed, that is a common position to hold, and supports a sharp distinction between facts and values. However, reflection on some of the considerations which have led people to take up anti-realist positions in limited areas has encouraged some to take up a kind of global anti-realism, though one very different from Berkeley's. In the next section I will set out a line of reasoning which may seem to support global anti-realism.

3 The 'language-game' argument for anti-realism

You might protest in advance that there must be something wrong with a theory which says 'These ordinary things – sticks and stones, cats and dogs, mountains and valleys – don't exist independently of our point of view, or of what we think or experience'. How can you take an anti-realist line quite generally? Those tempted by the sort of anti-realism I am about to describe will reply that the protest merely exhibits the prejudices of commonsense realism. What is needed is arguments, not bald restatements of the position to be defended. On the other side there are arguments. This one starts from Wittgenstein's thoughts about language and language-games. I am not suggesting Wittgenstein himself would have endorsed it: I feel sure he would not. Nor did he use the expression 'language-game' as it is used in this argument, to cover whole languages and all the practices associated with them.

Speaking a language is something we do. *How* we do it is not determined independently of the language-game itself. In that sense it is up to us. There are rules or norms; but we were not forced to adopt them. No doubt they

97

cater to our needs and interests; but people with different needs and interests would have had different rules or norms. People brought up in different cultures will speak different language-games, with different rules from ours. They think of the world from within their own language and culture; in some cases they have different interests and values, in which cases their culture leads them to direct their attention to different sorts of things from those salient in our culture. It is not as if the rules of our language-games were written in the book of nature. On the contrary, they are fixed by the custom and practice of communities in definite historical and social situations.

Not all language-games involve questions of truth or falsity.[10] But those which do, involve assertion. 'It's raining', 'The Battle of Hastings was in 1066', 'On the night of the murder I was at home': those are examples of assertion, and in particular of the sort we should ordinarily count as stating facts. Consider the language-games in which such utterances figure. Among the rules governing them are some which constitute standards of acceptability. Some examples: in general it is only acceptable to say 'It's raining here' in certain circumstances, when drops of water are falling from the sky, or when one may reasonably believe they are. It's only acceptable to say 'The Battle of Hastings was in 1066' if that statement coheres with the rest of our historical beliefs. It's only acceptable for someone to say 'I was at home on the night of the murder' if they *were* at home on the night of the murder. Using the principle we noticed in Chapter 2, if it is acceptable to make a certain assertion at all it is also acceptable to add the prefix 'It is true that' to it. Conversely, if an assertion with the prefix 'It is true that' is acceptable, so is the corresponding one without the prefix.

In that and related ways, language-games involving assertion link up acceptability and truth. Similarly they link up acceptability with descriptions such as 'saying how things really are'. For example, knowing how to play the language-game of ordinary 'fact-stating' assertion requires us to be ready to accept 'That is how things really are' in place of 'That is true', and vice versa. The argument concludes that *there is no more to truth than acceptability*. In that way what is true is inseparably dependent on what we think and experience.

That seems to imply a further conclusion: different communities may fix different systems of truth, which in turn seems to mean that *different communities may occupy different realities*. If nothing beyond language-

---

10 See *Philosophical Investigations*, §23, 'Review the multiplicity of language-games in the following examples, and in others:

Giving orders, and obeying them
Describing an object from its appearance, or from its measurements
Producing an object from a description
Reporting an event...'

games determines what is or is not acceptable, and truth is nothing but acceptability, then only language-games determine what is true or false. But we know that if it is true that p, then it's really the case that p. Given that different communities have widely different language-games which still purport to state the truth, differences between their respective language-games are enough to ensure differences in what is true and false, hence differences in the realities with which they deal. If one community includes 'The earth is bigger than the sun' among its acceptable statements, while ours includes 'The earth is much smaller than the sun' among *its* acceptable statements, we just have to accept that our realities differ: there is no independent source of correctness or incorrectness, of truth or falsity. You might object: 'Surely you can establish what's really and truly the case by *measuring* the earth and the sun'. But that suggestion plays into the anti-realists' hands. Measuring is itself a human activity, governed by its own community-established standards. In straightforward cases, such as the relative sizes or weights of apples or packets of breakfast cereal, there is little scope for significant cross-cultural disagreement. But measuring the sun and the earth requires us to use *theories* about the structure of the universe; and they are cultural constructions. For that and similar reasons, truth and reality are regarded, not as somehow standing outside the human activities involved in the various language-games of assertion, but as 'internal', as dependent on the rules governing them. (The fact that reality is not already classified may seem to provide support to these ideas: Chapter 2, section 8.) So there can be no such thing as appealing to measurement to establish 'what is really and truly the case' – unless that just means appealing to the standards and rules prevailing in one's society. If the argument works, then, truth and falsity, and with them reality itself, depend on what we think, on our point of view. So realism is wrong, and we have to accept anti-realism.[11]

Here is a rough outline of the argument:

(1) What a language-game is depends entirely on its rules (conventions, norms).

(2) Those rules depend on the custom and practice of the community; there is no higher standard to appeal to.

(3) Where a language-game involves questions of truth or falsity, there are rules governing the acceptability of assertions.

11 I do not know of a statement of this argument in quite the form presented here. Some components can be found in Kuhn's *The Structure of Scientific Revolutions*, some in Nelson Goodman's *Ways of Worldmaking*, some in Richard Rorty's *Philosophy and The Mirror of Nature*, and the general line of thought is widespread. I have tried to make the most persuasive case I can: I shall argue against it below.

(4) Those rules link up acceptability and truth, and with 'saying how things really are'.

(5) Therefore there is no more to truth than assertibility. An assertion's truth is just its acceptability in its own language-game.

(6) Further, different communities, with different kinds of 'fact-stating' discourse, each fixing a different system of truth, may occupy different realities.

The argument applies (if to anything) not just to what we may think of as 'fact-stating' discourse but to moral, religious and mathematical statements too, except for differences in the factors which make up acceptability. Not only the subject-matters of these different types of discourse are different; so is the amount of agreement they provide for. Moral discourse tends to allow for more disagreement than there is over what is acceptable in the area of ordinary fact-stating. We may agree that this man committed murder but disagree fiercely over whether he should be executed. However, according to the line of argument just set out, only the subject-matter, and in particular the amount of agreement there is, provides any basis for singling out ordinary fact-stating discourse from other types. Rorty puts it strongly: 'no distinction of kind separates the sciences from the crafts, from moral reflection, or from art'.[12]

You may object that there is something special about the rules of fact-stating discourse, and something even more special about those governing scientific statements, including the very general non-technical ones in the Core Scientific Story. Take 'The sun is much larger than the earth'. Surely it states a fact which holds quite independently of what we may think, whereas 'Capital punishment is wrong' or 'Democracy is a good thing' don't state facts but just express our attitudes? This objection is no more than a declaration of adherence to a form of realism, and a way of bringing out the difference between realism and anti-realism. Anti-realists don't deny there are differences; but they insist that the differences provide no justification for putting ordinary fact-stating discourse on a pedestal. *All we have to go on*, they insist, is community-established standards of acceptability. Answers to what we regard as straightforwardly factual questions, such as 'When was the battle of Hastings?' or 'How far away is the sun?' depend on our attitudes just as much as answers to questions like 'Is it right that abortion should be legal?' depend on our attitudes.

You protest that questions like the one about the distance of the sun can

---

12 R. Rorty, *Consequences of Pragmatism*, p.163. See also Chapter 11, section 7.

be settled objectively, by scientific procedures. How can they depend on our attitudes? The reply is that they depend on the scientific community's standards of rational acceptability. If those procedures conform to the standards, we regard the outcomes as matters of objective fact, otherwise not. But standards of rational acceptability are part of the community's value-system, and subject to modification – indeed, have actually been modified over the centuries.[13] Similarly, it is suggested by those who pursue this line of argument, many questions about what is good or right can be answered with only minimal disagreement by those who share much the same system of values. In some cases, they maintain, the answers have scarcely less claim to objectivity than those to straightforwardly factual questions. They don't deny that the scientific community's standards of rational acceptability are more uniform and more generally recognized than standards of moral or aesthetic value. They don't maintain there are no differences at all between matters of fact and matters of value. But they insist there is no sharp difference of kind. Thus what we still tend to call matters of fact depend on standards of acceptability in ways not essentially different from what we regard as unproblematically matters of value. In that sense, on their view, the truth itself depends on our values.

In other words there is no basis for favouring one type of discourse above others and going on to claim that it alone makes contact with objective, independent, reality. All types of assertion, 'fact-stating', moral, aesthetic, religious, or whatever, have to be regarded as being on an equal footing, since they are all just different kinds of language-games.

To ordinary realists the language-game argument's conclusions are outrageous, regardless of how fashionable they may be.

4 Failure of the language-game argument

In Chapter 4 I set out what I take to be the main lessons to be drawn from Wittgenstein's examples of language-games (sections 3, 4, 5 and 8). The argument in the previous section goes significantly beyond them. If it worked it would demolish commonsense realism (from now on, realism), the view that most of what we ordinarily and confidently take to exist does exist, independently of our thoughts or experiences. But realists can easily accept Wittgenstein's points about language-games. Indeed, his descriptions of language-games are naturally understood realistically and seem unintelligible otherwise. Players of language-games are ordinary human beings, born in the usual way, living in communities, interacting with one another and with the things in the world around them. They are trained to utter patterns

---

13 For a hugely influential presentation of this view see Kuhn, *The Structure of Scientific Revolutions*. Hilary Putnam says the essays in Part II of his *Realism with a Human Face*, especially ch. 11, aim 'to show that the fact/value dichotomy is no longer tenable' (p.xi).

of sounds, or to make patterns of marks on paper. Once trained, they find that performing those actions in the appropriate circumstances helps them to coordinate their behaviour with that of other people. All that is obviously consistent with realism. It presupposes there is a world with people in it and interacting with it. It is therefore consistent – to say the least – with the idea that truth is not the same as acceptability. For it is consistent with the idea that the world in which the language-game is being played is as it is *regardless* of whether the players themselves are clear about its nature. The realist will say there are truths about the world which hold independently of whether the participants in the language-game have the means to recognize them or even to state them. Exponents of the language-game argument will maintain that, when the realist makes such claims, that is done from within the realist's own language-game, so there is only the appearance of a mind-independent truth. But that claim takes us beyond the argument set out above. It does nothing to explain how there can *be* language-games not played by real people in a real world. How can people utter patterns of sounds in useful ways unless they are interacting in a world independent of their thoughts and experiences? If that is what they *are* doing, the existence of language-games, far from undermining realism, guarantees it. It guarantees that there are real matters of fact about the world in which people play language-games regardless of whether they themselves are aware of them or find their assertions acceptable. And if that is not what they are doing, the notion of language-games becomes impossible to understand, which demolishes the basis of the argument.[14]

Precisely which steps in the argument are faulty? The trouble just noted is pervasive, but affects particularly steps 1, 2, and 5. Contrary to step 1, it cannot be true that a language-game depends *entirely* on its rules. To some extent it must depend on the environment in which it is played. Contrary to step 2, therefore, features of that environment may themselves be appealed to if there is a question whether someone is following the rules; the outside world is independent of the language-game itself. (Whether the stranger used 'cow' correctly depends partly on whether the animal actually was a cow.) Those points ensure that step 5, even if it follows logically from the preceding steps, is not actually true.

Wittgenstein's ideas have encouraged people to see in them the ingredients of anti-realism. I have suggested that closer examination shows that to be a mistake, at least as far as his ideas on language-games are concerned. Obviously there is more to be said on that matter; essentially the above

---

14 You will have noticed that the conclusions of the language-game argument resemble true-for-me relativism, although they are reached by more sophisticated reasoning. In the end, the argument fails for essentially the same reasons as true-for-me relativism fails.

discussion will be taken up again in Chapter 9, in connection with Richard Rorty's 'postmodern' variety of pragmatism.

5 Is rationality relative?

The discussion of large-scale language-games involved the thought that people in different cultures may have very different ways of thinking and behaving. What people in non-Western cultures take to be appropriate frequently strikes Westerners as strange, if not irrational. To conclude the chapter I will consider a variety of sophisticated relativism which maintains that rationality itself is relative.

What is rationality after all? Is there a single absolute standard? (In which case, how can there be so much controversy about it?) Or is it relative to communities or even individuals? (In which case, why get more excited about it than we do about different traditions and tastes in music?)

For my purposes a good way into the topic is through a famous paper, 'Understanding a Primitive Society' by Peter Winch. He refers to work by the anthropologist E. E. Evans-Pritchard on the magical beliefs and practices of an African tribe, the Azande. Evans-Pritchard tells us how the Azande's magical practices form a system intimately enmeshed in the fabric of their everyday lives. Attempts by Europeans imbued with scientific attitudes to persuade them that they are mistaken only serve to reinforce their modes of thought:

> For their mystical notions are eminently coherent, being interrelated by a network of logical ties, and are so ordered that they never too crudely contradict sensory experience but, instead, experience seems to justify them. The Zande is immersed in a sea of mystical notions [the patterns of thought which introduce magic and witchcraft], and if he speaks about his poison oracle [a method of eliciting yes-or-no decisions on the basis of whether or not a chicken dies after being fed a special poison] he must speak in a mystical idiom.[15]

Winch parodies these remarks:

> For their scientific notions are eminently coherent, being interrelated by a network of logical ties, and are so ordered that they never too crudely contradict mystical experience but, instead, experience seems to justify them. The European is immersed in a sea of scientific notions, and if he speaks about the Zande poison oracle he must speak in a scientific idiom.[16]

15 E. E. Evans-Pritchard, *Witchcraft, Oracles, and Magic among the Azande*, p.319.
16 Winch, 'Understanding a Primitive Society', p.89.

Winch's main complaint is that Evans-Pritchard does not confine himself to describing the differences between what he calls 'the two concepts of reality involved':

> he wants to go further and say: our concept of reality is the correct one, the Azande are mistaken. But the difficulty is to see what 'correct' and 'mistaken' can mean in this case.[17]

Winch seems to think this is not just a difficulty, but an impossibility. He thinks there can be no basis for deciding between the two 'concepts of reality' and the associated 'standards of rationality'. He is not, of course, denying that we can observe the Azande's behaviour from outside and appraise it on the basis of our own concept of reality and our own standards of rationality, and – not surprisingly – find they are mistaken. That is precisely what he finds objectionable in Evans-Pritchard's discussions. In developing his objection he deploys considerations derived from Wittgenstein, some of which we have already discussed. The main hinge of his argument is the claim that standards of rationality and concepts of reality are inextricable from cultures and ways of life. They constitute the standards of reality, rationality and intelligibility for those who share a culture and way of life (or, in the very broad sense, a language-game) but they cannot be grasped except by those people. It seems to follow that those who approach a culture and way of life from outside cannot really understand its own standards of reality and rationality, hence can have no basis for criticizing them.

It seems certain that, if we wish to appraise the rationality and beliefs prevalent in a certain society, we must acquire the deepest understanding we can get of their culture and way of life. (The deepest we can get: our understanding can never be assimilated to the understanding which the members of that culture themselves have, because 'going native' would involve abandoning the project of appraisal.) But Winch goes crucially further. He seems to think that those who don't actually *share* the rationality and beliefs of a culture can't understand it and can't criticize its rationality or beliefs for that reason. Can that be right? There seem to be people who have started their lives sharing a particular culture but then have given it up and left it – but continued to criticize it. (What about St Francis, for example, or many hippies?) You don't have to be inside a culture to criticize it.

There is a more interesting objection to Winch's position. It concerns the claim that, as he puts it, 'standards of rationality in different societies do not always coincide'.[18] To be clear about the situation we must distinguish two

---

17 Op. cit., p.91.
18 Op. cit., p.97.

ideas that are easily bundled together. One is the idea of what rationality is, or of what it takes for a person to be rational. That, I shall argue, is not relative to culture. What it takes to be rational is the same among the Azande as in European society. In both cases, as I will try to make clear, being rational is doing whatever you suppose will tend to help you achieve whatever it is you want. The other is the idea of what it is rational for an individual to do or think in the circumstances, what makes particular actions or beliefs intelligible. That certainly is relative to culture and indeed to individual circumstances. If you were brought up among the Azande, then your beliefs and wants, hence your judgements about how to achieve whatever it is you want, will be very different from what they would have been if you had been brought up in Europe.

Suppose someone said, 'Rationality consists in eating as much as possible.' We can imagine situations where the remark would be intelligible: for example, if the speaker expected to be without food for a long period, or if they suffered from a psycho–physical condition like that of the shrew, whose nature compels it to spend its waking hours seeking and eating food. Failing such special circumstances, and assuming the speaker were not just expressing the scale of their gluttony, if the remark had to be taken as a statement of *what rationality is* in all circumstances, I suggest it would not be intelligible. We just could not count eating as much as possible as that which, in general, constitutes rationality, even though it may sometimes be a rational thing to do.

Why not? Because we have a certain conception of what rationality is, which rules out the possibility that rationality should consist in eating as much as possible. In spite of the vagueness of that conception, we know that for a person to be rational, as we understand the word, is something much more general.

It has to do with relations between their circumstances, knowledge and motivation on the one hand, and their behaviour or thoughts on the other. To be rational, thoughts and behaviour have to fit *appropriately* into the pattern provided by knowledge and motivation. If I want to eat an orange – if that is what I want to do now, all things considered – I will go into the kitchen. Why? Because I believe there are oranges there. If I were to go into the garden instead, even though I know there are no oranges there, my behaviour would be irrational. (It wouldn't be irrational if I had changed my mind; but the assumption is that at this moment I want an orange, all things considered.)

The background to the notion of rationality is certain general facts about all human beings. One fundamental fact is that we have needs and wants. Without needs or wants, no one would do anything at all: they constitute motivation. Another fundamental fact is that we acquire information: without information or beliefs about possible ways of satisfying needs and wants, action would be impossible. It is only when behaviour is directed at satisfying wants or needs on the basis of information about how that might be done that there is action. The notion of rationality bears on both these aspects: on the acquisition of information and on the initiation and control of action. We can be more or less rational both in our assessment of possible sources of information, given our wants, and in the means we adopt to satisfy our needs or wants, given our information. On this view of rationality, physiological and cultural differences are irrelevant. The Azande need be no less rational (or irrational) than Europeans. Even so, rationality could never consist in eating as much as possible. It is the wrong kind of thing: it has nothing to do with the systematic adjustment of behaviour on the basis of needs, desires and information.

You may object that, although that may be a widely shared view of what constitutes rationality, other cultures may have a different one. Does it really make sense to say so? To make good the claim that different cultures have a different concept of what constitutes rationality (as contrasted with what sorts of behaviour and thoughts are rational for them in their own special circumstances) it is necessary to be clear that the concept in question is still a concept of *rationality*. How could it be a concept of rationality if it diverged far from our own? We are, after all, perforce thinking in terms of our own concepts. The fact that they are our own concepts cuts two ways. First, it does indeed imply that other cultures may have different concepts. But second, it ensures that when we say we are talking about rationality it is our own use of this word – not that of other communities – which fixes what is to count as rational. We *cannot* count as rational something which diverges too far from our own concept. We ask the questions in our own language, so the answers must be in the same language. (If we wanted to study tigers, we should rightly be disappointed if some people who claimed there was a 'tiger' at the bottom of their garden turned out to be using that word as we use 'rabbit'.)

Suppose there were a community in other respects like ordinary human beings, but who spent most of their time eating as much as possible because, like shrews, they naturally needed to. We should not want to say they were acting irrationally. In the absence of countervailing factors, it is rational to satisfy one's needs. It would be irrational for them *not* to eat as much as possible, just as it would be irrational for us to starve ourselves until we were ill. However, that state of affairs would not show that, for them, rationality *consisted* in eating as much as possible. Nor, so far as I can see, could anything they said or did make it the case that they did think that. In order to have that thought they would have to have a concept of rationality. If that concept were much different from our own, we just wouldn't call it a concept of rationality at all. They might utter the sentence 'Rationality consists in eating as much as possible'. But there seems no way for us to be able to understand them to mean that they actually thought rationality consisted in eating as much as possible.

106

Apart from their unfortunate shrew-like drive to eat, the members of that community are like us. They still do certain things in order to achieve their objectives, and avoid others because they block their objectives. As with us, they still assess their situation in the world more or less accurately, they build up more or less reliable conceptions of their environment, and they manage their lives more or less efficiently. So there is nothing to stop them, *or us*, comparing them in respect of their ability to achieve their objectives given their culture, their beliefs and their other desires. Those are comparisons in respect of their rationality. Such comparisons are independent of the fact that pretty well everyone is eating as much as possible. Individuals among them whose need for food was less than the average might still be extremely rational; and vice versa. So here we have a conception of rationality – sometimes called 'instrumental' rationality – which can be applied across cultural differences. No doubt the notion is attenuated in comparison with some traditional ways of talking about rationality. But for our purposes it is extremely useful. It enables us to agree that the Azande, for example, are just as rational (or just as irrational) as Europeans. At the same time it leaves full scope for the obvious point that what it is rational to do typically depends on culture and circumstances, as well as on the individual's beliefs and motivation.[19]

It appears impossible to count any old thing whatever as constituting rationality. And we have a perfectly good, if limited, notion of rationality for making cross-cultural comparisons. Those considerations undermine the case for the total relativity of the concept of rationality.

MAIN POINTS IN CHAPTER 6

1   'Commonsense' and 'scientific' realism have been contrasted with two varieties of anti-realism: instrumentalism and Berkeleyan anti-realism, both hard to accept (section 1).
2   The language-game argument for anti-realism, supposedly based on Wittgenstein's ideas, has turned out not to be cogent (sections 4 and 5).
3   There is a useful sense in which rationality is not relative (section 5).

---

19 There are obviously questions about whether beliefs or information, and motivation, are themselves rational. Were they acquired in rational ways? Are they consistent?

CHAPTER 6: SUGGESTIONS FOR FURTHER READING

Berkeley. The *Dialogues between Hylas and Philonous* are readable and provide a good introduction to his approach. Ch. 15, 'Realism', in Adam Morton, *Philosophy in Practice*, helps to deepen understanding of what Berkeley is about. See also Jonathan Dancy, *Berkeley: an Introduction*. For more advanced discussions, see J. Bennett, *Locke, Berkeley, Hume: Central Themes*.

Realism and instrumentalism. Chapter 1 of F. Schmitt, *Truth: a primer*, introduces realism. J. J. C. Smart, *Philosophy and Scientific Realism*, is a classic and readable defence. Two advanced works, Bas Van Fraassen, *The Scientific Image*, and the related *Images of Science*, P. Churchland and C. Hooker (eds), discuss instrumentalist approaches.

The core of the **'language-game' argument** is to be found in Thomas S. Kuhn's classic, *The Structure of Scientific Revolutions* (2nd edn). Richard Rorty's *Philosophy and The Mirror of Nature* presents a highly readable account of philosophy in which, using essentially the same argument, he concludes in favour of what he calls 'edifying philosophy', whose point is 'to keep the conversation going rather than to find objective truth' (p.377).

There are several interesting discussions of **rationality** in Hollis and Lukes (eds), *Rationality and Relativism*. P. Winch, 'Understanding a Primitive Society', is in Brian Wilson (ed.), *Rationality*, which contains other useful material. For a highly readable discussion of many issues concerning rationality, see Martin Hollis, *The Cunning of Reason*.

7

FOUNDATIONS FOR KNOWLEDGE?

What if we could discover absolutely certain *foundations* for knowledge? We could apply logical reasoning to them and derive further solid knowledge, yielding a substantial stock of absolutely certain truths about reality. That would entitle us to disregard the language-game argument.

1 The idea of basing knowledge on foundations

The systematization of geometry is inspiring. You start off from a set of first principles, or 'axioms', as solid as anything possibly could be, and deduce any number of conclusions ('theorems') from them by unchallengeable logical steps. Plato was impressed by the work of Greek mathematicians along those lines, but bothered by the problem of how to establish the first principles themselves. His recommended solution reads well. By following a special kind of philosophical procedure (the 'dialectic') suitably selected and properly trained thinkers could, he suggested, reason from principles which at first were only provisional, but which would by gradual stages lead to a knowledge of the 'Form of the Good'. Having acquired that knowledge, they would be able to retrace the steps of their previous reasoning, and be brought to realize how the absolute truth of their provisional assumptions had finally been established. The idea is impressive – but deeply obscure.[1] (It is interesting that the culmination of the dialectic – encountering the Form of the Good – is described in terms comparable to those of reports of mystical experience.)

2 Descartes' 'method of doubt'

Another great philosopher who attempted to build knowledge on absolutely certain foundations was René Descartes (1596–1650). His approach was a great deal clearer than Plato's. (Although Descartes is a huge landmark in

---

1 Plato, *Republic*, books vi and vii. To be fair, Plato represents Socrates as finding it hard to explain his project.

philosophy, he was also a mathematician of the very highest rank.[2]) Impressed by human fallibility, he devised a special method for acquiring knowledge. This was his famous 'method of doubt'.

Descartes was worried by the thoughts which tend to lead to *scepticism*, the view that nothing can be known. We think we know many things, including matters of fact about the world around us, and also mathematical and logical truths. Yet quite often we are misled by our senses; and we can easily make mistakes in our calculations in mathematics and logic. If both our senses and our abstract intelligence are subject to error, how can there be genuine knowledge at all? He eventually hit on a method. He would examine all his beliefs, and provisionally give up all that could possibly be doubted until, proceeding with the utmost caution, he found some beliefs that were immune to doubt. Then he would build on those foundations, and either acquire new knowledge, or provide absolutely certain support for the beliefs that had been provisionally suspended. In his words:

> My whole aim was to reach certainty, and to reject loose earth and sand so as to find rock or clay.[3]

As he proceeded with this 'method of doubt' he found he was able to doubt all beliefs that depended on the evidence of his senses. Since his senses often led to mistakes, all such evidence was unreliable. Indeed, a 'malicious demon' might even be causing him to have experiences that were exactly like normal experiences of the world, but illusory. As when we dream, yet seem to be in a real world different from the real world, so what we regard as our genuine waking experiences might all be caused not by our encounters with external reality, but by the operations of the demon. Even when it appeared to Descartes that he was reasoning impeccably, as with his mathematical investigations, it might be that his thinking was being systematically distorted by that same malicious demon.

One thing he found he could not possibly doubt: that he existed: *Cogito, ergo sum* (I think, therefore I am). In order to engage in his method of systematic doubt, he could not rationally doubt that he was thinking, or that, in order to think, he must exist. That was the indubitable foundation for his subsequent reasoning. His next major move was to argue from his own existence, as a doubting and therefore imperfect being, to the existence of a perfect being, God. He could *conceive* of a perfect being, yet (so he

---

2 It has been urged that it is in mathematics that Descartes's greatest work lies. 'It is given to but few men to renovate a whole department of human thought', says E. T. Bell. 'Descartes was one of those few....Descartes [by his development of coordinate geometry] remade geometry and made modern geometry possible' (Bell, *Men of Mathematics*, p.56).
3 Descartes, *Discourse on the Method*, Part III.

argued), being imperfect himself, could not have originated that idea: only that perfect being could have produced it. To cut short a disconcertingly weak train of reasoning, he argued that God would not allow someone who 'clearly and distinctly' recognized that something was the case to be systematically deceived. In that way, he believed, most of what we regard as knowledge can be reinstated.

Descartes's own pursuit of his remarkable project has been influential in spite of the unsatisfactory character of the reasoning at that vital stage and elsewhere. He himself used a mix of abstract argument and experience to construct the foundations of his system. Others have attempted to use one or other of those resources exclusively. It will be useful briefly to consider them.

3 Can knowledge be based on purely a priori foundations?

One approach attempts to found knowledge on purely 'a priori' premises (premises we can know without knowing anything about how the world happens to be). We saw that Parmenides, that hero of archaic philosophy, attempted to establish the truth about reality by a priori argument, starting from the splendidly stark premiss (difficult to deny) IT IS OR IT IS NOT. In spite of its failure, his example might inspire us. If we worked at the task hard and intelligently enough, perhaps we could establish a priori foundations for a knowledge of reality.

Perhaps pigs could fly. The trouble is that the premises of an a priori argument must themselves be a priori. That means they are knowable without taking account of how things are in the world; so they can't depend on how the world happens to be. Unless it is impossible that the world should have been other than it actually is, therefore, a priori reasoning cannot tell us any particular facts about it. Take for example the statement that $2 + 2 = 4$. It is knowable a priori if anything is. It is 'true in any possible world'. That means it cannot provide any useful information about the world we actually live in – our own reality. Regardless of what reality is like, two plus two would still be equal to four. Another example: Kant thought we could know a priori that *every event has a cause*. If he was right, that would certainly help us to get from one piece of knowledge about the world to another. If we knew that long ago the dinosaurs suddenly became extinct, it would enable us to infer that something must have caused them to become extinct. But it would be no use as a basis for learning any particular facts about the world in the first place – it would not help us to discover *whether* dinosaurs really did suddenly become extinct. A priori principles are remarkably useful if you have some facts to start from; they can serve as premises for surprising conclusions. But they cannot yield factual starting points.

In order to think, we need certain capacities and propensities, possibly even certain concepts. (I take it that *concepts* are ways of classifying and thinking about things, and that they are necessarily involved in having beliefs.) It seems roughly true that thinking just *is* the application of concepts. Conceivably, then, there are truths about our concepts which can be arrived at a priori. (That was Kant's big idea.) Even so, it provides no basis for acquiring beliefs or theories about the world to which those concepts are supposed to apply. The very assumption that those concepts are not acquired through experience, but are innate, or at any rate supply necessary conditions for all possible thought, makes that clear. If all possible thought is constrained by those concepts, then their implications hold in all thinkable worlds. What we want to know about, however, is the actual world, the world where woodlice invade houses and bread falls buttered side down. This actual world is only one of infinitely many thinkable worlds.

For those and similar reasons the suggestion that knowledge of reality could be built on purely a priori foundations has lost whatever appeal it once had, in spite of stalwart efforts by philosophers such as Spinoza and Leibniz. (Spinoza (1632–1677) is the most consistent exponent of this approach. In his *Ethics* he purported to use the 'geometrical method' – definitions, axioms, proofs of theorems – to establish a number of results about the nature of God, freedom, and the world (not, for the most part, ethical results in spite of his title).)

4 Can knowledge be based on foundations provided by experience?

The rival approach is that solid, certain knowledge of reality might be founded on sense experience. It may well seem more attractive. Since the time of the ancient Greeks many philosophers have adopted it. If the Core Scientific Story is true, the evolutionary function of eyes, ears and other perceptual equipment is to allow us to gather information about our environment. How could sense experience fail to provide a solid foundation for our knowledge of matters of fact?

We have already noticed one difficulty. The senses can mislead us; not everything we take to be the evidence of our senses could possibly amount to a solid foundation for knowledge. True, it seems the only way we could possibly check on what our senses tell us is by further experience. In practice it seems that when we are alert in full daylight and things are in full view, we scarcely ever make mistakes. The fact that we *can* do so doesn't automatically prevent sense experience from yielding very solid knowledge indeed. All the same, the fallibility of the senses remains an obstacle if we are looking for absolutely solid foundations.

Another difficulty is this. Even if what our senses told us about our surroundings were absolutely trustworthy, we should still have to go beyond that evidence in order to build up knowledge of the rest of reality. At least that is so if we assume there is more to the world than what our senses tell us about our immediate surroundings – and that is an assumption which is hard to challenge. It has underlain scientific theorizing since the time of the Greek atomists. We can distinguish two broad ways in which there is 'more to reality'. One is that there are regions of space and time beyond the reach of our senses, yet which our unaided senses *could* have enabled us to find out about if it had been possible for us to be there then. The other is that there are aspects of reality which we should be incapable of detecting by our senses even if we were in the right place at the right time. As human culture has developed, we have elaborated theories which purport to describe such aspects of reality. Protons are invisible even if we use powerful microscopes; vast numbers of stars and other cosmic entities are invisible even with the aid of powerful telescopes, or so we are told. Since in both ways there is more to reality than what our senses convey, we have to make inferences and formulate theories. Yet – this is a further difficulty – those inferences and theories cannot be absolutely guaranteed to be correct. We have evidence about how things *have* behaved in the past. But as David Hume disconcertingly pointed out, no amount of such evidence will establish, beyond the possibility of error, how things will behave in the future. (That is the famous 'problem of induction'.[4])

The difficulty of finding solid support for theories about matters beyond the reach of our senses may seem to give some advantage to theories which deny there is anything 'out there' to be right or wrong about. One such theory is Berkeley's. If nothing else is involved in the existence of ordinary material objects than our having 'ideas' of them in our minds (or God's having such ideas), then where there are no ideas there is no reality anyway; and if there are no independently existing objects, objects have no fine structure to be right or wrong about. The trouble is that if you accept that doctrine, you still have to provide a good reason to accept it; and the reasons available are not compelling.

An apparently less demanding doctrine is *phenomenalism*. It seems to offer the advantages of Berkeleyanism without God. It is an interestingly different way in which one might attempt to found knowledge of reality on experience, without commitment to things having a fine structure undetectable by the senses. Phenomenalists claim that statements about objects 'out there', such as sticks, stones and tomatoes, can be 'analysed' in terms of statements about actual or possible *experiences*.[5] ('Analysis' here usually involves finding equivalent statements that are also informative. An equivalent statement would necessarily be true or false in exactly the same circumstances as the original statement.)

4 See David Hume, *A Treatise of Human Nature*, Book I, sections xii and xiii.
5 See A. J. Ayer, *Language, Truth, and Logic*.

Take for example the statement:

(1) There is a woodpecker in the garden.

Phenomenalists would hope to be able to produce an equivalent to (1) in terms of possible experiences. A first stab might be:

(2) If anyone were in a suitable place in the garden they would have woodpecker-experiences.

But that wouldn't work because it leaves the notions of 'place' and 'garden' to be understood in the ordinary way, as things 'out there'. An attempt to improve on it might go: 'If there were the right sort of garden-experiences they would include woodpecker-experiences'. One difficulty is that this presupposes all sorts of conditions are satisfied: the observer must have normal sense perception; there must be normal conditions in the garden; the woodpecker must not be dressed up as a rabbit;…. Another difficulty is that, in order for the conditional (if–then) statement (2) to be true, something must presumably *make* it true. What can that something be except a real garden and a real woodpecker 'out there' – independently of possible experiences of them? If that is right, the phenomenalist project is doomed from the start: it presupposes the outside world exists independently of experiences, and so for that reason cannot be analysed in terms of them. Phenomenalism is indeed hard to defend.

5 Wittgenstein on private language

A possible explanation of the failure of phenomenalism may be found in Wittgenstein's famous 'private language argument'. What follows, however, can be only a brief glance at a complex skein of argumentation, much interpreted and debated.

We can start from the point that phenomenalism needs a special 'phenomenal language' dealing exclusively in terms of experiences. Arguably, anyone who assumes that the only certain knowledge we have is of our experiences and sensations is committed to something of the sort. If you aim to build up your knowledge of the external world from foundations derived from experience, you have to assume you can know about the latter while remaining uncertain about the former. It is a short step to accepting that you can *talk* about the latter in ways that other people might not be able to know about.

Such a language would have to be capable of being understood by the person whose experiences they were, even though no one else could possibly understand it. In a very strong sense of the phrase, then, it would have to be a 'private language'. It would not just be a sort of code – like the shorthand

114

Pepys used for his diary – that other people could understand if only they knew the key; it must be a language others could never hope to understand because they could not know what experiences its expressions referred to.

Wittgenstein sets out a battery of considerations which appear to show that a private language of that particular sort is impossible. The starting-point is that any language whatever must have rules. As we saw in Chapter 4, sections 4 and 8, no linguistic expression is *intrinsically* meaningful. It derives its meaning from being used in accordance with rules, conventions or norms. Wittgenstein reasons that, in the case of a language that was private in the special sense just described, there would be no way for the user to tell whether they were following its rules. Indeed there would be no way even to set up the rules in the first place. In order for there to be rules, there has to be a contrast between following them and not following them; between getting it right and getting it wrong. But if no one else could tell what the words of the language meant, there would be no possibility of a contrast between using the language in accordance with its rules and only seeming to do so. In Wittgenstein's words: 'One would like to say: whatever is going to seem right to me is right. And that only means that here we can't talk about "right".'[6] There could be no following the rules at all, hence no language.

If that reasoning is successful, it is fatal to the project of building up knowledge of the rest of the world from foundations derived solely from knowledge of our own experience.

6 A general difficulty for foundationalist views: Neurath's boat

To conclude the chapter I will mention a general difficulty that applies to all kinds of 'foundationalist' proposals. Those proposals require us to put all our present beliefs on one side, pretending we know nothing, and build up our knowledge again from scratch. That would involve 'standing outside' our own beliefs – which is an impossible project.

In order to make decisions about what to do, we need *some* beliefs and concepts. Imagine I had decided to follow Descartes' example and magically succeeded in putting all my current beliefs in suspension, so that now I had no actual beliefs at all. Then in particular I would have no beliefs about what I was aiming to do, no beliefs about whether I was trying to acquire knowledge. That would quickly put paid to my foundational project. Evidently, if we have decided to build up our knowledge from scratch, we have no hope of succeeding unless we retain some idea of what knowledge is, and of what we are aiming to achieve. That means we need some *beliefs* on those matters. Another example: suppose I wanted to decide whether or not to accept the belief *that I exist*. I would be helpless if I had no beliefs

---

6 *Philosophical Investigations*, sec. 258.

about what are good reasons for accepting a given suggestion and what are bad ones. It would defeat the whole project if those beliefs had to be given up as well. So there is simply no way in which we could 'stand outside' all our beliefs.

You might suggest that it isn't really beliefs, or even concepts, that we need to have in order to be able to make decisions about which suggestions to accept and which to reject: it would be enough if we had a suitable set of tendencies and inclinations. But that would not work. The project of building up knowledge from foundations demands conscious attention to principles, and that inevitably commits you to some beliefs about what those principles are and to having concepts in terms of which to think about them. Descartes adopted the principle that he would accept no belief unless he could 'clearly and distinctly' perceive it to be true; so among other beliefs he had the belief that it was a sound principle. Without attending to the principles on which one is operating, and the resulting beliefs about them, there would be nothing to distinguish someone attempting to base knowledge on foundations from someone just getting on with the ordinary business of living, without giving any consideration to questions of justification.

Couldn't someone tinker with our brains so that we were left completely free of all beliefs and concepts? Perhaps. But think what the result would be: you would be rather like a new-born baby. You would not be able to think to much effect at all until you had learnt a language, and picked up *from others* a fresh set of concepts, ways of thinking and beliefs. Then you would be back essentially where you had started from. Like it or not, there is no way out of this situation. If we want to revise our system of beliefs and theories, even our concepts, then we can certainly do so. But we have to start from where we are; and we have to use some of the beliefs we already have. There could not be such a thing as standing outside all theories, all 'conceptual schemes', and starting from scratch. The point is emphasized by both Wittgenstein and Quine, who uses Otto Neurath's words on the topic as an epigraph to his book *Word and Object*:

> We are like sailors who have to rebuild their ship on the open sea, without ever being able to dismantle it in a dock and reconstruct it from the best components.

Notice there are two aspects to this thought. There is an inward-looking one, concerning the implications which the project of revising beliefs has for the belief-system itself. (We must leave enough timbers in place to keep the boat seaworthy while we replace others.) There is also an outward-looking one: there cannot be such a thing as facing a reality that is naked and unconceptualized; we can only face it on the basis of the beliefs and concepts we have. (To keep sailing at all, we need some kind of boat.)

You might perhaps think I have been making heavy weather of something straightforward. Can't the world just impress its nature on us directly, without the mediation of concepts, beliefs or theories?[7] The idea does have a certain appeal: let reality itself, undistorted by conceptual lenses, reveal itself. But difficulties jump out as soon as we consider what 'we' must be like in order to be open to such disclosures. It is not as if any old thing were capable of the necessary sort of intelligent receptivity. Sensitivity alone is not enough. Litmus paper is sensitive to acids and alkalis, but we can't say the nature of fluids is 'revealed' to the litmus paper. Nor is it enough just to be capable of receiving and holding impressions. The world doesn't reveal itself to sealing wax. Only a special kind of thing is capable of the right kind of intelligent sensitivity. It must be capable not only of having experiences, but of dealing appropriately with experiences. That means it has to be capable of classifying and ordering things, and going for one sort of thing rather than another. In other words, it has to have concepts, even if only rudimentary ones. Having concepts inevitably involves having theories, even if they are half-formed or primitive. That takes us back to the last paragraph.

It seemed we might have been able to settle the dispute between realism and anti-realism by basing knowledge on foundations. The results have not been encouraging: that project is open to serious objections. However, the failure of the language-game argument for anti-realism does not finally settle matters. There is a more sophisticated variety of anti-realism to be considered.

MAIN POINTS IN CHAPTER 7

1   The idea of basing knowledge on foundations has been pursued by Descartes and others, some of whom have attempted to do so on purely a priori foundations, others on foundations derived from experience. All appear unsuccessful (sections 1–4).
2   Wittgenstein's 'private language argument' appears to demolish the whole project of basing knowledge of the rest of the world on indubitable knowledge of our own experiences (section 5).
3   A general difficulty for foundationalist approaches is that we cannot conduct any project at all without some beliefs, concepts and theories. Looking at it from a different angle, we cannot confront a naked and unconceptualized reality. There seems no way to escape the predicament of Neurath's sailors (section 6).

---

7 Some people detect an implication to this effect in Heidegger's thoughts on truth as 'disclosure'. See his *Being and Time*, and H. Dreyfus's *Being-in-the-World: a Commentary*. I do not think that interpretation does him justice. In any case, he did not explain how to get round the considerations just mentioned.

CHAPTER 7: SUGGESTIONS FOR FURTHER READING

Foundationalism. J. Dancy, *An Introduction to Contemporary Epistemology*, chs 4 and 5, provides clear introductory exposition and discussion. A classic text, though not in detail always easy to follow, is W. Sellars, *Science, Perception and Reality*, ch. 5.

For **Wittgenstein on private language** the primary text is his *Philosophical Investigations*, §§243–317. A. Kenny, *Wittgenstein*, and Marie McGinn, *Wittgenstein and the* Philosophical Investigations, offer useful introductions. For more advanced discussion see David Pears, *The False Prison*, vol. ii. Saul Kripke, *Wittgenstein on Rules and Private Language*, presents an advanced, controversial, but very readable interpretation.

On **Descartes**, his own *Discourse on the Method* and *Meditations* are the best introduction. Bernard Williams, *Descartes: the Project of Pure Enquiry*, is not easy, but full of interest.

8

DUMMETT'S ANTI-REALISM

This variety of anti-realism, like the one based on the idea of language-games, has Wittgensteinian roots. It starts from one of Wittgenstein's main topics: understanding statements.

1 Truth conditions, understanding and mathematical truth

What is it to understand a statement? One widely accepted suggestion is that it is to know its 'truth conditions': the conditions under which it would be true. We understand the statement 'It rained here yesterday', for example, just in case we know what conditions must be satisfied for it to have rained here yesterday. If we don't know what those conditions are, it is hard to claim we really understand it; and if we do, what more could be required? (Truth conditions are not to be confused with truth value – whether the statement in question is true or false. Supposedly, a statement has the same truth conditions regardless of whether it is true or false: they are the conditions in which it *would* be true.)

There is at least one field where that suggestion gets us into trouble: mathematics. We tend to assume that if mathematical statements are true at all, they are true in *all* conditions – in all 'possible worlds'. Suppose we were trying to get someone who had missed out on mathematics to understand '2 + 2 = 4', and simply said 'It's true no matter what: true in all possible worlds – rain, shine, Hell or high water'. That would be useless as an explanation of what '2 + 2 = 4' means. The same 'explanation' would apply to '5 – 3 = 2', together with all other true mathematical statements as well, including 'There is no greatest prime number'.

Presumably understanding a given statement is the same as knowing what it means. If understanding it were just a matter of knowing in what conditions it is true, we should have to conclude that all true mathematical statements meant the same. Given minimal assumptions about meaning, we know they do *not* all mean the same. (We can know the meaning of '2 + 2 = 4' without also knowing the meaning of 'There is no greatest prime number'.) So it seems that understanding mathematical statements cannot be just a matter of knowing their truth conditions.

Recall a suggestion noticed earlier, to the effect that for the case of mathematical statements, truth is *provability* (and falsity is disprovability). If acceptable, it seems to get us over the difficulty. It enables us to say that to understand a mathematical statement is to know what would constitute a proof of it. On that basis, since knowing what would be a proof of '2 + 2 = 4' is clearly not the same as knowing what would be a proof of 'There is no greatest prime number', the difficulty posed by the truth conditions theory would not arise.

2 Dummettian anti-realism

That approach to meaning and understanding has some appeal in connection with mathematical statements. Michael Dummett has been exploring the possibility of extending it to all statements in general. This is a special variety of anti-realism. Other varieties, for example instrumentalism about the theoretical entities of physics, emphasize the question of what exists. They tell us that some class of things assumed to exist does not really exist. Dummett's anti-realism, in contrast, emphasizes questions of understanding and truth. What is it to understand statements of the kinds in question? What is it for them to be true? There are two central ideas.

The first is that understanding a statement is knowing the conditions in which it may correctly be *asserted*, rather than the conditions in which it is *true*. Meaning and understanding are to be explained in terms of 'assertion conditions' (or 'assertibility conditions') rather than 'truth conditions'.

Connectedly, the second central idea is that a statement's being true depends essentially on our ability to *tell* that it may correctly be asserted. Where the mathematical kind of anti-realism uses the notion of provability as its version of truth, the general kind uses correct or warranted assertibility. So if we cannot tell whether or not a certain statement is assertible, it lacks a truth value.

At first that last implication might not seem too disturbing. We are familiar with cases where we are not sure whether a certain description applies. (Is that book red or not? Well, it's on the borderline: surely it doesn't have to be determinately one or the other?) They are beside the point for Dummett's anti-realism. It is concerned with all statements, including those we regard as on the one hand straightforwardly factual but on the other hand beyond our powers warrantedly to assert or deny. Examples include many statements about the remote past or remote regions of space. We ordinarily tend to take a realist view of such statements. We assume they *are* either true or false even if we have no way to decide which. Take for example the following:

(1) Just before we came into this room, that fly was moving towards the window.

(2) In that galaxy there are exactly three stars that have exactly three planets.

(3) Four thousand years ago a bear coughed here.

We assume such statements have truth values (we assume they are true or false) even though we may have no grounds for asserting them, and negligible chances of discovering whether they actually are true or false. A statement's being true or false is one thing, we assume; being able to discover its truth value is something else. To be justified in asserting a statement does not, according to the realist, ensure that it is true: there is a gap between justified assertibility and truth. The anti-realist denies those assumptions. Consider the statement:

(3) Four thousand years ago a bear coughed here.

There might have been evidence either for or against it. There might have been evidence that, at the time in question, this region lay beneath the sea, in which case we could justifiably deny that there had been bears here at all, coughing or not. On the other hand we might have discovered the remains of bears showing evidence of tuberculosis, in which case we could justifiably have asserted the statement. But suppose that today, as it happens, there is no evidence either for or against it. The Dummettian anti-realist appears to be committed to maintain that the statement has no truth value.[1] But for reasons we have noticed already, truth cannot be supposed to be insulated from reality. So the anti-realist implies that in this case, as in countless similar ones, *reality itself is indeterminate*, in the sense that it is neither the case that a bear coughed here 4,000 years ago, nor not the case. There is no fact of the matter, either way.[2] (That seems to bring significant implications for logic. If reality itself is indeterminate in certain cases, the assumption that any statement is either true or false has to be given up. In that case there appears to be no backing for the logical law of Excluded Middle which states that, for any proposition p, either p or not-p.

---

1 In that situation you might find it natural to say that the statement was neither true nor false. However, Dummett distinguishes between that and saying that the statement in question lacks a truth value. See *Truth and Other Enigmas*, pp.xviif.

2 For a region of reality to be indeterminate appears to be different from its being filled with 'cosmic porridge'. If there are regions of cosmic porridge, their existence – as patches of an indeterminate sort of stuff – is a hard matter of fact. If reality is indeterminate, there are *no* such facts about it.

Dummett's investigations have led him to pursue the question of alternatives to 'classical' logic.)

I will set out, and then discuss, what I take to be the main features of the case for Dummettian anti-realism. This kind of anti-realism is more sophisticated, more interesting and better defended than the varieties we have looked at so far. (Dummett insists, by the way, that exploring different varieties of anti-realism is for him a research programme: he is not to be understood as advocating anti-realism.)

3 The case for Dummettian anti-realism

The background is familiar from our discussion of Wittgenstein's ideas on language-games. Following Wittgenstein, the Dummettian anti-realist holds that the meaningfulness of a linguistic expression consists in its being used in accordance with rules. Assuming that any human being can learn a human language, this type of anti-realist points out that we pick up our knowledge of our language by sharing in its use with others who already know it. So it seems there can be no more to knowing the meanings of sentences than can be somehow picked up from their use by others. How does the infant learn to use, hence understand, sentences such as 'It's raining', 'I like ice-cream', 'There were two rabbits in the garden', if not by associating with other people using either those very sentences, or others with similar patterns, in appropriate circumstances? Everything involved in knowing the language must be available to any learner (though it has to be assumed that learners and speakers share the same 'form of life': Chapter 4, section 9). That seems to amount to saying that those other speakers must be able to demonstrate or manifest their understanding. So any account of understanding, meaning and truth has to be able to explain those two related facts: that we can *acquire* an understanding of the sentences of our language, and that we can *manifest* that understanding in use.

The Dummettian anti-realist is now in a position to challenge at least some varieties of realism, including the common realist assumption that we understand statements about remote regions of space and time in such a way that they may perfectly well *be* true even if it is beyond our powers to *discover* that they are true. It is agreed on all sides that we understand statement (3) (about the bear). But suppose there is no evidence either for or against it. The realist will insist that it still *has* a truth value; but the anti-realist challenges that assumption, and wants to know how it could possibly be so.

The challenge is for the realist to explain how we can have any idea of what it is for a statement such as 'Four thousand years ago a bear coughed here' to be 'realistically' true – true in the way the realist supposes, not just assertible – if there is no way to recognize that it is true. So at the same time the challenge is to explain how it is possible to *understand* such a statement. The Dummettian anti-realist argues as follows.[3] We have to be able to manifest our understanding of 'true' just as we do for any other word. For any given statement, the correct use of 'true' in connection with that statement must be capable of being shown in its actual use; and (it is assumed) the only way that is possible is if the circumstances in which 'true' *is* correctly used of it are ones that can be recognized as such. Those circumstances are ones where we have evidence for the truth or falsity of the given statement. However, if the statement happens to be one where there is *no* recognizable evidence for its truth or falsity, then in those circumstances there is no way for the use of 'true' (or 'false') to be connected to it. In Dummett's words: 'We could not, in any context, gain a notion of truth as attaching to statements independently of our means of recognizing them as true.'[4] In those circumstances, according to him, it is impossible for the statement to be intelligibly said to be true or false. If it cannot intelligibly be said to be true or false, then, according to Dummett, two important consequences follow. First, the statement is not true or false: it lacks a truth value. Second, because in the circumstances envisaged we could not recognize that it was true or false, we could not attach to it the sort of meaning the realist assumes it has. We could not associate it with the sort of 'truth conditions' the realist supposes are necessary for it to mean what it does: 'verification-transcendent' truth conditions, ones not necessarily recognizable as such. So we could not *manifest* our grasp of those truth conditions. In that way, the realist's assumptions appear to lead to the conclusion that we do not even understand the statements in question. Since we clearly do understand them, the realist's conception of what it is for them to be true must be mistaken.

Now consider the statement

(4) All mice are mortal.

We certainly understand it. Yet since it applies to all the mice that will ever have existed, there could hardly be such a thing as *recognizing* a situation in which it was (realistically) true. We can recognize a dead mouse, but how could we similarly recognize that it was the last mouse? It is hard to see how a learner of the language could pick up an idea of what it is for the state-

---

3 This is my own attempt to present the kernel of the case for Dummettian anti-realism. I believe it to be as clear and compelling as any that have been presented by Dummett himself; but that may be disputed. In what follows the qualification 'Dummettian' is sometimes omitted.

4 Dummett, 'The Reality of the Past', reproduced in his *Truth and Other Enigmas*, p.367. As Crispin Wright puts it: 'The anti-realist challenges the realist satisfactorily to explain how we could come by, and distinctively display, an idea of what it would be for a statement to be true independently of the existence of any means for our determining its truth' (Wright, *Realism, Meaning and Truth*, pp.178f.).

ment to be true – of its truth conditions – in so far as its being true is taken (as the realist takes it) to be different from its being assertible. How can it be connected to its supposed truth conditions? In the apparent absence of a satisfactory realist answer, the anti-realist maintains that there can be no satisfactory explanation of its having the sort of meaning the realist takes it to have, and of our understanding it in a realist way. That is why the anti-realist suggests that to understand a statement is to know the conditions in which it is *assertible*, rather than those in which it would be *true*. We can recognize the conditions in which a related statement, such as 'This mouse was mortal', is true. But (the anti-realist maintains) we cannot similarly recognize the conditions in which (4) itself is supposed to be true. If, on the other hand, understanding that statement requires only that we can recognize conditions in which we are justified in asserting it, there is no such difficulty – though in that case there is no more to the statement's being true than there is to the existence of evidence justifying its assertion. Its being true in this anti-realist way is very different from its being true in the way the realist has in mind – a point that will become clearer in the following sections.

4 Possible realist replies

Dummettian anti-realism has two distinct components. One is a critique of a particular account of understanding, the one according to which understanding a sentence is knowing its truth conditions. The other is a positive doctrine, which includes the claim that understanding a sentence is knowing its assertibility conditions, and in particular the claim that 'we could not, in any context, gain a notion of truth as attaching to statements independently of our means of recognizing them as true'. For the anti-realist, according to Dummett, *the truth of a statement can consist only in the existence of evidence justifying its assertion.*[5] (Recall the comparison of his kind of anti-realism with the suggestion that mathematical truth is just provability.)

The most promising strategy for realists seems to be to undermine the anti-realist's assumptions about the ways in which it is possible for sentences to be associated with knowledge of their truth conditions. Dummett seems

5 In 'Realism' (1963) he says: 'For the anti-realist, an understanding of such a statement [viz. one of those we tend to think of realistically but whose truth values we cannot recognize] consists in knowing what counts as evidence adequate for the assertion of the statement, and the truth of the statement can consist only in the existence of such evidence' (*Truth and Other Enigmas*, p.155). He is sometimes more cautious, e.g. in his 'What is a Theory of Meaning? II', in *The Seas of Language*, where he says 'the notion of truth, when it is introduced, must be explained, in some manner, in terms of our capacity to recognize statements as true, and not in terms of a condition which transcends human capacities' (p.75).

to assume that we could only acquire or manifest knowledge of the truth conditions for a sentence by being faced with a situation satisfying the truth condition when the sentence was uttered, as we can be faced with snow when 'It's snowing' is uttered, or with a dead mouse when 'This mouse was mortal' is uttered. The realist had better argue, then, that a knowledge of truth conditions may be acquired indirectly.

Here is one way. The realist can point out that we acquire our first language by degrees. Successive stages of understanding are built on earlier ones. Encounters with dogs, cats, mice and many other things enable us to connect words such as 'dog', 'cat', 'mouse', with particular types of things or situations. Then we learn how sentences are constructed from such components with the aid of words such as 'is', 'not', 'and', and words such as 'some' and 'all'. So it seems possible that we pick up a grasp of the truth conditions of sentences such as 'This mouse was mortal' by being directly brought up against situations in which it is true, and then pick up a grasp of the truth conditions of sentences such as 'All mice are mortal' indirectly, by learning the significance of constructions including such words as 'all'. Similarly, we learn more or less directly the truth conditions of sentences such as 'The distance from here to there is one mile', and then indirectly learn the truth conditions for the results of substituting larger numbers for 'one'.

When Dummett is discussing such replies he makes an interesting assumption. He assumes the realist has to 'make a surreptitious appeal to the conception of an ability to determine, by inspection, the truth of a sentence of the new kind in the same general way as we determine the truth of one of the old kind. Such an ability comprises the capacity to view at will any region of space-time, so that all are accessible.' He concludes that the realist has to form, 'by analogy with our own faculties, the conception of a being with superhuman powers' (the 'God's Eye View').[6] If that is right the realist is in trouble. But it is far from clear that the realist has to accept that account. Why concede that in every possible case the truth value of a statement has to be discoverable at all? Even if that were to be conceded, why concede also that the method of discovery must be 'inspection'? (See the rest of this section, and Chapter 9, section 3.)

Of course Dummett does not deny that the gradual build-up of our knowledge of our language provides some understanding of problematic sentences such as 'All mice are mortal'. His objection is that there seems no way to explain what the truth conditions for that sentence are except, trivially, by means of that sentence itself; for example:

6 Dummett, *The Logical Basis of Metaphysics*, p.345.

(5) 'All mice are mortal' is true if and only if all mice are mortal.

That is certainly a true statement. The trouble seems to be, from Dummett's position, that (5) could not be used to inform someone of (4)'s truth conditions because the right-hand side of (5) is the same as (4) itself, and so could be understood only by someone who *already* understood (4). Nor would it be enough just to know that (5) was true. To see the point, notice that you could know the following sentence was true – I assure you it is! – without understanding it or knowing it means the same as (5):

(6) Si quis 'All mice are mortal' ait, verum solum dicit si omnes mures mortales sunt.

However, realists can appeal to more fundamental considerations. They can maintain that Dummett has failed to do justice to the fact that we deliberately produce theories covering more of the world than is immediately accessible. Anaximander's theory, Greek atomism, the Core Scientific Story – all offer frameworks in terms of which the truth or falsity of some statements is inevitably hard for us to establish, perhaps impossible. Yet grasping the theory seems to enable us to understand such statements in spite of our inability to recognize situations where they are true. Indeed, it is an important feature of such theories that they include the means to explain how it is that some facts are inaccessible to us.

Equally important, such theories explain how there may be varying amounts of *evidence* for some statements even when there is no way to establish whether they are true or false. We acquire a grasp of what counts as evidence, and of how to assess the strength of evidence, at the same time as we acquire a grasp of the theory itself. Recall Quine's remarks about theories (Chapter 5, sections 4–7). According to his conception, a statement's truth value can never be 'determined' beyond the possibility of revision. Nor can truth values generally be 'recognized' or discovered 'by inspection'. Instead, what constitutes our ability to understand individual statements is our grasp of the theories in which they are incorporated. Perceptual evidence never absolutely compels us to accept or reject a statement: there are always varying degrees of justification. In some cases, such as 'That flower is red' or 'This mouse is dead', the justification will be overwhelming and not in practice disputable. Yet the normality of circumstances is only a matter of degree; so even in those cases it would be a misrepresentation to maintain that there was no possibility of error. In other cases, the interdependence of the components of our theory and the corresponding interdependence of our justifications for accepting and rejecting statements rule out a statement's ever being assertible beyond the possibility of challenge – even when there are very strong grounds for asserting it.

Realists taking that approach do not seem to be committed to the possibility of a being with superhuman powers who could 'determine' the truth of a sentence 'by inspection'. *No* statement is such that its truth is determinable 'by inspection' alone: some weight must always be given to the surrounding theory. So Dummett's counter to the first reply is not compelling. (See also Chapter 9, section 3.)

Dummett does discuss Quinean holism. When he does, he is not focusing on issues of assertibility. He is concerned to argue that a thoroughgoing holism cannot account for the facts of language-learning. However, you don't have to be a thoroughgoing holist to press the above reply to anti-realism. You can be moderate. Moderate holism will be to the effect that for many areas of the language, understanding some sentences requires knowing a good deal of theory, more or less as a whole. Nor does this point apply only to the higher levels of scientific theory. It is obvious that we can't understand the biological term 'gene', for example, without some knowledge of the associated theory of reproduction. But the same general point holds for most, if not all, of our everyday language. Even understanding common words such as 'bread', 'house', 'arm', involves webs of more or less closely interlocking beliefs, which may be regarded as partly constituting our theories of bread, houses, bodily parts and so on. So it does not seem that the anti-realist can escape Quinean attack by maintaining that theoretical language is distinct from the rest. On the contrary, it seems that being able to have beliefs at all depends on a network of theory, however homespun.

A moderate amount of theoretical interrelatedness is enough to ensure that in many, perhaps most, cases there can be no unchallengeable basis for claiming that a statement is true, and that 'inspection' is never enough by itself. To repeat, if that is right, one of anti-realism's main bases for attacking realism has crumbled. The realist is not forced to concede that understanding what it is for a statement to be true depends generally on our being able to recognize situations in which it is true, if it is.

Dummett has interesting ideas about the disputes between various kinds of realism and anti-realism. These have run on over centuries, everyone knows all the moves, but 'No knock-out blow has been delivered. The decision must be given on points; and we do not know how to award points.' The opposing theses, realist and anti-realist, are at present no better than 'pictures': 'the principal difficulty is that, while one or another of the competing pictures may appear compelling, we have no way to explain in non-pictorial terms what accepting it amounts to'.[7] The strategy he recommends is to approach the problems 'bottom up'. That is, to ignore metaphysical problems at the outset, and start off by examining the disagreements between realist and anti-realist over the 'correct model of

---

7 Both quotations are from *The Logical Basis of Metaphysics*, p.12. For more on Dummett's assumptions about how sense can be made of realism, see the next section.

meaning' for the problematic statements (such as statements about remote regions of space and time, those involving infinite domains, and 'counterfactual conditionals' – statements such as 'If the house had had proper foundations, there wouldn't have been these cracks'). It is worth emphasizing how far-reaching Dummett's claim is. A description of how language functions on the lines he envisages, a 'meaning-theory' of a special kind, 'will resolve these controversies without residue: there will be no further, properly metaphysical, question to be determined'.[8] Many philosophers disagree. Elaborating the above suggestions about the role of theory will enable us to see how realists might reply.

5 Dummettian anti-realism and theory

Dummett remarks:

> Realism about the past entails that there are numerous true propositions forever in principle unknowable. The effects of a past event may simply dissipate....To the realist, this is just part of the human condition; the anti-realist feels unknowability in principle to be intolerable and prefers to view our evidence for and memory of the past as constitutive of it. For him, there cannot be a past fact no evidence for which exists to be discovered, because it is the existence of such evidence that would make it a fact, if it were one.[9]

That is shocking to any realist. But to counter it, what is needed is arguments, not expressions of repugnance. Arguments are hard to come by if Dummett is right. As we have seen, he thinks that in spite of a strong undertow towards realism, realism and anti-realism are no better than competing 'pictures', and their exponents are at present doomed to engage in a futile pillow-fight. However, for reasons I will mention shortly, it is hard to see how realism can be regarded as just a 'picture'.

Consider the following story. Until yesterday there were beneath the ground, but undiscovered, the remains of bears with evidence that they had lived 4,000 years ago and suffered from tuberculosis. So until yesterday anti-realists, if they had come across the evidence, would have agreed with realists that it was a fact that 4,000 years ago a bear coughed here. But yesterday work began on the foundations of a new building, totally destroying that evidence. According to the anti-realist position sketched by Dummett in the passage just quoted, what was a fact until yesterday is no longer a fact. Realists will object that what happened here yesterday cannot

---

8 Op. cit., p.14.
9 Dummett, *The Logical Basis of Metaphysics*, p.7. As we saw earlier, he has made more cautious statements about the links between evidence and truth.

be relevant to whether or not a bear coughed here 4,000 years ago. They will insist that the only things relevant to that question are what happened at that time. If there was a coughing bear here then, the effects of its presence may or may not have persisted until yesterday or today. But realists will regard it as absurd to suggest that the actual existence of the coughing bear – the original cause of any persisting traces – depends at all on whether such traces still exist. They will see the suggestion as symptomatic of a failure to acknowledge the conception of reality we actually share.

Dummettian anti-realists will probably reply that those considerations only appear to have force if we question-beggingly rely on the realist assumption that any statement is either true or false (the 'Principle of Bivalence'). We have seen that Dummett himself maintains that we cannot settle the matter without a thorough investigation into our actual use of language, and of the conditions that must be satisfied for sentences to be capable of being understood as they are. The eventual outcome of such investigations might be that our use of language does not warrant our assumption of the validity of that principle.

But is what the realist says about the bear really based on such high-level assumptions? It is not adherence to an abstract Principle of Bivalence which makes us think that what happened in the course of yesterday's excavations is irrelevant to the question of whether a bear coughed here 4,000 years ago: we may never have considered any such principle. It is our understanding of words such as 'fact', 'true', 'cause', 'effect' and many others, cooperating in our everyday conception of the world. Dummett does not deny we *are* thus realistically inclined. What can be questioned is his claim that what does the work, what predisposes us in favour of realism, is an abstract principle rather than our understanding of the point of those central features of our everyday language and its associated theories.

He might reply that this still begs the question. Even if it is our understanding of everyday language, rather than any assumed logical or semantic principles, which inclines us to accept a realist interpretation of the story about the bear, still, to construe everyday language as realist is itself question-begging. Realists will dispute that reply. It might have worked if the theory that realists assume to be incorporated into everyday language were just a 'picture', as Dummett claims, and if there were no basis for deciding between it and anti-realism until we knew the outcome of further investigations into the correct model of meaning for the problematic statements. But that does not seem to be the situation. I will mention three considerations to the contrary.

First, realism seems to be inculcated by normal language-learning. Our everyday conception of the world encourages the idea that events have occurred of which there are now no traces. Indeed it seems to imply that such things happen. (Otherwise, why do burglars bother to wear gloves?) As a result of normal language-learning we assume, among many other things, that the world has existed for a long time, and that myriads of past events have caused other events, which in turn have caused others (one example: the breeding of countless generations of flies), yet that for many of the more remote individual events (such as the exact movements of an individual fly at a particular time and place a million years ago) there is no surviving evidence whatever. Our everyday conception includes notions of 'event', 'fact' and 'cause' which enable us to conceive of real events as related in space and time, and also by causality, in such ways that events in what is from our present point of view the past are by no means 'constituted' by present evidence and memories, but independent of them. That everyday conception supports a realist interpretation of the story about the evidence of tuberculous bears. It does not appear to beg the question against the anti-realist to regard our everyday conception of things as realist.

Suppose that is still somehow a mistake. The realist can point to a second consideration. We have available a powerful and self-consciously realist theory: the Core Scientific Story. That theory does not *seem* like a mere 'picture'. It seems like an attempt to tell the literal truth about the world. Certainly that is what it is intended to be. If it is said to be just a picture, one wonders how anything could qualify as an attempt to state the literal truth. The Core Scientific Story is as literal and non-metaphorical as any statement can be. It is precisely the sort of thing that pictures and metaphors can be contrasted with. Dummett's assertion that realism is just a picture is at best puzzling.

In any case – this is the third consideration – realists can suggest that the Core Scientific Story offers a satisfying scheme of description and explanation for our present situation, and the anti-realist has nothing comparable to offer. That is why Dummett's claim that we shall have no basis for deciding between realism and anti-realism until we have conducted a penetrating investigation into our actual use of language is so problematic. Anti-realists have to regard the complex structure of their experience at each moment as a sort of brute inexplicable datum. If present evidence for and memories of the past are 'constitutive' of it, as suggested in the quoted passage, then the idea that past states of the world can explain its present state is a chimera. What is *constituted* merely by present evidence and memories cannot conceivably have had a causal role in bringing about that evidence or memories. It follows that the existence of that evidence and those memories remains mysterious. Nor is it just the existence of evidence and memories that is puzzling on the anti-realist conception. The very existence of thinkers and users of language is itself deprived of any plausible explanation. That is something else which has to be accepted as an inexplicable datum. In contrast, the Core Scientific Story has persuasive explanations for all those things, and more. Of course any account of the world has to treat some things as basic and inexplicable (the Big Bang, for example). The trouble, realists will complain, is that what the anti-realist is willing to accept as basic and inexplicable is so much more complicated and mysterious even than the Big Bang.

6 Anti-realist truth and reality

Realists are shocked by the suggestion that what makes statements like the one about the bear true or false is the situation on the basis of which we judge them.[10] There are ways in which one might attempt to soften the effects of this claim.

One would be to decouple truth from reality. Recall the principle noted earlier (Chapter 2, section 7):

It is true that p just in case p

for any proposition p (at any rate for reasonably clear statements). Why shouldn't we give up that principle and allow a statement to lack a truth value, without having to conclude that reality is indeterminate? Well, suppose that (a) the statement about the bear lacks a truth value, but (b) the relevant aspects of reality are determinate. Suppose further that the relevant aspects of that determinate reality include a bear actually having coughed here 4,000 years ago. Then *it was the case* that the bear coughed here at that time, but *it is not true* that the bear coughed. I see no way to make sense of that. The same goes for the related suggestion: that (c) the statement about the bear is true, but (d) either no bear actually coughed here 4,000 years ago, or the relevant aspects of reality are indeterminate. The consequences of giving up that principle seem no less strange than those of the original anti-realist suggestion itself.

Another way of softening that suggestion would be to allow the situation on the basis of which the relevant judgements are made to extend into the past and the future. If the evidence is not restricted to what is available to us here and now, but includes what *would* have been available if we had been, or were going to be, in the right place at the right time, then anti-realists can agree with realists over vastly more. Reality would be much less indeterminate. For example, we could conceivably have been here 4,000 years ago, when we could have checked on any local bears. The statement about the bear would have had a definite truth value after all. But consider the assumptions necessary for Dummettian anti-realists to make sense of that concession. They would have to admit that there are facts about what is

---

10 Dummett has recently stated that idea explicitly: 'The anti-realist accuses the realist of interpreting those statements [such as the one about the bear] in the light of a conception of mythical states of affairs, not directly observable by us, rendering them true or false. According to the anti-realist, what makes them true or false are the observable states of affairs on the basis of which we judge of their truth-value' (*The Seas of Language*, p.469).

observable over vast stretches of the past and future – facts independent of what is accessible to us here and now! It is hard to see how that could fail to count as a commitment to realism. Apart from that, the concession would deprive anti-realism of one of its greatest attractions. This is that it promises to dispose of scepticism. If truth is essentially linked with discoverability by us here and now, as full-strength Dummettian anti-realism has it, we cannot be seriously mistaken about the world. But if anti-realists follow the present suggestion and concede there are truths that we could not discover here and now, but only if we had been or had been going to be in the right place at whatever the right time was, Dummettian anti-realism seems scarcely better placed to repel scepticism than ordinary realism.

MAIN POINTS IN CHAPTER 8

1 The case for Dummettian 'anti-realism' faces serious difficulties (sections 4–6).
2 Recognition of the role and nature of theory and the explanatory power of the Core Scientific Story gives the realist ammunition against Dummettian anti-realism (section 5). Decoupling truth from reality does not seem to help anti-realism; nor does extending the spatiotemporal range of evidence (section 6).

CHAPTER 8: SUGGESTIONS FOR FURTHER READING

The difficulty of the ideas introduced in this chapter is aggravated by the generally difficult style of the main authors. **Dummett** manages to present a reasonably accessible introduction in the paper 'Realism and Anti-Realism', to be found in his *The Seas of Language*. Similarly accessible is 'The Reality of the Past' in his *Truth and Other Enigmas*.

In a succession of stimulating and readable publications **Hilary Putnam** has developed something akin to Dummettian anti-realism which he calls 'internal realism' and which he contrasts with 'metaphysical realism' (note that both views are different from the kind of realism proposed here). See his *Reason, Truth and History*, chs 1 and 3; also his collection *Realism with a Human Face*, in which the following items are specially useful: his own Preface; the paper of the same title (which discusses Rorty's views); and 'A Defense of Internal Realism'.

Crispin Wright is a follower of Dummett who has developed his own approach. The introduction to his *Realism, Meaning and Truth* may be found helpful; the papers in the body of that book, like the rest of Dummett's, are hard going.

For **critical discussion** see A. C. Grayling, *An Introduction to Philosophical Logic*. A reasonably accessible critical article is Colin McGinn, 'Truth and Use', in *Reference, Truth and Reality*, ed. M. Platts. There is advanced discussion in Michael Devitt, *Realism and Truth* (2nd edn), ch. 14.

9

RORTY'S 'POSTMODERN' PRAGMATISM

Richard Rorty is influenced by the American pragmatists. He also endorses Wittgenstein's views about language-games and Quine's rejection of a sharp distinction between the 'analytic' and the 'synthetic'. He agrees with both philosophers in rejecting the idea that knowledge can be built on foundations, but he goes well beyond their positions. He sometimes calls his variety of pragmatism 'postmodernism'. It will be instructive to consider it.

1 Rorty's pragmatism

Rorty likes William James's definition of 'the true' as 'what is good in the way of belief';[1] and indeed his position is close to James's (though Dewey is the pragmatist he seems to admire the most). I will focus on one or two places where Rorty's pragmatism appears to conflict with realism. Discussing them will help to define both views more sharply, as well as improving our grip on the problems. I will say briefly what those points of conflict are, then examine them more closely.

Recall to begin with a remark of Rorty's quoted in Chapter 1: 'Truth cannot be out there – cannot exist independently of the human mind'.[2] That is puzzling if you understand it as it seems to be intended, to mean that somehow *the truth – and with it reality – depends on us*.

The remark could be taken differently, to mean that, since the things that are true – beliefs, statements and theories – have to be expressed in terms of our own concepts, when those concepts depend on our interests, languages and imaginations, then *it depends on us what truths we can express*. If that is his point, how could anyone dispute it? He is saying that what you can express depends on what you can express. However, plenty that he says – plenty on top of his Wittgensteinian, Deweyan and Quinean inheritance – seems to add up to a lot more than that.

1 W. James, *Pragmatism: a New Name for Some Old Ways of Thinking*, p.42.
2 R. Rorty, *Contingency, Irony, and Solidarity*, p.5.

One thing he says is that he favours a coherence theory of truth. Such theories, you will recall, make the truth of a statement or theory a matter of its coherence – its freedom from inconsistencies, its explanatory interconnections and so on (Chapter 2, section 9). But Rorty's is a puzzling version of the coherence theory. He sees no incompatibility between it and a version of the correspondence theory. In one sense of 'world', he claims,

> – the sense in which (except for a few fringe cases like gods, neutrinos, and natural rights) we now know perfectly well what the world is like and could not possibly be wrong about it – there is no argument about the point that it is the world that determines truth. All that 'determination' comes to is that our belief that snow is white is true because snow is white, that our beliefs about the stars are true because of the way the stars are laid out, and so on.[3]

If we take that passage at face value it looks like a commitment to a strong realism, of a kind that actually rules out any normal sort of coherence theory of truth. However, it is not enough for what he would count as an interesting realism. The interesting kind of realism, according to him, calls for a special philosophical sense of 'true' according to which it might turn out that none of the things we thought we were talking about really existed. He thinks that entails the untenable 'cosmic porridge' doctrine, to which I will return.

Another point of difference emerges in Rorty's views about large-scale language-games, which he calls 'vocabularies'. In his view these 'alternative vocabularies' are to be regarded as more like alternative tools than competing accounts of how things are.

That claim is closely connected to another. Rorty's pragmatism rejects the idea that the world has an 'intrinsic nature'. This puzzling claim will serve to focus the main discussion, for it highlights a stark contrast between postmodern pragmatism and realism.

2 Does the world have an intrinsic nature?

Realists don't have to be entirely happy with the phrase 'intrinsic nature'. If you accept that nature does not determine our concepts, you don't have to suppose it makes sense to say that the world has a 'nature' except in terms of some theory. We are forced to accept that it is only from within some theory that it makes sense to speak of something having a nature. Rorty puts this point tellingly: 'The world ... cannot propose a language for us to speak'.[4]

---

3 Rorty, 'The World Well Lost', in his *Consequences of Pragmatism*, p.14. He expresses similar views elsewhere in that collection, e.g. p.162.
4 Rorty, *Contingency, Irony, and Solidarity*, p.6.

135

That is the uncontroversial 'Neurath's boat' point: we cannot have any thoughts at all except in terms of some conceptual scheme, some system of ways of thinking, which inevitably includes something like a theory (Chapter 7, section 6).

So far, then, realists have no quarrel with Rorty's postmodern pragmatism. If that were all he meant there would be no disagreement. But they will also insist that it is a question of objective fact – independent of what anyone thinks – whether this or that aspect of the world is as specified in such and such a theory. Chemical theory, for example, articulates a system in terms of which the fine structures of different substances can be specified. Astronomical theory deals with the large-scale nature and arrangements of bodies distributed in space and time. In terms of both theories we can describe objective features of the world – or so realists like to think. For example, around us there are large quantities of a substance whose molecules have the composition specified by the formula 'H_2O'; the solar system consists of the sun and nine planets; there are vast numbers of galaxies, each containing vast numbers of stars. Such statements illustrate a reasonably clear sense in which, contrary to what Rorty seems to claim, the world can properly be said to have an intrinsic nature. Those large amounts of water, the structure of the solar system, and the numbers and distribution of the galaxies, are all independent of us, even though – of course – we cannot describe them except in terms of theories we have thought up. So how can it be right that 'the notion of "accurate representation" is simply an automatic and empty compliment which we pay to those beliefs which are successful in helping us do what we want to do'?[5] Let us look more closely at Rorty's reasoning.

He asserts that the idea that the world has an intrinsic nature 'is a remnant of the idea that the world is a divine creation'. I will examine his main reason for this colourful suggestion in the next section. But one consideration is that 'the cash value of that phrase is just that some vocabularies are better representations of the world than others, as opposed to being better tools for dealing with the world for one or another purpose'.[6] That is a strongly pragmatist assertion. Rorty seems to think that only confusion results from adding to the claim that some theories are better *tools* than others for some purpose, the further claim that they *represent* the world better, that they are closer to getting things right. That clearly conflicts with realism.

In ordinary talk we distinguish sharply between whether a belief or theory is useful and whether it is true. If I have just found a wallet with a thousand pounds in it and I need the money, it would be useful to believe

---

5 Rorty, *Philosophy and The Mirror of Nature*, p.10. Cf. his *Contingency, Irony, and Solidarity*, p.4.
6 Rorty, *Contingency, Irony, and Solidarity*, p.21.

nobody would mind if I kept it. But that wouldn't make the belief true. Being a useful tool is one thing; being true is something else. Pragmatists are prepared for that sort of attack. When James said the true is 'what is good in the way of belief' he was not thinking of ordinary usefulness-for-me. He explained that 'what is better for us to believe' must not clash with other beliefs.[7] My belief that nobody would mind if I kept the money doesn't fit coherently into the rest of my theory of the world: people do tend to mind if they lose a thousand pounds. That belief would hardly count as good in the way of belief. Still, we do make the distinction between what is useful and what is true. Can Rorty's pragmatism obliterate it?

We can devise a more sophisticated version of the objection, using again the example of undiscovered evidence of coughing bears having lived here 4,000 years ago. Suppose that yesterday all that evidence was destroyed by bulldozers, without anyone knowing that it had been there. Commonsense realism says the story is perfectly intelligible, and that it is still either true or false that there *were* bears that coughed here all those years ago. Dummettian anti-realism, in contrast, says that when there is no evidence, the statement is neither true nor false. (Recall that according to Dummettian anti-realism 'there cannot be a past fact no evidence for which exists to be discovered, because it is the existence of such evidence that would make it a fact, if it were one'.[8]) What does Rorty's pragmatism say? If there is no evidence of any kind one way or the other – as this story has it – then from the point of view of what is good or useful by way of belief, there is nothing to choose between saying it is true that there were coughing bears here then, and saying it is false. In this particular case, then, it seems that Rorty goes along with Dummettian anti-realism: the statement lacks a truth value. Now let us change the story slightly. Suppose there are factors at work here and now that would make believing the statement false more beneficial than believing it true. In that case Rorty's account would appear to require it to be false. It would require it to be false even if those factors have nothing to do with anything that happened 4,000 years ago! (Perhaps believing there were no tuberculous bears would make people more cheerful and so more resistant to disease.)

A further point: whether a belief *is* useful or beneficial or otherwise practically valuable is a matter of fact.[9] It seems to be so regardless of whether it would be useful to believe *that* it was useful. If so, the pragmatic idea of truth undermines itself.

Rorty cannot deny that his position conflicts with our commonsense assumptions about truth, even with our ordinary *concept* of truth. So much the worse, he may say, for that ordinary concept. Postmodern pragmatism is

---

7 James, op. cit., p.43.
8 M. Dummett, *The Logical Basis of Metaphysics*, p.7.
9 As Plato makes Socrates point out when discussing Protagoras' ideas, *Theaetetus*, pp.177c ff.

not bound to accept that all our ordinary concepts are in order as they are.[10] But now he faces a crucial question. Why should we accept the recommendation to ditch our ordinary assumptions about truth? What are the advantages? Here, it seems to me, the case for postmodern pragmatism is at its weakest. Paradoxically, it is vulnerable for reasons pragmatists ought to accept as sound. You begin to suspect there are powerful pragmatic reasons to accept realism.

According to the commonsense realist assumption, what makes it a fact that bears coughed here 4,000 years ago is what happened at that time, not the present existence of evidence to that effect. It seems to make perfect sense to tell a story about events in the remote past causing later events, each of which in turn caused many other events, the chains of causes and effects continuing until the present day – yet to maintain that vast numbers of those events are no longer within our power to detect. The Core Scientific Story is such a story.[11] Undeniably it has great explanatory power. Giving up the idea that facts about the past depend on what actually happened in the past, and adopting instead the view that they depend on whatever evidence there may be in the present, would therefore be a radical upheaval in our ways of thinking. It would be even more of an upheaval to include among the 'evidence' factors whose only connection with the past was that they made certain beliefs beneficial to us now – they were just useful tools. What good reasons are there to give up our ordinary idea? Earlier I suggested we had not been given a good reason by Dummett. I will now argue that none is forthcoming from Rorty either.

He seems to have two main objections. One is that he thinks the claim that one theory is a better 'representation' than another, or comes closer to getting things right, only seems to make sense because we assume a 'God's Eye' point of view is available. (Dummett and Putnam make the same assumption.[12]) The other is that he assumes any non-trivial realism is bound to fall into the 'cosmic porridge' trap. I think it is possible to see that both assumptions are mistaken. Ironically, it looks as if his own ideas are hopelessly stuck in the cosmic porridge.

10 Contrary to Wittgenstein's position, according to which philosophy 'leaves everything as it is', *Philosophical Investigations*, §124.
11 All the evidence I have strongly suggests that most people do in fact accept a realist story of this sort. It doesn't seem to be something dreamed up by obsessed philosophers. As Berkeley lamented, 'It is indeed an opinion strangely prevailing amongst men, that houses, mountains, rivers, and in a word all sensible objects have an existence natural or real, distinct from their being perceived by the understanding' (*Principles of Human Knowledge*, Pt. I, sec. iv).
12 See p.125 above, and H. Putnam, *Reason, Truth and History*, pp.49f. Putnam sometimes seems to put much more into the idea of a God's Eye View than I am assuming. See, e.g., his *Realism with a Human Face*, p.17.

3 Does realism imply a God's Eye View?

Realism does not have to imply that a God's Eye View is possible. On the contrary, it seems to imply that it is impossible. At any rate, if we accept anything like the Core Scientific Story, no one – not even a being with super-human powers – could get into a position where they could simply 'read off' how things were by directly inspecting the world. The whole idea of 'inspecting' bits of the world appears intelligible only so far as it involves something like ordinary perception. Ordinary perception, however, always has some point of view, some position in space and time. If the observer is located in space and time, some parts of the world will be closer than others, from which it follows that the observer will have access to less information about what lies further away. That follows from the fact that, in order to acquire the information, something has to travel from what is perceived to the perceiver – light, for example. The further away something is from a given point, the less light from it reaches that point, hence the less informa-tion. Admittedly the idea of a God's Eye View does not have to be that a single observer should be able to find out about everything at once. It need only be that, for any given truth, a suitably equipped observer could discover it. In that case the idea is *nothing but* a picturesque way of expressing the assumption that every truth is in principle discoverable, to which I will return shortly. But the above considerations still apply. Take for example the statement:

All mice are mortal.

There can be no sort of 'inspection' capable of assuring the observer that it is true. Nor will it help if we imagine the observer moving about in space or time. Observing many dead mice at one place leaves open the possibility of a mouse surviving somewhere else. Realism, far from implying the possibility of a God's Eye View, actually rules it out.

It will be objected that in that case realism implies both the possibility and the impossibility of a God's Eye View – a contradiction. However, we have been given no reasons to accept the crucial claim that realism implies the God's Eye View *is* possible. Rorty offers none, so presumably he is making hidden assumptions. We discussed a couple of likely assumptions in connection with Dummettian anti-realism. One has just been mentioned: the assumption that every truth is in principle discoverable. Dummett calls it 'the absurdity of supposing that a statement of any kind could be true if it was in principle impossible to know that it was true'.[13] But that assumption is question-begging. Realists will probably concede that vast numbers of interesting truths about the world can indeed be known (in the sense that we

13 Dummett, *The Logical Basis of Metaphysics*, p.345.

can have good reasons for believing them). That goes even for such dramatic one-off truths as those about the Big Bang. But why must they also concede that the same goes for *all* truths? Why should they not maintain, as is implied by the Core Scientific Story, that some truths – for example those about the exact movements of flies millions of years ago – cannot be discovered by us? No non-question-begging reason shows up.

Here are two other assumptions – they may underlie Rorty's reasoning:

(1) If truth is independent of observers, then the conceptualization of reality is independent of thinkers: reality imposes concepts on us.

(2) If truth is independent of observers, then a theory of the world must somehow be capable of being compared with naked unconceptualized reality.

There are good reasons to go along with Rorty's rejection of the right-hand sides of each of these statements. Reality does not impose concepts on us: there is some degree of conceptual autonomy (Chapter 2, section 8); and our theory of the world cannot be compared with naked unconceptualized reality (Neurath's boat: Chapter 7, section 6). Rorty may assume it is impossible to be a genuine realist without accepting both those views as well. But that is a mistake. Realists can accept both conceptual autonomy and that we are in Neurath's boat. In the concluding chapter I will try to make clear that both ideas are compatible with strong realism. Nothing forces realists to accept the possibility of a God's Eye View.[14]

There have been rivals to the Core Scientific Story. Anaximander's account of the origins of the solar system is one; Democritus' atomism is another – an impressive one at that. If Rorty's first, 'God's Eye View' objection to the idea that one theory may be a better representation of the world than another is to work at all, it must work in these cases. Our preference for the CSS both over Anaximander's story of the cosmic egg and the fiery star-rings encased in fog, and over Democritus' uncuttably solid fundamental particles, must be either no more than a mere recognition that the CSS does better work, or else it must depend on a nonsensical positing of a God's Eye View. The second alternative has been rejected. But the first is inconsistent with the CSS itself. If you endorse the CSS, you thereby commit yourself to a realistic story of the world in which things and events occur independently of whether or not anyone believes they do. According to the CSS itself, it tells us about the intrinsic nature of the world. Rorty

---

14 Putnam assumes that 'the whole content of Realism [note the capital 'R'] lies in the claim that it makes sense to think of a God's-Eye View' (*Realism with a Human Face*, p.23); so what he means by 'Realism' is something rich and strange, and not at all what I or most people mean by 'realism'.

must either show there is something internally inconsistent in the CSS, or give us a reason for rejecting it in favour of a story according to which it is neither true nor false that events for which we lack evidence have occurred or will occur. I know of no such reason. Certainly nothing Rorty offers looks like one. On the contrary, pragmatic considerations seem to drive us to realism! The most useful theory has it that reality is independent of human minds and interests.

That might seem too quick. What if he replied that there is *no more* to the CSS's truth than that it is useful? He does, after all, insist that 'there is no pragmatic difference, no difference that makes a difference, between "it works because it's true" and "it's true because it works" '.[15] To this the realist can reply that such remarks appear to be an attempt to evade the force of the reasoning in this section and the last. Either he has to claim there is no difference in *meaning* between 'it's true' and 'it works', or not. If he does claim there is no difference in meaning, I submit that the reasoning in this chapter makes clear both that there is a difference, and what that difference is. The CSS describes a reality, much of it knowable by us here and now, much of it not; and the CSS provides a satisfying explanation of many things, including that we are here now, and that the CSS itself 'works'. It works because of the nature of the reality it describes. That justifies the distinction between 'it's true' and 'it works'. If on the other hand Rorty accepts there *is* a difference of meaning between those two expressions, I submit that the reasoning in this chapter directly disproves his claim that there is no difference between 'it works because it's true' and 'it's true because it works': it supports the former claim but not the latter. Notice, finally, that the realist can easily agree that which 'theory of the world' we accept is a matter to be decided on pragmatic grounds. (That is what Quine recommends, for example.) But that is not at all the same as conceding that once you have accepted a particular theory of the world, for example the CSS, you can somehow stop short of regarding it as a description of an independent reality. How can you accept a theory which says, for example, that the stars exist independently of us and our ways of thinking, and still maintain that the truth about the stars 'cannot exist independently of the human mind'?[16]

---

15 Rorty, *Consequences of Pragmatism*, p.xxix.

16 You can still insist that how we talk about the stars depends on our language; but every sane person will accept that. Rorty himself makes it difficult to tell what he thinks by sometimes appearing to accept realism, as when he says 'we now know perfectly well what the world is like and could not possibly be wrong about it': *Consequences of Pragmatism*, p.14. To set against that, we have, for example, the following: 'The intuitive realist…thinks that, deep down beneath all the texts, there is something which is not just one more text but that to which various texts are trying to be "adequate". The pragmatist does not think that there is anything like that' (op. cit., p.xxxvii).

4 Realists can keep out of the cosmic porridge

Rorty's second main objection to the idea that one theory may be a better representation than another is that any non-trivial realism is committed to regarding truth as correspondence in a sense in which 'the world might, for all we know, prove to contain none of the things we have always thought we were talking about'. He goes on to say that such a notion of 'world' would have to be 'of something *completely* unspecified and unspecifiable'.[17] In other words it would have to endorse the 'cosmic porridge' doctrine, which we know is untenable.

Why should realism, to avoid the reproach of triviality, have to adopt such a ridiculous position? Why shouldn't it maintain that, although the world contains most of the things we have always thought we were talking about, there is still room for our theories about other aspects of reality to be right or wrong – theories about the fine structure of things, and theories about events remote in time or space? In the previous section I argued that Rorty has given us no reason to reject the view that Democritus' atomism was mistaken in spite of being a powerful and impressive theory. When we say that, we are not *just* saying it is an inferior instrument to today's physics. We are saying it is a less accurate representation of how the world really is. If that is right, we can be non-trivial realists while keeping clear of the cosmic porridge.

It seems that Rorty has not offered persuasive reasons to prefer his pragmatism to realism. The alternatives he presents us with – to accept his own position and reject the idea that the world has an intrinsic nature, or to plunge absurdly into the cosmic porridge – are not exhaustive. There is a non-trivial realist way out. He has given us no good reason to accept the view that alternative theories are to be regarded as more like alternative tools than competing accounts of how things are. A coherence theory of truth is not an option. Yet that by no means compels us to adopt any strong variety of correspondence theory. Realists may still follow Quine (and indeed Rorty himself) and adopt a 'redundancy' theory of truth (Chapter 2, section 7).

There is another interesting consideration. According to Rorty the pragmatist 'drops the notion of truth as correspondence with reality altogether, and says that modern science does not enable us to cope because it corresponds, it just plain enables us to cope'.[18] Cope with what? It makes no sense to say we can cope unless there is something or other to cope *with*. Is what we have to cope with a world with an intrinsic nature and features that we can represent to ourselves more or less accurately? Or is it something without any intrinsic nature and no features of any intelligible kind? Rorty has explicitly ruled out the first horn of this dilemma: it is supposed to be a mistake to think

17 Rorty, *Consequences of Pragmatism*, p.14. See also pp.xvii, xxiv–xxv.
18 Rorty, *Consequences of Pragmatism*, p.xvii.

the world has an intrinsic nature. Given his assumptions, that seems to force him to accept the second – the cosmic porridge idea. I leave it as an exercise for the reader to think up ways in which he might reply.

5 What's so special about science?

We have noted reasons for rejecting a variety of assaults on commonsense realism. In Chapter 3 some simple varieties of relativism were examined and found to fail. In Chapters 6, 8 and 9 some more sophisticated varieties of relativism and anti-realism were criticized. However, here and earlier I have appealed to what I call the Core Scientific Story as an example of a realist 'theory of the world'. That may have worried or even repelled some readers. Am I recommending slavish acceptance of Western science? Doesn't science leave out the most important aspects of life – those which give meaning to our existence? I will try to meet those worries in the next chapter.

MAIN POINTS IN CHAPTER 9

1   Rorty rejects the idea that 'the world has an intrinsic nature', and with it the claim that one theory may be a better representation of reality than another (section 1).
2   Both claims appear unjustifiable (sections 2, 3 and 4).
3   Rorty assumes realism commits you to the possibility of a 'God's Eye View'; but that, too, is an unwarranted claim (section 3).
4   His claim that any non-trivial realism is committed to the 'cosmic porridge' doctrine appears to be based on assuming realists are committed to two views they can and ought to accept: that reality is not already labelled with conceptual divisions; and that we cannot compare our theory with naked unconceptualized reality (sections 3 and 4).

CHAPTER 9: SUGGESTIONS FOR FURTHER READING

The main text is Rorty's *Philosophy and The Mirror of Nature*; but a good idea of his approach can be derived from the 'Introduction' to his *Consequences of Pragmatism*, and 'The World Well Lost' in that collection. See also his *Contingency, Irony, and Solidarity*.

For **criticism** see the two collections, *Reading Rorty*, ed. A. R. Malachowski, and *Rorty and Pragmatism*, ed. H. J. Saatkamp. See also Michael Devitt, *Realism and Truth* (2nd edn), ch. 11.

10

SCIENCE AND THE WORLD OF
EVERYDAY LIFE

The world around us is full of meaning. Those are not just sheets of paper over there: they are a draft of my book; that is not just a lump of metal: it is a radiator which is helping to keep me warm in this icy weather; that sound is my wife's voice: she is telling me a friend is on the phone; those dark clouds mean more snow is on the way; the flat surface outside is a road; the moving shapes are children throwing snowballs. Those things may not mean the same to you as to me; but they will still mean something. In general the things around us are not, for us, just occupants of space and time. They are enmeshed in the needs, interests, plans, hopes, anxieties, desires and memories that help to structure our lives.

If we consider how the world is described in terms of particle physics, we seem faced by something very different. In that restricted scientific vocabulary there is no room for descriptions of the colours, sounds, smells, tastes or feels of things. Still less does it provide for descriptions that will connect things with those needs, interests and so on. Not only that: physics tells us much that actually seems to conflict with our experience. For example, what we think of as solid objects turn out to consist mainly of empty space. Even atoms, we learn, are not only not solid themselves; they are in other ways very different from the sorts of things we encounter in ordinary life, and their constituents are weird. Yet that narrow vocabulary of particle physics is apparently capable of specifying, in its own way, everything that happens in the entire universe.

It can look as if science leaves out everything that matters. It can even look as if what science tells us about is a different reality from the world of everyday life. Can we come to a satisfactory view about the relations between these two 'images'?[1] That would be wildly ambitious in a book of this kind; I will limit myself to an attempt to clarify some main issues. I shall

1 Wilfrid Sellars wrote that the philosopher is confronted 'by *two* pictures of essentially the same order of complexity, each of which purports to be a complete picture of man-in-the-world, and which, after separate scrutiny, he must fuse into one vision' ('Philosophy and the Scientific Image of Man', 1962, in his *Science, Perception and Reality*, p.4). He refers to the 'manifest image' and the 'scientific image'.

be particularly concerned to make clear that adherence to the Core Scientific Story by no means commits us to giving a secondary place in the scheme of things to whatever makes life meaningful.

1 The idea that science devalues the world of everyday life

An extreme position about the relations between science and reality was adopted by the German philosopher Edmund Husserl (1859–1938). In Husserl's later work the villain was Galileo, who allegedly 'replaced' the world we actually live in with a world of abstractions. What occurred was:

> The surreptitious substitution of the mathematically substructured world of idealities for the only real world, the one that is actually given through perception, that is ever experienced and experience-able – our everyday life-world [*Lebenswelt*].[2]

Worse, Galileo taught that sensory qualities (colours, sounds and the rest) were purely subjective. Experiences of them were in the subject only as 'causal results of events taking place in true nature, which events exist only with mathematical properties'.[3] According to Husserl, the mathematization of science had the effect that all truths about our pre-scientific and non-scientific lives were 'devalued'. The idea that the objective world was a closed world of causally interacting bodies prepared the way for Descartes's dualism. The result was that the world was split in two: on the one hand physical nature; on the other the world of the mind.[4]

It is undeniable that descriptions of the world purely in terms of the distribution and states of atoms and sub-atomic particles are hard to link up with the world as we experience it. Yet we normally think and act in terms of the world as we experience it. There is a genuine problem about how the two sets of descriptions – two sets of truths – are related. Pursuing that problem, as we shall be doing shortly, forces us into philosophical investigations.

Husserl's claims raise further questions. I will briefly note one or two of them.

One question is whether he is right to suppose that the mathematization of science has a tendency to 'devalue' pre-scientific and non-scientific truths.

---

2 E. Husserl, *The Crisis of European Sciences and Transcendental Phenomenology*, pp.48f.
3 Op. cit., p.54.
4 The intellectual history hereabouts is interesting. It was Husserl's sometime pupil Heidegger who first laid stress on the mental–physical split allegedly inaugurated by Descartes. Husserl himself was guilty of a philosophical approach ('phenomenology', which he founded) which depended absolutely on the existence of just such a 'split'. Husserl ignores the much earlier but closely related contribution of Democritus: 'Conventionally there is colour, conventionally there is sweetness, conventionally there is bitterness; but in truth there are atoms and empty space'.

To the extent that there is such a tendency, it presumably arises from such facts as that some things are easier to quantify than others. For example it is easier to collect statistics on the costs of maintaining parks in cities than to assess the value of those green spaces. However, to put a higher importance on the quantifiable just because it is quantifiable is not scientific. It is a symptom of 'scientism', which Popper once characterized as 'dogmatic methodological naturalism'.[5] Blaming science for the perversions of scientism seems no better than blaming Marconi for radio talk-shows.

Another question is raised by Husserl's claim that the conception of the 'objective' world as a world of causally interacting bodies prepared the way for Cartesian dualism. Perhaps that is so: it is a question of historical fact. Certainly Descartes was influenced by that conception. However, I suggest that the philosophically interesting question is whether that conception of the world leaves no alternative to dualism. It does not seem to do so. That was suggested, indeed, by the ancient Greek inventors of the atomic theory themselves, who were stalwart anti-dualists. For them, mental activities were among the processes fully accounted for by the motions of atoms in space. Today it is very common for philosophers to accept that the world 'out there' is a world of interacting bodies and impersonal physical forces, but at the same time to reject dualism, insisting that mental states and processes are just one kind of physical process. (See section 8 below, and the end of the final chapter.)

Finally, there are questions about the special notion Husserl introduces as his contribution to avoiding the problems raised by other approaches: the notion of the 'life-world' (*Lebenswelt*). Some of his remarks suggest that this life-world is none other than the world of everyday life, in which case the life-world must include things like sticks and stones, stars and starfish, which occupy time and space. Other remarks make that interpretation hard to sustain. For example, he says the life-world is 'built up' by us. There would be no problem if Husserl were merely stating the view that what is 'built up' is not reality, but our *conceptions* of reality. As we saw earlier, that is Berger and Luckmann's view, even though their way of putting it suggests something more exciting.[6] But that deflationary reading of Husserl is problematic. However, if the main points to be developed in this chapter are right, we can do without his technical apparatus.

2 Different descriptions of a single reality?

Realists, both commonsense and scientific, will tend to maintain that in spite of the differences between scientific and everyday descriptions and

---

5 K. R. Popper, *The Poverty of Historicism*, pp.60 and 105n. He said he used the word 'as a name for the imitation of *what certain people mistake* for the method and language of science'.

6 See Chapter 3, section 9.

explanations of the world, there is no serious problem. Both apply to the same reality. There is no plurality of realities, only of perceivers, with their different points of view.

Let me elaborate. Each species has its own sensory equipment and its own cognitive and intellectual capacities. Each has its own way of perceiving the world. Unlike us, snakes are sensitive to infra-red radiation; bees are sensitive to ultra-violet radiation and the polarization of light; and so on. That gives an unproblematic sense to the suggestion that each species occupies its own world: it is merely a vivid way of saying that each perceives the world – the same world – in its own way. Typically there will be areas of reality which it ignores completely, but they will still be there, in spite of not being perceived by that species. Ultra-violet radiation is not annihilated by the fact that we have no sense-organ for detecting it.

Similarly, each individual within a species has a different history from any other, and – certainly in the case of human beings – different preferences and interests. Very likely each individual perceives the world differently from any other. Indeed, the same person may perceive the world differently at different times. As Wittgenstein put it in the *Tractatus*, 'The world of the happy is a different one from that of the unhappy'.[7] We are quite ready to talk of people inhabiting different worlds on account of their different attitudes, moods, interests, social circumstances, states of mental and physical health, ages, sexes. But although realists can go along with that way of talking, they will insist that such differences are consistent with the view that literally there is only one world, one reality: it is just that different people perceive it differently.

There is a complication when we take account of theory-construction. There are commonsense theories of the world and there are scientific ones. But the realist idea still seems to work: the two kinds of theories and their associated descriptions both apply to the same reality.

There would not even appear to be a problem with this idea if the different theories applied to different parts or aspects of the one reality: one telling us about the elephant's trunk, another about its tusks, another about its tail. But that is not just trivial but beside the point. What realists say is that a scientific description and a commonsense description can perfectly well both be of the same thing. Here it may seem that there are difficulties.

Consider these two replies to the question, 'What's in that glass?':

'Water'

'H_2O'.

Those replies are either both true or both false (they are 'truth-functionally equivalent'). There is no question of their being in conflict. However, they

7 L. Wittgenstein, *Tractatus*, §6.43.

don't *mean* the same. You may wonder how they can both be about the same thing. As we noticed, it is only if they are both about the same thing that there seems to be a difficulty. A little reflection shows there is no real difficulty. The first reply tells us the stuff is water; the second specifies the chemical composition of that same stuff. The second reply doesn't mean the same as the first because it tells us something the first does not; but it is not about something different. The second is in a way more informative. We were able to learn the meaning of 'water' without at the same time learning the chemical theory which enables us to understand the formula 'H_2O'; when we learned the theory, we thereby learned more about water.

That illustrates the realist's claim that a scientific description and an everyday description can both be true of the same thing, in this case the contents of a glass of water. It is natural to suggest that this is so because they are used for different purposes and therefore, typically, in different contexts. There is no implication that the scientific scheme is superior to the everyday scheme for all purposes. It is superior for the special purpose of describing and explaining structures and processes to which we ordinarily have no access. But it seems to have nothing to say about other things that matter to us.

The sensible realist sees no problem there. Science says nothing about most of the things that matter to us because what matters depends on our needs, interests, plans, hopes, anxieties, desires and memories – conceived of by us in terms of those attitudes, and as the ones who have them, not as observers of ourselves as objects of laboratory investigation.

One type of opposition to this ecumenical position has already been noted. It consists of maintaining that the scientific scheme is inadequate because it leaves out everything of value in human life. At the other extreme, opposition comes from those who expect the scientific scheme to be capable of displacing the everyday one. The thought is that the scientific scheme is superior to the everyday scheme, which is likely to embody primitive misconceptions. 'Eliminativism' of this kind is most strikingly advocated in the philosophy of mind. The eliminativist maintains that 'folk psychology' – our everyday scheme of psychological description and explanation in terms of beliefs, desires, wishes, hopes and the rest – is likely to be not just inferior to a developed scheme of explanation based on the neurosciences, but actually false. One reason offered for this view is that it seems highly unlikely that everyday psychology is capable of being 'reduced' to the new neuroscientific scheme.[8] I shall return to this issue.

There seems to be an unexamined assumption behind both those contrasting positions. It is that there can be only one true theory of the world.

---

8 See, for example, Paul M. Churchland, *Scientific Realism and the Plasticity of Mind*.

3 Does realism require a single true theory of the world?

What Putnam has labelled 'Metaphysical Realism' is to the effect that there is just one 'true and complete' description of the way the world is.[9] We noticed in the first chapter that Aristotle seems to have been committed to that claim. Here I will try to show that realism in general is not. In particular, commonsense realism is not committed to it; and there are good reasons to reject it.

What would it be for a description of the world to be 'complete'? One natural suggestion is that it would be complete just in case it included every truth about the world. There is more than one thing wrong with that suggestion. A subtle thing wrong with it is that there are arguments which seem to show that we cannot talk coherently about 'all truths'. (I call it 'subtle' because the arguments depend on some technical logic.[10]) Another thing wrong with it is this. There can be truths only where there are concepts: patterns of thinking. But concepts are in general dependent on conceivers. The identity of a concept cannot be determined independently of the type of creature we suppose to be using it. Apart from other considerations, there are Wittgenstein's points about 'form of life' to be taken into account (Chapter 4, section 9). Human beings are able to acquire human languages, and with them human concepts, because as a species we share certain built-in predispositions, capacities, intellectual and sensory aptitudes, tendencies to find certain things salient. Any human infant can learn any human language. But conceivably there are intelligent species which do not share exactly our form of life, in this important sense of the phrase. In that case they may have difficulty acquiring our languages and our concepts, and we may have difficulty acquiring theirs. It might even be impossible to do so. Yet why should they not be perfectly capable of stating and discovering truths in terms of their own concepts?[11] If they could do that, then at least some truths statable in their language would not be statable in ours, and vice versa. So there could not be a single theory incorporating all truths statable in either language. If theories taken from both languages were to be conjoined, no one would be able to understand more than part of the result. They would remain distinct theories, not one theory. (Because the dispositions, tendencies and aptitudes required for understanding the one part would, by assumption, exclude those required

---

9 H. Putnam, *Reason, Truth and History*, pp.49f.
10 See P. Grim, *The Incomplete Universe*.
11 There is a line of argument purporting to show that, unless a community's utterances were translatable into English, they could not be counted as using a language at all. See D. Davidson, 'The Very Idea of a Conceptual Scheme', in his *Inquiries into Truth and Interpretation*. For the reason just noted I find the argument unpersuasive.

for understanding the other.[12]) The conceivable multiplicity of forms of life threatens the project of constructing a theory whose 'completeness' consisted of its including all truths.

Let us leave aside that rather special possibility, and concentrate on truths comprehensible to human beings – who all share a single form of life in the relevant sense. Even so, the project of incorporating all those truths in a single theory is problematic. It is not as if different human cultures all shared the same concepts. On the contrary, there seem to be wide differences in conceptual scheme from culture to culture (concepts of kinship and of colour are two famous examples). Each different conceptual scheme provides for a different set of truths statable in its own terms, and there seems no limit to the number of different schemes that there could be. If that is right, there is no way for a single theory to encapsulate all the truths each of which could be stated in terms of *some* humanly intelligible theory. That is the main reason for concluding that the suggested explanation of what a 'complete' theory might be is misconceived. Certainly we can learn more than one language, pick up foreign cultures, and thereby make ourselves able to state truths using all the languages we have learnt. But even ignoring the constraints of time and memory, the fact that there is no limit to the number of *possible* human languages and conceptual schemes would frustrate the project. No one could know all possible human languages. At any rate, that is so if we make the reasonable assumption that exact translation from one language into others is not generally possible.

There are, however, linguists and psychologists who maintain that there is a set of primitive conceptual 'atoms' with which every human infant is provided innately. If they are right, every concept that a human being can conceivably acquire can be represented in terms of that innate set of conceptual atoms, rather as any molecule can be constructed from atoms belonging to the basic kinds recognized in chemistry. Again if they are right, the last paragraph does not after all rule out the possibility of a single theory incorporating all humanly intelligible truths. I must say I am not persuaded by their reasoning. In any case it does nothing to undermine the considerations about different forms of life.

A commonsense realist impressed by the above considerations will reject the assumption that there could be such a thing as a single 'complete' theory of the world in the suggested sense. Such a realist will maintain that there is no limit to the number of different theories of the world, formulated in terms of different conceptual schemes, yet all objectively true. But to put the position in those terms is misleading. Let us grant that the completeness of

12 You might insist that it's just a single big theory, only nobody knows or understands more than a part of it. That would be a forced use of the expression 'one theory', though, if only because nobody *could* understand more than a part of it. It couldn't be fitted into a single mind because, by definition, that one mind would have to have contradictory features.

a theory of the world cannot consist in its explicitly incorporating all truths. There would still not be much point in saying there could be many different theories of the world if each of them were incomplete in the sense that it left something out. In that case, as we noticed earlier, the differences between the theories might be simply that they covered different aspects of the world. One might be biological, another astrophysical. (One would have nothing to say about planets; the other nothing to say about plants.) The point of discussing realism in terms of 'complete' theories of the world is to avoid such trivialities. 'Completeness' does not seem definable in the way just considered. Perhaps, however, the point is just that the theory must not leave anything out. How should we understand that requirement?

To get clearer about it let us consider, to start with, commonsense realism. I have roughly defined it as the view that the things we ordinarily and confidently suppose to exist do exist, independently of what we may think or experience. Now, we have to agree that it can only be in terms of our own languages and conceptual schemes that we suppose things to exist. There could be no such thing as standing outside all conceptual schemes and judging reality untrammelled by any (Neurath's boat). But different languages and their associated conceptual schemes classify things differently. The linguist John Lyons, discussing the difficulty of translating 'The cat sat on the mat' into French, remarks that none of the French words *tapis*, *paillasse*, *carpette* and so on applies to the same things respectively as English 'mat', 'rug', 'carpet' and so on.[13] When I, as an English speaker, say 'There are mats, rugs, carpets...', a French speaker will say 'Il y a des tapis, des paillasses, des carpettes...'. In view of the fact that the French classify floor-coverings differently from English speakers, do I have to say the French speaker has left something out? Surely not. A French inventory of the floor-coverings in a certain building will have different headings from an English one; but each complete inventory will include all the floor-coverings in the building. In that sense each inventory is complete. Here, perhaps, we have a useful analogy with the case of commonsense realist 'theories of the world'. English-speaking commonsense realists can list what there is in the world in terms of their conceptual scheme, and French-, Turkish- and Chinese-speaking commonsense realists can list what there is in terms of their respective schemes; and it is quite possible that each list leaves nothing out – in spite of differences between the schemes.

Consider further the relations between English and French inventories of floor-coverings in the building. Suppose someone who speaks both English and French is presented with the *English* inventory on its own. (It consists of a series of headings – 'mat', 'rug', 'carpet',...– each with a number indicating how many items fall under that heading.) Does it supply enough

13 J. Lyons, *Semantics*, pp.237f.

information by itself to enable them to construct an accurate French inventory? Not necessarily. The reason is the fact which made that example helpful in the first place: there is cross-classification. Two items which both fall under a single English heading may fall under different French ones. In general, *the English inventory doesn't fix what the French one should be.* It doesn't provide enough information to determine the contents of all other possible commonsense schemes for classifying floor-coverings. In its *own* terms the English inventory leaves nothing out. It is complete in that sense – the sense in which to alter any of the numbers under the various headings would be to falsify the inventory. But it does not, and should not be expected to, fix how a different scheme of classification would describe the situation it describes.

That example helps to show how a commonsense realist can on the one hand maintain that a theory of the world in English might be complete in the sense that it left nothing out, and on the other hand concede that it wouldn't say everything about the world that could be said, even at a commonsense level – that is, without invoking scientific schemes of description – and so would be compatible with other, different, theories of the world also being true. Let us now try to spell out what completeness in the required sense is.

A 'theory of the world' is an attempt to describe what there is in the world, and how the things in it behave. The Core Scientific Story is thus a small but vital component of one such total theory of the world. In practice, of course, we never formulate more than fragments even of what we believe to be a true theory of the world. But let us indulge in a little idealization and pretend we can deal in terms of a theory covering the whole of space and time. Then we can think of something roughly analogous to the complete inventory of floor-coverings in the building. In place of the inventory's headings we can have a special set of statement-making sentences. In place of the inventory's numbers we can have the words 'true' and 'false'.

The special sentences must be restricted to all those statement-making sentences whose truth or falsity does not depend on their context. We exclude sentences such as 'The gate is open' and 'It's raining'; but we include sentences of the forms 'All A are B' and 'Some A are B', and sentences which start off by pinning themselves down to a location in time and space. We can pretend we have a universal scheme of coordinates for fixing statements to particular times and places, so that sentences like 'At x,y,z,t, the gate is open' are included. A theory of the world in a given language can now be defined to be *complete* just in case, for each of those chosen statement-making sentences, *either that statement or its negation is included in the theory of the world.*

It should now be clear that a commonsense realist, at any rate, does not have to maintain that there is only one 'true and complete' description of the way the world is. Instead, they can maintain that there is any number of true and complete descriptions in terms of any number of different languages and conceptual schemes. The theories of the world that people actually hold include many false statements, of course, so there will inevitably be conflict between the theories actually held true. But that is beside the point, which is that according to the realist there *is* at least one true theory, regardless of whether anyone actually holds it true. In view of the potential infinity of different conceptual schemes (the commonsense realist can maintain), there is any number of different, yet still true, theories of the world, all complete in the sense just explained.

Can this kind of realism escape being sucked into the 'cosmic porridge' doctrine? If realists deny there is just one true and complete theory of the world, doesn't that imply that it is up to us how we slice the world? Not at all. The realist who concedes there are many true theories takes seriously the claim that those theories are *all true*. They describe objectively real features of the world, features 'out there', not ones that depend on our decisions. Just how that is so will, I hope, become clear in the course of the discussion.

Another objection may have occurred to you. If two theories of the world both leave nothing out, isn't the realist bound to say that at least one of them is in some respect false, or else that they are not genuinely different, but just different ways of saying the same things, mere 'notational variants'? Here the example of the English and French expressions for floor-coverings is helpful. It suggests that the realist can resist this line of reasoning. Two theories would be notational variants of each other if they were straightforwardly intertranslatable. But the words for types of floor-covering, we are assuming, are not thus intertranslatable. (They are still intertranslatable *roughly*; but there are no *exact* equivalents.) The point is further illustrated by the fact that the English inventory by itself does not automatically determine what the French one will be – precisely because the concepts are not intertranslatable. At the same time the two inventories are not mutually contradictory: certainly not, because they both describe the same reality, though in different but compatible ways. What goes for the inventories goes for theories of the world: it was differences between the English and French *languages* that made the inventory example work. It looks as if the realist can consistently maintain that there can be many different true theories of the world, all compatible with one another.

4 Scientific theory and reality

You might be willing to concede the point to the extent that it applies to commonsense descriptions. But, you might suggest, it is part of commonsense realism to hold that the ordinary things it says exists – people, houses, pots and pans, the sun, other stars – are constructed in certain ways from certain kinds of stuff, about which certain things are true. Common sense won't tell us the details of the fine structure of things. That is the task of science. Nevertheless there are truths about their structure. It may seem that those truths hold purely because of the nature of the fine structure of things themselves, and not at all because of the interests or culture or language of the scientists who find out about them. To the extent that our scientific descriptions are correct, the joints and connections between our concepts will correspond accurately to the joints and connections between the things themselves. In that case, even though there will be many different but mutually compatible true commonsense theories of the world, none leaving anything out in its own terms, the same cannot be said for the scientific truth. When we get down to the rock-bottom details of the nature of things, as investigated by a realistic fundamental science, a true and complete theory will mirror nature (you may think) so that there cannot be more than one true and complete scientific theory of the world. Of course there could be different versions of that theory in different languages. But if there appeared to be two different theories, then at least one of them would be false, or they would just be alternative ways of saying the same thing – mere notational variants.[14]

That argument has some appeal, but is at best incomplete. One reason is now familiar: it disregards Wittgenstein's points about 'forms of life'. Intelligent beings with a different form of life from ours might have radically different scientific theories from any we could possibly have. Perhaps that idea is just mistaken (though if it is I know of no refutation of it). That is one gap in the argument. Another is that it does nothing to show that a *complete* theory of the world is possible at all. There seems no a priori reason why the world should not be complex in ways that defied description even in principle. (There are mathematical ways of specifying how that might be so.) However, although that is certainly a gap in the argument, it is not important from the point of view of an interest in realism. If the world really is complex in those ways, our best theories will also have to be incomplete for that very reason. No matter how detailed they may be, there will always be more still to be described. In any case, the difficulty can be sidestepped. The argument in the last paragraph can be taken to apply only to what a scientific theory of the world can truly and accurately say. There are two other things wrong with it, which I think are more important.

The first is that it fails to take account of the fact that any scientific theory of the nature of things has to be thought up. We noted early on that even our ordinary concepts of things, such as people, animals and plants, are not forced upon us by the world, but depend on our sensory and intellectual capacities, and our natural tendencies and aptitudes. There is some

14 See Bernard Williams, *Descartes*, for discussion of what he calls 'the absolute conception': the idea of 'what the world is like independent of any knowledge or representation in thought' (p.65). The absolute conception appears to imply a single true theory. See also R. Rorty, *Consequences of Pragmatism*, pp.191–5.

'conceptual autonomy'. That remains true even though people, animals, plants and so on interact with us very directly. We can't help seeing, hearing, touching, smelling, and in some cases eating them. But the idea that all these things have more or less complicated internal structures, the fine details of which are hidden from us even when we survey their innards when they have been cut open, is not an obvious one. Possibly it did not occur to anyone before, say, the sixth century BC. That whole project had to be thought up first; and then people had to think up ways of carrying it out. As we saw, the original version of the atomic theory was devised with very little reference to anything but the most generally noticeable facts about change, such as combustion, decay and growth. In order for the argument two paragraphs back to work, it needs to show that when scientists have thought up ways of characterizing the fine structures of things, including ways of explaining their behaviour, somehow the things themselves will compel the developing theories to converge on a single theory. But why shouldn't there be scope for conceptual differences even between theories that are true and complete?

You may suggest that unless there were convergence there would be no content to the scientific realist's claim. How could science tell us what there really is if there could also be an alternative science telling us that what there really is is something different? At first that objection seems unanswerable. But recall what was said earlier about commonsense realism. We saw no reason to reject the idea that there could be any number of different languages and conceptual schemes, all capable of telling the truth about commonsense reality, all compatible with one another. Why shouldn't the same go for scientific theories? Why shouldn't Martian scientists produce a theory of the world formulated in terms of concepts different from those of terrestrial scientists, while both theories were equally true and complete? Why shouldn't both theories tell us 'what there really is', each in its own terms? When one says 'This is what there really is', it need not – must not – be taken to imply that there is no alternative way to describe what there is – any more than an English inventory of the floor-coverings in a certain building excludes a French inventory in terms of different concepts.

You might be tempted to object that it is surely an objective matter of fact what things and properties there are. If so, surely the uniquely correct theory will be the one which specifies precisely those things and properties. But if that point is to be relevant, there must be a uniquely correct way to specify those things and properties. To assume there is such a uniquely correct way of specifying them would beg the question. It would amount to assuming the correctness of Aristotelian realism in the first place.

We noted an apparently more compelling objection. If both theories are true and complete, how can they fail to be equivalent to one another, hence intertranslatable or mutually 'reducible', just alternative ways of saying the same thing? Let us look more closely at that suggestion.

5 Possible relations between theories. Reduction and 'strict implication'

Chemistry seems to be in some sense reducible to physics. In recent years much controversy and confusion have been caused by failures to make clear what is meant here by 'reducible'. One suggestion has been that reduction requires the statements of one theory to be translatable into statements of the other. Another, not quite so demanding, is that they must be logically equivalent to statements in the reducing theory. (A statement is translatable into another just in case they both mean the same; two statements are logically equivalent just in case it is necessarily the case that they are either both true or both false.)

Should we understand the reducibility of chemistry to physics to mean that the truths of chemistry are translatable into truths of physics? Not necessarily. In translation we have to use the concepts of the two theories; and in general there is no reason to expect that the concepts of chemistry will be composed of 'conceptual atoms' provided by the concepts of physics. Why should they be? Certainly chemists want their theories to be compatible with physics. They need no persuading that in some sense *no more is involved* in chemical processes than is involved in the underlying physical ones. At the same time chemists have a degree of autonomy. It is for them, not for physicists, to determine which substances and processes are of interest to them, which experimental procedures are appropriate, and which ways of classifying substances and processes are most relevant to their aims. Conceivably, then, people whose interests were in some ways similar to, but in some ways slightly different from, those of today's chemists might devise a scheme of concepts that would still have to be counted as chemical in a broad sense, yet was not identical with the one prevailing in today's chemistry. In that way chemistry is in some respects dependent on physics, in some respects autonomous. That gives us one reason to be suspicious of the original idea of reducibility, which had the objective of *eliminating* the 'reduced' science by means of the 'reducing' one. The thought was that what had originally appeared to be a messy multiplicity of different sciences was actually a disguised unity. The basic science was to be physics, because it is at least plausible to maintain, with Quine, that 'nothing happens in the world, not the flutter of an eyelid, not the flicker of a thought, without some redistribution of microphysical states'.[15] But we can agree with that dictum without denying that chemistry is to some extent autonomous in the way just indicated.

Given a degree of autonomy for chemistry, there seems no particular reason to expect that the truths of chemistry must have translations, or even

15 W. V. Quine, *Theories and Things*, p.98.

logical equivalents, in terms of physics. Granting that chemical processes involve nothing but processes which in any particular instance have physical descriptions, it doesn't follow that for each true sentence of chemistry there is a true sentence of physics which accurately translates it, or even one logically equivalent to it. Certainly for each particular chemical truth there must be particular physical truths which guarantee that it holds: truths describing the particular circumstances, and general physical laws. That must be so if no more is involved in chemical processes than physical ones. But in order for there also to be translatability or logical equivalence, all chemical *types* would have to coincide with types specifiable in purely physical terms. I know of no good reason to suppose that that is so.[16]

The same goes for relations between truths statable in terms of physics and truths statable in terms of everyday psychology. In this case it is glaringly clear that the two sets of conceptual schemes were devised independently and with very different purposes. Unlike the concepts of physics, for example, those of everyday psychology – intention, desire, belief, emotion and so on – were not devised primarily with a view to being able to describe and explain the fine structure of the systems to which they apply. On the contrary, they were developed to enable us to understand other whole human beings and ourselves in spite of our almost total ignorance of our fine structure. Again, although dynamics is a component of physics, and likewise unconcerned about the fine structure of the systems to which it applies, dynamics cannot be said to have been devised with a view to 'understanding' systems in the same sense as everyday psychology aims at understanding people. Psychological explanations are in many ways unlike ordinary physical ones. (One conspicuous difference is that, while ideas like 'appropriate' or 'reasonable' often figure in psychological explanations, nothing analogous occurs in physical ones.) Given that the two sets of concepts and explanatory schemes were devised for such different purposes, it is not surprising that there seems no prospect of being able to find physical translations or logical equivalents to the truths of psychology.

A once-standard way of providing for the 'reduction' of one theory by another was by means of 'bridge laws': laws stating equivalences between pairs of sentences from each of the two theories. To take an old (though inaccurate) example, the following would be a possible bridge law connecting psychology and biology:

(BL) An organism is in pain if and only if its C-fibres are firing.

---

16 Some philosophers would urge that there must be such translations, even if they include infinite sequences of physical sentences. But it is not clear that the idea of such infinite sequences is intelligible, unlike the chemical ones they were purportedly equivalent to. Much more could be said.

Either the statements on each side of 'if and only if' are supposed to be *logical* equivalents, or not. If they are supposed to be logical equivalents, there is no problem – apart from the last two paragraphs, which suggest such equivalences are not to be found. If the statements connected by a bridge law are *not* logical equivalents, what makes them true at all? In the example of (BL), the concept of C-fibres is biological. Is (BL) a law of biology? It had better not be, since the concept of pain is not a concept of biology but of everyday psychology – and the whole idea was to get rid of those concepts in favour of biological ones. It seems (BL) must instead be a law of psychology (or perhaps of some other non-biological science). The trouble is that in that case it cannot contribute to reducing psychology to biology! If non-logically necessary bridge laws are the best we can hope for, there is no reduction in the sense called for. Non-logically necessary bridge laws turn out to be a thoroughly unsatisfactory approach to reduction. What to do?

It makes sense to speak of one theory being reduced to another if all its truths can be translated into those of the other, and also if all its truths have logical equivalents in the other. Unfortunately such equivalents seem unlikely to hold. On the other hand you can't claim to have got rid of one theory in favour of another if the best you can do is produce non-logically necessary bridge laws. However, there are other useful ways in which the truths of one theory can be related to those of another.

The sort of relation that concerns us is one where *no more is involved in* the things and events described in terms of one theory than is involved in those describable in terms of another. An example will make the idea clearer. Think of mountains, valleys, rivers and other features of the landscape. I take it these involve nothing beyond the sorts of things that could (though with huge difficulty) be described in terms of particle physics. For, perhaps regrettably, we have given up believing in river gods, tree spirits and so on. Let us pretend there exists an actual specification of the physical universe as it is, purely in terms of particle physics. This vast specification – I will call it *P* – pins down every detail of every particle throughout the entire actual history of the universe, past, present and future. Also – a vital point – it specifies the physical laws according to which those particles behave. Now imagine God at the moment of creation. He has devised this blueprint *P* and creates a physical universe in accordance with it. Having done so, does he have any further work to do in order to ensure that there are mountains, valleys, rivers and so on?[17] Clearly not. Having created a physical universe in accordance with *P* (which includes statements of physical laws), he has thereby created mountains, valleys and the rest. There is *no more* to the existence of such things than is involved in the distribution and states of

---

17 This illuminating way of dramatizing the issues is due to Saul Kripke.

physical particles throughout space and time, behaving according to the laws of physics. It is not just a coincidence that no more is involved. It is (we can say) a logical matter. There is absolutely no possibility whatever that there should have been a physical universe as specified by *P*, and that the landscape in all its details should have been other than it actually is. Landscape descriptions are not included in *P*, since it is strictly in terms of particle physics. Yet *P* fixes, in the most absolute way possible, the truths that can be stated in terms of landscape features. In a very clear sense, then, descriptions of features of the landscape apply to exactly the same reality as is specified by *P*. It seems highly unlikely that there should be translations or logical equivalences between landscape statements and statements in terms of *P*.

A convenient technical expression is to say that *P strictly implies* the truths about the landscape. (One statement strictly implies another if it is absolutely impossible for the first to be true and the second false.) There seems every reason to suppose that this relation holds between the truths of physics and those of chemistry. If all chemical events and processes involve nothing but physical events and processes, all chemical descriptions are descriptions of processes which, individually at least, have full physical descriptions too. In that case it is impossible that all actually true physical descriptions should hold and some chemical description (which is actually true) should fail to hold; so the totality of physical truths strictly implies all chemical truths. That may well be so even though it is impossible to find translations or logical equivalents for all chemical truths in terms of physics. (Incidentally, any true 'bridge laws' will themselves be strictly implied by the totality of physical truths.)

In the previous section we looked at the idea that there might be many different true and complete scientific theories of the world. We considered the suggestion that if two scientific theories of the world were both true and complete they would have to be, if not intertranslatable, then logically equivalent or otherwise 'reducible' to one another. We can now see why that is not necessarily so. Pretend each theory consists of a long compound sentence: a string of sentences conjoined by many occurrences of 'and'. Each will include (as *P* does) statements of the laws of the theory together with a vast number of factual statements in terms of the theory. It seems that, if each theory strictly implies the other, each may be both true and complete in its own terms, yet not translatable or equivalent to the other, or even 'reducible' in any but the weakest sense. Strict implication does not entail translatability or even logical equivalences between statements of the two theories.[18]

18 I must mention a notion related to strict implication: *supervenience*. There is a considerable literature on this notion. However, for my purposes I find strict implication, as explained above, more useful. If you prefer to talk of supervenience, note that it must be 'logical' supervenience. It is not just a matter of natural law, but of absolute necessity, that when the arrangement of atoms and molecules in the universe has been fixed, so have all the mountains.

Of course that does not settle the matter. But it does forestall any quick move to the conclusion that there could be only one true and complete scientific theory of the world.

6 Does science establish what is real?

Quine maintains that it is the business of 'scientists, in the broadest sense' to surmise what reality is like; 'and what there is, what is real, is part of that question'. That is a version of scientific realism. According to some versions of scientific realism, not only do scientists surmise what reality is like: if a certain kind of discourse doesn't tie in with science, it doesn't tell us about reality. Or, even more strongly, if something isn't explicitly provided for by science, it doesn't exist at all. Those are kinds of 'eliminativism'.

Scientific realism doesn't commit you to reject commonsense realism. Of course commonsense realism is a vague position. Conceivably what the majority of people confidently suppose to exist includes some things ruled out by science, though I don't know of any clear examples. In any case, the fact that commonsense concepts are usually different from scientific ones does nothing to undermine the existence of the things we ordinarily suppose to exist. The landscape example reinforces that claim.

If we take a very narrow view of science and allow only physics, chemistry and biology to count as science, then science in this sense doesn't include landscape concepts. It clearly doesn't include them explicitly; and it seems unlikely that it even provides the means to translate or provide logical equivalents for them. The system of landscape concepts seems to be, in that sense, *incommensurable* with the system of narrowly scientific concepts. Some hard-nosed theorists would see in that fact (if it is a fact) a reason to consign landscape talk to the intellectual dustbin, along with talk about witches, magic and phlogiston. According to that approach, if it has no counterpart in scientific talk it doesn't describe reality. But that conclusion is perverse. As we have noticed, all truths about the landscape are strictly implied by the truths that could be stated in terms of particle physics alone. Landscape descriptions are just *alternative ways of talking* about parts of the same physical universe specified by *P*. Mountains don't fail to exist just because they happen to be made up of molecules! The reality of the universe as specified in purely physical terms automatically *guarantees* the reality of mountains, valleys, rivers and the rest. (Not that we needed any such guarantee. Any sensible realism recognizes that our grip on reality comes from our ordinary ways of interacting with the world, not from science. If scientific discoveries, or philosophical argument, appeared to show we must give up believing in the existence of mountains and valleys, that would be a reason to question the scientific or philosophical reasoning.)

You may wonder what's so special about science anyway. Why should we give any privilege to what scientists say? Why should it be a scientific theory, physics, which provides the vocabulary for an account of the world, *P*, which strictly implies other truths? In reply I have another question. Does anyone know any better way than by science to discover both the fine structure of reality and the facts about what is remote from us in space and time? We briefly noticed the scope and depth of the sciences at the beginning of Chapter 2. Their success in practical life is too familiar to need emphasis. Nor is there anything mysterious about that success – provided we adopt a realistic viewpoint and assume there is a reality 'out there' to be discovered. On that assumption the increasing success of the sciences is not surprising. They are increasingly successful because they are discovering more and more details about the world.

Keep in mind how the sciences have become more and more sensitive to what is out there. The ancient Greeks' brilliant version of the atomic theory was devised in spite of their having to rely almost exclusively on a priori reasoning, given that they were puzzled by the obvious empirical facts of change, decay, combustion and the like. They had no instruments, and no tradition of using instruments to test their hypotheses and devise increasingly sophisticated methods of 'putting nature to the question'. Their whole approach was deficient in that kind of sensitivity to nature. Today's sciences stand in conspicuous contrast. They are extraordinarily sensitive to nature because of three things: scientists' ability to use both a huge array of extremely sensitive instruments and machines; their ability to deploy an array of sophisticated mathematical methods; and the availability of theories constructed from within a tradition of detailed, painstaking work.

It is our ordinary experience of the world from birth, and perhaps from before birth, which provides us with our basic grip on reality. It was not on the basis of some scientific theory that we learned to find our way around. But a physical specification of the universe not only guarantees the existence of the commonsense world of everyday life in the way we have noticed. It provides for much more besides. Notably it provides for the fine structure of the things around us and for the existence and nature of things remote in time and space. Granted our grip on the main conspicuous features of reality comes from ordinary non-scientific interactions, it would seem irrational to deny that the sciences provide our best possible means of finding out about things beyond what is immediately accessible to us.

7 Relating science and common sense: (a) theoretically

The question I raised at the beginning of this chapter was: How is the world as presented to us by science, and notably by physics, related to the meaning-dense world of everyday life? In section 2 I sketched a realist answer: science and common sense are different ways of describing and explaining exactly the same reality. For example, 'Water' and 'H_2O' are respectively common-sense and scientific answers to the question of what is in the glass. But that suggestion left several worries outstanding.

If realism is correct, doesn't it imply that there is a single true theory of the world? If so, how could scientific and commonsense descriptions both be true? I offered reasons why there is no such implication; on the contrary, there are reasons to think that realism is consistent with there being indefinitely many different true theories of what there is (providing they are just different, and do not actually contradict one another). Another suggestion (not a worry) was that, even if there could be many true commonsense theories, there could be only one true *scientific* theory. I argued to the contrary. Then we faced the question of whether, if both commonsense and scientific theories might be true, one kind had to be *eliminated* in favour of the other. Again I argued that it is not necessarily so. Finally we considered the suggestion that one of the two must be *reducible* to the other. Having considered various senses of 'reducible', I argued that realism does not call for reducibility. I described a relation, strict implication, which can hold between theories when neither is reducible to the other. Applied to the case of a scientific theory of the world on the one hand and our commonsense theory on the other, the suggestion is that the former strictly implies the latter: it is absolutely impossible that the former should be true and the latter false. Let us take another look at that suggestion.

Recall that enormous conjunction P of truths stated in terms of particle physics (section 5). P includes the laws of physics, but also all truths about the positions and states of elementary particles throughout the whole of space and time. In that sense it specifies the entire physical universe, past, present and future. P is stated in a narrow vocabulary which excludes all the vocabularies in terms of which we characterize reality from our different points of view as individuals, with our own needs, interests, hopes, fears, memories, habits and the rest.

Any *scientific* realist – anyone who accepts that most of what science tells us about the world is true – must agree that if there are any truths other than those actually included in P, then they are strictly implied by P. That is, it is absolutely impossible that P should be true and any of those other statements false. The reason is that, in effect, scientific realists are committed to the view that there is *nothing there* beyond what can be described in scientific terms. Scientific realists who are also eliminativists may refuse to accept that there are any further truths. They may deny that what can be said in non-scientific vocabularies describes anything that really exists. But, as we saw, that position is perverse and certainly not compulsory. (It would imply there were no mountains.) In any case, all scientific realists who are not eliminativists must agree that such further truths are strictly implied by P.[19] So truths such as that

19 Strictly, they should make one exception. They will hold that among the actual truths is the truth (X) that nothing exists other than what is strictly implied by P – no angels, for example. But (X) itself does not seem to be strictly implied by P, so (X) needs to be added to the statement of their position.

Napoleon had a headache on 1 January 1800; that those sheets of paper are a draft of my book; that the radiator feels warm; that my wife is telling me a friend is on the phone; that those dark clouds mean more snow is on the way – the non-eliminative scientific realist had better hold that all those and other meaning-impregnated truths are strictly implied by *P*.

All of which helps to explain how it is that scientific realism need not involve any devaluation of the world of everyday life. It does not conflict with human values. In particular it does not usurp everyday psychological explanations in terms of our beliefs, desires, intentions, hopes, fears and the rest. Indeed, as we have noticed, it allows a fair amount of autonomy to psychology. For that reason it imposes only a light constraint on morality, aesthetics, politics and other characteristically human kinds of discourse. The constraint is simply that scientific truth must be reckoned with as far as it is known.

The scientific story – at any rate the story as told in terms of physics – does not itself include any treatment of *how the world strikes us* from our various individual points of view. It does not *treat* things as enmeshed in our attitudes of likes and dislikes, needs, interests and so on. It says nothing – in those terms – about headaches, warm radiators, friends or snowball fights. There is a sense in which it 'leaves out' those things. But then it does not set out to treat things in that way. In its own way it provides for the existence of all of them. It does so in the sense that the scientific story cannot be true while any of those other statements is false. The scientific realist does not have to claim that those other statements are reducible to truths of physics, only that they are strictly implied by the latter. In other words, the reality covered by science is the very same reality as is covered, though in different ways, by those other truths.

8 Relating science and common sense: (b) non-theoretically

The attention I have been giving to theories may have conveyed a wrong impression. One complaint against 'rationalistic' philosophers such as Plato and Descartes is that they give a distorted picture of our relations to the world. They represent us as related to reality via theories, when in fact things are utterly different. Heidegger emphasizes that our ordinary everyday existence depends chiefly on our relationships with other people and with such things as clothing, houses, pots and pans: things we think of in terms of our dealings with them. He attempts to undermine what he regards as mistaken assumptions about these complex relationships. According to the view he attacks, these relationships have two main components. There is the human mind, which is the source of the meaning we give to things; and there are those things themselves. Still according to that traditional type of theorizing, the significance things have for us is just a product of the way our minds operate on those things. Here is Hubert Dreyfus's account of Heidegger's view to the contrary:

The traditional misunderstanding of human being starts with Plato's fascination with theory. The idea that one could understand the universe in a detached way, by discovering the principles that underlie the profusion of phenomena, was, indeed, the most powerful and exciting idea since fire and language. But Plato and our tradition go off on the wrong track by thinking that one could have a theory of everything – even human beings and their world – and that the way human beings relate to things is to have an implicit theory about them.[20]

According to Heidegger those everyday relationships are emphatically not the product of our 'mental' activity. They are constituted by our practices – by our ordinary everyday activity in the world, including especially our interaction with others, and our ways of using things. We have always had dealings with other people, and we have always had dealings with various kinds of equipment. People and things have meaning for us because of these long-standing relationships, not as a result of some earlier theoretical activity. Essentially the same point is made in Wittgenstein's *On Certainty*. For example he remarks, 'Children do not learn that books exist, that armchairs exist, etc. etc., – they learn to fetch books, sit in armchairs, etc., etc.'[21]

Whether or not that view is right (and I happen to agree with most of it) it does not conflict with the line I have been taking. The view I have been sketching in this chapter does not imply that, in Dreyfus's words, 'the way human beings relate to things is to have an implicit theory about them'. Certainly we *have* theories, which cover all the kinds of things we have dealings with. But that is not to say that our relationships with other people and things are based on theory in the way Heidegger and Wittgenstein both reject. My claim about the strict implication of other truths by the narrowly physical truths is entirely consistent with the insight that the ways we understand other people and the world in general depend on interacting with them and it, not purely on mental activity.

What I have said so far does, however, ignore an enormous and pressing problem. How to explain the ways in which the physical truths encapsulated by *P* strictly imply the rest? We may be willing to accept that they are strictly implied by *P* while having no clue as to how that could be so. The Core Scientific Story gives us a start. It offers the outline of an account of how there have come to be sentient, intelligent beings. The animal world evolved from inanimate life-forms, which had themselves evolved from simpler systems. Human beings in turn evolved from other, less developed species.

---

20 Hubert Dreyfus, *Being-in-the-World*, p.1.
21 L. Wittgenstein, *On Certainty*, §476.

As intelligent creatures with complex sensory systems, living in communities which have developed rich cultures, including language, we experience the world from a wide range of different perspectives, and come to see the things about us as enmeshed in networks of significance. The Core Scientific Story at least begins to explain how there can be beings to whom things matter, and who devise non-scientific vocabularies for talking about what matters to them.

There are large gaps to be filled. But non-eliminative scientific realists hope that philosophical work will eventually fill them. The necessary explanations will show how a certain class of *objects* – complex physical organisms with the power of perception – are at the same time *subjects* – perceivers, centres of consciousness with their own individual perspectives on the world, with memories, habits, values, preferences, and a rich social existence, interacting with other people and things. A satisfactory account must include a solution to the various aspects of the mind–body problem, which obviously I am not attempting here. But no one, to my knowledge, has produced compelling reasons to suppose that the project cannot eventually succeed.

Those philosophical explanations would, among other things, explain the fact that we have developed the everyday vocabularies in terms of which, in contrast to the vocabularies of the sciences, we habitually express our feelings and values. In that way the explanations would make clear why the Husserlian claim that science devalues the world of everyday life springs from misconceptions.

MAIN POINTS IN CHAPTER 10

1   Does science devalue the world we live in? (section 1). No (sections 2, 7 and 8).
2   Does realism require there to be only a single true 'complete' theory of the world? No (sections 3–5).
3   Is non-eliminative scientific realism committed to the 'reducibility' of commonsense truths to scientific ones? No. It is committed only to hold that the totality of narrowly physical truths *strictly implies* all commonsense truths (sections 5, 7 and 8).
4   Science does not uniquely establish what is real. At the same time it is the best way we have of finding out about the fine structure of the physical world, and about what is remote in time and space (section 6).
5   None of this implies that our understanding of other people and the world around us is a matter of having *theories* about them (section 8).

CHAPTER 10: SUGGESTIONS FOR FURTHER READING

For a **general** elementary introduction to the issues, see Adam Morton, *Philosophy in Practice*, ch. 15, 'Realism'. Christopher Hookway, *Quine*, chs 4, 11 and 12, has excellent discussions of many of the issues. Chapter 7 of Michael Devitt's *Realism and Truth* (2nd edn) defends scientific realism.

Reductionism. Two articles in the *Oxford Companion to Philosophy* provide background: Michael Ruse, 'Reductionism' (pp.750f.) and Jaegwon Kim, 'Mental Reductionism' (pp.751f.).

Heidegger. Hubert Dreyfus, *Being-in-the-World: a Commentary on Heidegger's Being and Time, division I*, provides a readable introduction to the most relevant work by Heidegger.

11

A STRONG REALISM

Relativism is weirdly seductive. In our sane moments we know perfectly well that the world doesn't depend on us. Yet we – some of us anyway – are easily excited by statements like 'even reality is relative'.[1] Perhaps we get intoxicated by the suggestion that we have the power to construct our own reality. Certainly the ways we *think* about the world depend on us: on our capacities, interests, values, temperaments, points of view. The world really does strike different people in different ways. We really do think up our own theories. All that is admitted by any sensible realist. But it provides no grounds for relativism.

Simple varieties of relativism were rejected in Chapter 3. More sophisticated varieties were criticized in Chapters 6, 8 and 9. In this final chapter I will set out a strong kind of realism, and try to make clear how it is consistent with the main ideas which seem to nudge us towards relativism. To bring out the character of the realism I recommend, I will contrast it with some features of Rorty's pragmatism.

1 The main apparently relativizing ideas

We can say goodbye to at least three varieties of relativism. Subjectivism is the most exciting and primitive. According to it, what is true is whatever is actually held true; but many of us hold that subjectivism itself is false; so if it is true it is false; therefore it is false (for no statement could be both true and false).[2]

Protagorean or 'true-for-me' relativism is more subtle. It cannily rules out there being such a thing as a statement which is true or false full-stop. It insists that the only thing there is in the way of truth is truth-for-someone-at-a-time. But, as we noticed, in order for there to be truth-for-someone, someone must exist independently of whatever anyone may think – even if the sole thinker has peculiar ideas about existence. That someone exists is

1 Nelson Goodman, *Ways of Worldmaking*, p.20.
2 Chapter 3, section 2.

therefore true independently of what anyone may think. So Protagorean relativism, according to which there is no such truth at all, is false (full-stop) for that reason alone, apart from other reasons we noticed. Everyone has to be a realist about something.

The third relativizing doctrine which I think has been refuted is the 'cosmic porridge' idea, about which enough has been said, perhaps, in the course of the book.

Four other main views *appear* to drive us towards relativism but, I think, do not. In any case they have strong reasons on their side and must be accepted by any sensible realist. The first is Wittgenstein's ideas about language-games. That broad comparison of the use of patterns of sound (or marks on paper) with playing games is brilliantly illuminating. If language is to work at all there must be rules or norms, analogous to the rules of a game, which provide the framework in terms of which we can assess the appropriateness or correctness of linguistic acts in the contexts of their utterance. Just as we can pick up the rules of games by joining in, so we can pick up the rules of a language-game (or a whole language) by taking part in the activity of speaking and writing it. Just as there is an indefinitely large variety of different kinds of games, so there is an indefinitely large variety of kinds of use of language. Just as the ability to play a game depends on being the right sort of creature (nothing anyone does could teach our cat to play chess), so the ability to be trained to use a language depends on belonging to the right 'form of life' – sharing with its users the same natural abilities and predispositions to count certain patterns of behaviour as 'going on in the same way', others as not.

The idea of language-games is quite commonly supposed to force us into relativism – a sophisticated version of true-for-me relativism. The 'language-game argument' summarized the reasoning. It turned out to be a failure. But that does nothing to undermine the idea of language-games itself; it just rests on mistaken inferences from it. The idea of language-games will be touched on again in the course of this chapter; but I assume it has already been shown to be entirely compatible with realism.[3]

The second of the four main views which appear to have a relativizing tendency, but which again there are good reasons for realists to accept, is Quine's general doctrine of posits and theories of the world. Shortly I will explain why it is no threat even to a strong realism.

The third main relativizing view is summed up by Neurath's boat. We cannot stand outside all theories and compare what a theory says with naked, unconceptualized reality. Thinking and theorizing are necessarily conducted on the basis of one's own theory, with its own particular system

---

3 Chapter 6, section 4.

of concepts. That fits in with Quine's doctrine of theories of the world. It, too, is consistent with strong realism.

The fourth view, 'conceptual autonomy',[4] is that the world outside us cannot fix our concepts. Contrary to what Aristotle assumed, the world does not determine how we think; at least not completely. In the previous chapter I considered an argument which began to look as if it might lead to the conclusion that the world *could* fix our scientific concepts. I offered reasons for rejecting it, though I do not claim to have refuted it. If what follows is right, conceptual autonomy, too, is consistent with strong realism.

2 'To call a posit a posit is not to patronize it'

Let us return to Quine's ideas about theories of the world and 'posits'. Positing, you remember, is something we do just by saying 'There are so-and-so's; the things we say exist are posits.

That entails it is up to us which posits there are in our theory of the world. If we don't posit so-and-so's, they are not posits and not included in our theory; if we do, they are. At a superficial glance that may appear to commit Quine to the view that whether or not there are rabbits, for example, depends on us – which is absurd. The realist view is that, although it is up to us whether or not we have the concept rabbit, and whether or not we think there are rabbits, that has no bearing on whether or not there are rabbits. You and I think there are rabbits, while Bodo, for some peculiar reason, thinks there are none; but that has no bearing at all on whether or not there really are rabbits.

We need to be careful, though. There is one sense in which it may be said – confusedly but not stupidly – that the existence of things depends on us. Cats (to change the example) exist just in case it is true that they exist; it is true they exist just in case the statement 'There are cats' is true; whether or not that statement is true depends on how the words in it, notably 'cat', are used; and how those words are used depends on us. So whether cats exist can be said to depend on us in that sense: it depends on our language, our use of words. (If you prefer not to treat truth in terms of language, there is a parallel argument in terms of concepts. It is true that cats exist just in case the concept *cat* applies to them; concepts depend on people; so the existence of cats depends on people.) But that sense in which we might say the existence of things 'depends on us' is beside the point. Certainly it is up to us which words or concepts we use. But that doesn't mean it is up to us whether or not those words or concepts actually apply to anything. We have indeed devised the concept *cat*. But we cannot fix whether or not there actually are cats: that depends on how things are in the world.

---

4 Chapter 2, section 8.

That is a commonsense line of thought. You might object that it introduces its own confusions. To posit cats, you may say, is not just to have a word or concept at our disposal. It is to commit ourselves to the existence of cats. We commit ourselves to being willing to assent when asked questions like 'Are there cats?' And the theory of the world in which cats are posits is ours. Since it is, after all, we who are speaking – we who say 'There are cats' and mean it – the upshot may seem to be, when we speak from within our theory of the world, that *there are cats*. For we are speaking as people who posit cats. That is a less superficial way in which Quine's position may appear to commit him to the view that the existence of cats depends on us: a kind of anti-realism or idealism.

There are some who interpret Quine in that way. I will try to make clear that they have missed the interesting and important character of his position. He has said that 'To call a posit a posit is not to patronize it....Everything to which we concede existence is a posit from the standpoint of a description of the theory-building process, and simultaneously real from the standpoint of the theory that is being built.'[5] But those remarks are not as clear as they might be: further explanation is needed. The idea of a 'theory-building process' is clear enough: we encountered it at the start of this book and have been discussing aspects of it ever since. But what does he mean by 'real from the standpoint of the theory'? The least he can mean is that those whose theory it is believe there really are things of the kinds they posit. However, that is consistent with someone saying that what is posited in someone else's theory does not exist. You may believe in ghosts; I don't. So I will say your posited ghosts don't exist. That may still seem to reinforce the suspicion that Quine's remarks support a relativism according to which there is no more to the existence of anything than that it is posited. He has an answer:

> Have we now so far lowered our sights as to settle for a relativistic doctrine of truth – rating the statements of each theory as true for that theory, and brooking no higher criticism? Not so. The saving consideration is that we continue to take seriously our own particular aggregate science, our own particular world-theory....Within our own total evolving doctrine, we can judge truth as earnestly and absolutely as can be...[6]

That sounds encouraging to realists, but again needs interpretation. First, what can he mean by saying 'we continue to take seriously' our own particular theory? There is a sense in which we could take a theory seriously

---

5 W. V. Quine, *Word and Object*, p.22.
6 Op. cit., p.24. For further discussions of these and related matters see C. Hookway, *Quine*.

without necessarily holding it true. (The police have evidence that the murderer got in through the window. Taking that theory seriously would not automatically commit them to accepting it as true.) Quine goes on to say 'we can judge truth as earnestly and absolutely as can be'; so it seems he means 'take seriously' to be equivalent to 'hold true'. Still, since he clearly thinks each of us has a slightly different total theory, and these theories conflict with each other, can he really avoid being a relativist?

There is no threat of relativism here. I take it the idea is this. Everyone has their own theory of the world. When we judge what is or is not the case, we cannot help doing so on the basis of our own theory. My theory includes as posits other people and cats but not ghosts. Yours may share my positing of people and cats but include ghosts. I agree there are people and cats; but when you say 'There are ghosts' I disagree. And I am really disagreeing, not just saying 'I have decided not to posit ghosts' or, 'For me, there are no ghosts' (as if it were like 'I don't happen to like Stilton cheese'). I am saying you are *objectively* mistaken about what there is. I am being as strongly and thoroughly realist as it is possible to be. After all, my theory – like any theory that people actually hold – is a theory about what there is! That is a logical point. Everyone is a realist about what their own theory posits, precisely because that is the point of the theory: to say what there is, what really exists.

You may worry that we might be confident our theory was correct yet still be mistaken. Of course. So far as I know there is no way to guarantee that one's theory is correct beyond all possibility of error. That can hardly come as a terrible shock. If anyone thought there was some way to guarantee their beliefs were true beyond even the possibility of error, they were over-optimistic. In any case, the possibility of being wrong cannot rule out the possibility of being right. On the contrary: if error is possible, so is correctness. Insisting one is right while conceding the possibility that one is mistaken provides no foothold for relativism. It is ordinary intellectual decency.

Those points become even clearer when we recall that positing is only part of what goes into constructing (or rather reconstructing) a world-theory. Much of the theory doesn't consist just of statements that various things exist, but of descriptions of various aspects of the world and accounts of how things are related. 'There are rabbits' slots into a web of statements of everyday information, natural history and biology, including accounts of rabbit-warrens, something about long furry ears and fluffy white tails, preferences in food, propensity for swift breeding, alarm signals, and much else. Further, except for the very special cases of Berkeley and others whose theory of the world is self-consciously anti-realist, the web of statements that make up a person's theory of the world will include ones such as 'The existence of ordinary physical objects does not depend on whether anyone believes they exist'. Such statements are very firm components of many people's theory – including my own. At the same time I broadly accept Quine's remarks about positing. So there seems no good reason to think he is committed to relativism or anti-realism. On the contrary, he has made clear how we can be strong realists while accepting his views about theories of the world.

The same considerations also show that the thoughts epitomized by Neurath's boat have no tendency to force us into relativism. That follows immediately from the terms of the above discussion, where it is assumed that we always have some theory on the basis of which we assess other people's theories. There is no reason why realists should find that embarrassing. Realists, like relativists, are inducted into a human way of life from the start of their lives, and pick up the language and theories of those around them. If they come to think self-consciously about their current theories, they have to do so in terms of those very theories, even if they don't realize it. But all along, their theories are aimed at representing how things really are in a mind-independent world.

3 Realism and conceptual autonomy

'Conceptual autonomy' is the name I am giving to the point that the world does not force us to adopt any particular concepts: we have some freedom in the matter. We are creatures of a certain particular kind, with certain particular needs and certain particular sensory and intellectual capacities. Things in the world do not come ready-labelled. We devise the 'labels' or concepts to suit our needs and interests – or rather, it is as if we had devised them. The point is that it is our own natures, not only the world, which largely determine which concepts we adopt.

Conceptual autonomy may appear to provide support for relativism. That appearance springs from the same confusion as that which produced the misconception that Quine's ideas about posits support relativism. Realists can accept that our conceptual schemes are up to us while insisting that it is up to the world to determine whether or not anything happens to fall under a given concept. How we came by our concept *cat* is one thing; whether anything satisfies it – whether there actually are any cats – is something else.

The four main ideas with an apparently relativizing tendency were the language-game idea, Quine's views on posits and theories of the world, Neurath's boat, and conceptual autonomy. We have seen they are all consistent with a strong realism.

4 Does the language-game idea make philosophy a waste of time?

It will now be instructive to examine an interesting line of thought suggested by Richard Rorty in connection with what he calls 'vocabularies' – large-scale language-games or theories. It partly concerns the idea of reduction. If he is right, much of philosophy is a waste of time, including discussions about relating scientific theories and everyday talk.

We noted in the previous chapter that some philosophers have held that, if two theories both apply to the same subject-matter, one of them must be either *eliminable* in favour of the other, or else *reducible* to it. We also noted that some scientific realists have looked forward to an eventual single grand theory – presumably physics – capable of describing and explaining every-thing. I offered reasons against both those positions. In their place I suggested a helpful application of the notion of strict implication. One theory may strictly imply another without being reducible to it in any strong sense. The implied theory may retain a considerable degree of autonomy as far as its conceptual scheme is concerned; yet both may be about the same reality.

Rorty warns against the assumption that 'all vocabularies are dispensable, or reducible to other vocabularies, or capable of being united with all other vocabularies in one grand unified super vocabulary'. To that extent realists can agree. But he goes further, claiming that if we avoid that assumption 'we shall not be inclined to ask questions like "What is the place of conscious-ness in a world of molecules?"…"What is the place of value in a world of fact?"…' (that is, questions a lot of philosophers have spent a lot of time and effort discussing). 'We should not try to answer such questions', he says. Instead, 'we should restrict ourselves to questions like "Does our use of these words get in the way of our use of those other words?"'[7]

The underlying thought is essentially the same as the one used in the 'language-game' argument in Chapter 6, and as Winch's main point about rationality, discussed in the same chapter (section 5). It is to the effect that, since language-games or 'vocabularies' are ultimately just ways of behaving, there is no interesting way to relate one of them to others except on the basis of how far they get in each other's way. They are, it is said, 'incommensu-rable'. Playing tennis might get in the way of playing chess, but it would be absurd to ask questions like 'How does your backhand relate to your skill in deploying your Knights?' However, there is only a tenuous analogy between that case and the case of language-games. Contrary to what Rorty seems to have assumed, language-games may be intimately linked in a variety of ways.

He claims that if we follow his advice we shall not be inclined to ask questions like 'What is the place of consciousness in a world of molecules?' He thinks such questions spring from misconceptions. Nothing to get excited about: just find out whether our use of words to do with conscious-ness and our use of physical and chemical descriptions of things get in each

7 R. Rorty, *Contingency, Irony, and Solidarity*, pp.11f.

other's way. But that is puzzling. Has anyone ever thought that those vocabularies get in one another's way? The truth is that when we reflect on these matters we can hardly avoid wondering how physical facts bear on psychological facts. What has perplexed people from at least the time of Descartes is the question of how (what we think of as) truths expressed in the language of consciousness on the one hand, and truths expressed in the language of physical objects on the other, actually *are* related. Nor are we being confused. It is reasonable to assume that the psychological facts and the physicochemical facts both hold of *us*. We assume that the same organisms – those complex physical structures – are also what have experiences; and we want to understand how that can be so. When you put things like that, Rorty's advice seems perverse.

Imagine someone asks 'What is the place of mountains in a world of molecules?' If that question is taken literally (for it does sound a little poetic), there is no difficulty at all. Mountains are *made* of molecules. They consist mainly of rock-formations, assembled by gradual large-scale processes on the surface of the earth; rocks consist of minerals; minerals consist of molecules in various configurations. And that's it. (Incidentally, that explanation also makes clear how truths about mountains are strictly implied by truths about molecules.) The reason the corresponding question about consciousness still puzzles us is that we lack a comparably satisfying answer, based on a complete understanding of what it takes for something to be conscious. Does consciousness require a special kind of substance, completely unlike ordinary physical things, as Descartes maintained? If not, as is widely supposed by many of today's philosophers, just what is it about certain physical systems which ensures that they have conscious experiences when other physical systems do not? It is not that attempts to find satisfying answers to the question have been completely fruitless. But none of the accounts on offer so far has evoked wide assent.

That doesn't mean the whole idea is a waste of time, as I will try to show with the help of an example. Philosophical behaviourism offers an account of the mental which, although it has not satisfactorily answered the question about consciousness, has helped us get much clearer about what is involved.[8] ('The mental', by the way, can be taken to be the wide range of activities involved in different kinds of thinking and experiencing.) A closer look at philosophical behaviourism will help to show how far Rorty's approach is misleading. It will also illustrate the utility of the notion of strict implication of one theory by another.

---

8 Behaviourism as a methodology for *psychology*, which attempted to make psychology scientific by finding explanations of behaviour purely in terms of inputs and outputs, is not in question here.

5 Philosophical behaviourism

Philosophical behaviourism starts from the compelling thought that when we learn how to talk about one another's thoughts and experiences we depend on how people behave. It goes on to claim that philosophers from Descartes onwards have been completely mistaken in their assumption that the phrase 'the mind' refers to a sort of ethereal theatre whose performances each of us enjoys in private, while others can only guess at what goes on. They deny there is any such thing as a 'mind' in that sense. They call attention to the way the form of our utterances may be misleading. The sentence 'I have a mind' has the same form as 'I have a book'. So we are tempted to assume that, just as having a book is being related to an object (the book), so having a mind is being related to a special thing, a mind. Behaviourists say that is a mistake – as much of a mistake as it would be to assume that, because a certain car's performance is good, there is a special entity, its performance, to which the car is related. The fact is, of course, that, for a car, having a good performance is just behaving in certain ways, or being disposed to do so. Similarly, say the behaviourists, having a mind is having the right total pattern of dispositions.[9]

Recall the explanation of dispositions in Chapter 5, section 2. Something is disposed to do something if it would actually do it when certain conditions were satisfied; but a thing may have many dispositions never manifested in actual behaviour. Philosophical behaviourists maintain that human beings have much more complicated systems of dispositions even than those provided by sophisticated computer programs. Their main point is that what we call mental states – having thoughts and experiences of all kinds – are complicated dispositional states of the system, nothing more. Just what those dispositions are is not obvious; and working them out is not a trivial task. A couple of crude examples will give some idea of a behaviourist approach, though they are certainly too simple. To be angry might be said to be just a matter of going red in the face, shouting, banging the table energetically – or, if not actually doing any of these things, being disposed to do them. Similarly, to believe it's raining might be to be disposed, if you go out, to put on a raincoat, take an umbrella and so on, and if you hear the question 'Is it raining?', to reply 'Yes'.

Contrary to vulgar prejudice, behaviourists do not deny that there are conscious states. What they say is that philosophers have been thoroughly confused about their nature. To have conscious states, they maintain, is just a matter of acquiring (or having) certain kinds of dispositions. Having a headache, to give one more example, might consist in acquiring dispositions

9 G. Ryle, *The Concept of Mind*, offers powerful and readable considerations to this effect.

to wince, frown, hold the hands to the head, reply 'Yes' when asked 'Does it hurt?', and so on.

In such ways behaviourism offers a reply to the question 'What is the place of consciousness in a world of molecules?' Perhaps surprisingly, it explains consciousness in terms of bodies and behaviour. Against Rorty's injunction not to waste our time on such matters, it shows how the language-game or 'vocabulary' of everyday psychology might be related to those of biology, chemistry and physics, which can also be applied to human beings.

6 No reduction and no unity

Philosophical behaviourism is not widely accepted, although it still has a number of influential adherents. In spite of what my remarks may have suggested, I think it is badly mistaken. One thing wrong with it is precisely its failure to deal convincingly with conscious experience. (Can having a toothache, for example, be just a matter of being disposed to act in the ways we tend to assume are *caused* by the toothache?) However, philosophical behaviourism has been a fruitful and influential way of approaching a whole complex of questions surrounding the mental. At the very least it offers valuable clues about how we can talk about other people's mental states: we can do so because we can learn what dispositions are typically involved in what mental states. We could hardly have come to talk about mental states at all if they had not been linked with patterns of behaviour in something approaching the ways behaviourism suggests.

If psychologists and philosophers had followed Rorty's advice to give up asking questions like the one about the place of consciousness, they would not have bothered to think up behaviourism. The result would have been that we should have been deprived of a fruitful, if flawed, source of insights into the nature of psychological states. So I think that example gives us good reasons to ignore Rorty's advice. The kind of philosophical behaviourism I have been discussing also helps to undermine Rorty's assumption mentioned earlier: that to reject his advice commits you either to the dogma that one theory is eliminable or reducible to another, or to the dogma that all theories can be united in a single super theory. Again, as in the case of realism and truth, he tries to force us to choose between repellent alternatives which do not exhaust the options available. In connection with the behaviourist answer to the question about consciousness, Rorty's assumption would require mental language to be eliminable, or reducible to talk of behavioural dispositions, or else to belong together with such talk in a 'grand unified super theory'. We can now see that his assumption is mistaken.

That sort of behaviourism makes no claims of reducibility. It is not committed to the view that mental statements are translatable or logically equivalent to statements in terms of dispositions. Just as well, since there are excellent reasons to think no such equivalents could possibly be produced.[10] Yet there is no reason to go to the other extreme and conclude that, if a behaviouristic approach answers the question, we must be able to link up behavioural talk and molecule talk in a 'grand synthesis'. As we saw earlier, when discussing the relation of strict implication, our psychological scheme of description and explanation was devised (if that is the right word: 'cobbled together' might be more apt) independently of, and for different purposes from, physics and chemistry. That, together with other reasons, suggests they could not be combined to make a single theory. At the same time, if human beings are purely physical organisms with no non-physical extras, then our psychological language-games apply to the same things as those to which physical and chemical statements also apply. The notion of strict implication enables us to clarify a possible relation *between* language-games or 'vocabularies', a relation that philosophical work may be able to make intelligible in particular cases. The philosophical work carried out in connection with the behaviourist project has contributed to making it intelligible that psychological language applies to organisms which consist of nothing but molecules. It proposes a way in which we might be able to understand how truths statable in terms of molecules may strictly imply truths in psychological terms.

Those two language-games – of everyday psychology and of molecules – are very different; yet, after all, they are both concerned with human beings. Compare the way in which the chemical language-game that is played with formulas such as 'H_2O' and our ordinary use of the word 'water' are both concerned with the same stuff. The chemical language-game, though it was developed in vastly different ways from our ordinary use of 'water', was nevertheless developed in harmony with the latter. The two language-games are not totally disconnected, as chess and tennis are. Similarly, we cannot just sidestep the question of how truths about the physical and chemical composition of our bodies are related to psychological truths. The attempt to discover what those relations are is a fascinating part of the attempt to discover the nature of human beings.

7 Fact-stating and other language-games

The example of behaviourism shows how two different fact-stating language-games – the physical and the psychological – might be illuminat-

---

10 The central objection to such views is that how we are disposed to behave depends on our total mental state at the time, not just on some particular belief, desire or feeling. If I believe it's going to rain, for example, I may well take an umbrella when going out – but only if I'm not so parched that I want a thorough soaking. See, e.g., D. Armstrong, *A Materialist Theory of the Mind*, ch. 3.

ingly brought into relation with one another. It would be marvellous if we could make clear not only *that* the totality of truths statable in terms of the former strictly implies truths statable in terms of the latter, but *how* that is so: what it is about the psychological facts which ensures they are strictly implied by the physical ones (assuming they actually are strictly implied). To do that would be to solve the so-called 'mind–body' problem. Earlier we noticed two other pairs of fact-stating language-games which appear to stand in the same relation of one-way strict implication. The totality of truths statable in terms of physics seems very likely strictly to imply the totality of truths statable in terms of chemistry, though the converse is not true. Similarly, the same physical totality strictly implies all truths about the landscape, but the converse is not true. Yet, as with the psychological example, that does not require the statements thus strictly implied to be also *translatable* in terms of those which strictly imply them, or even in terms logically equivalent to them. The truths strictly implied by the first members of each of these pairs retain some autonomy, even if the relevant theorists know that the strict implication relation holds. Psychologists, chemists and describers of the landscape, for example, still use their own special methods independently of the methods of physics; and they still retain their own special interests and are free to devise and revise their own concepts. Those pairs of language-games remain distinct, yet not so distinct that they cannot intelligibly be supposed to deal with the same things.

To conclude this section I must deal with a possible query about my use of the phrase 'fact-stating' to describe the statements of physics, psychology and chemistry, together with ordinary talk about other people, the stars, sticks and stones. Again it will be useful to mention a claim by Rorty. He sees it as part of pragmatism that there are no intellectually respectable distinctions to be drawn between the cognitive and the moral:

> …a second characterization of pragmatism might go like this: there is no epistemological difference between truth about what ought to be and truth about what is, nor any metaphysical difference between facts and values, nor any methodological difference between morality and science.[11]

Have I provided any reason to reject that component of pragmatism? It is hard to draw sharp lines; but it is not hard to point to typical, central or 'paradigmatic' cases of factual language. The statements in the Core Scientific Story, such as 'The earth is a planet of the sun', are examples. So are everyday statements about sticks and stones, reports on such matters as the weather and the traffic, and most if not all news items. Granted that

---

11 Rorty, *Consequences of Pragmatism*, p.163.

much, there seems no reason why realists should have to maintain that there are sharp lines to be drawn. It is consistent with the kind of realism sketched in this chapter that there should be a whole range of cases: from neutral factual discourse, through factual discourse expressing the speaker's attitude, to types of discourse which are more concerned to express values or just tastes; and then on to kinds which don't even look factual – allowing also for discourse which looks factual, except that the writer or speaker is only pretending: fiction.

We have a wide choice of more or less neutral terms in which to make what are still factual assertions. We also have a range of terms expressing attitudes as well as stating facts. ('I saw you in your old banger yesterday': that statement is factual, even though the choice of words manifests an attitude to my car.) We have no difficulty with the idea, either, that statements which are little more than expressions of taste should be dressed up in the form of factual statements. We don't feel compelled to regard statements like 'That colour's revolting' as factual, for example. There are difficult questions about how far it may be appropriate to regard moral and aesthetic statements as factual or as objective; but I shall not pursue them. We have seen why such difficulties need not undermine a solid kind of realism.

8 Conclusion

In this book we have seen how the project of devising a 'theory of the world' was approached (in remarkably different ways) by thinkers in ancient Greece. We have considered various suggestions about what it would be for such a theory to be true. We have seen reasons to reject the simpler varieties of relativism, and to accept that we are all realists about something. We have examined some of the most powerful and impressive thinking of the twentieth century on these matters, from Wittgenstein and Quine among others. We have also examined some sophisticated varieties of relativism and antirealism, though they have not stood up well to criticism. Finally we have seen how four ideas that at first glance appeared to push us towards relativism are compatible with a strong realism. There seems to be no limit to the range of different conceptual schemes on the basis of which we could represent reality; and it is largely up to us which conceptual scheme we use. But that does not mean the truths we conceptualize depend on us to the slightest extent.

MAIN POINTS IN CHAPTER 11

1 Four strongly supported views – Wittgenstein's on language-games, Quine's on theories of the world, Neurath's boat, conceptual autonomy – may appear relativistic, but are not (whole chapter).
2 Quine's views on positing and theories of the world provide for a strong kind of realism (section 2).
3 Philosophical behaviourism, though flawed, illustrates a way in which physical and psychological language-games or 'vocabularies' can be fruitfully related (sections 5 and 6).
4 Rorty's injunctions to avoid certain philosophical questions are unwarranted; and, contrary to his assumptions, different language-games can be related in ways entirely consistent with the sort of realism described here (sections 4, 6).

CHAPTER 11: SUGGESTIONS FOR FURTHER READING

Quine's 'Two Dogmas of Empiricism' is the classic text for his realism and his views on **posits and theories of the world**; section 6 is the most relevant to our interests. See also his *Word and Object*, ch. 1. For background and discussion see Christopher Hookway, *Quine*, especially chs 2 and 3.

In his *Reality and Truth* (2nd edn), a book in many ways congenial to the present one though much more advanced and detailed, Michael Devitt defends a robust **realism**. In his highly readable book, *The Last Word*, Thomas Nagel defends a strong realism against several varieties of relativism; it, too, presupposes a fair amount of philosophical background.

On **philosophical behaviourism**, an attractive classic text is G. Ryle, *The Concept of Mind* (though his behaviourism is qualified). Wittgenstein has sometimes been thought to take a behaviourist line in *Philosophical Investigations*, although that reading is contentious. D. C. Dennett in *Consciousness Explained* is strongly behaviouristic in spite of his protestations to the contrary. For standard objections to philosophical behaviourism see D. M. Armstrong, *A Materialist Theory of the Mind*, ch. 5.

GLOSSARY

(Sections where the listed topic is mentioned are referred to in brackets.)

Analytic; analytic-synthetic distinction Traditionally, analytic truths are supposed to hold purely on account of relations among concepts or the meanings of words, e.g. '2 + 2 = 4', 'Bachelors are unmarried'. All other truths count as 'synthetic'. (5.7, 5.8)

A priori Knowledge or reasoning is said to be a priori if guaranteed by reason alone, independently of sensory evidence. (1.3; 7.3)

Assertion An assertion is an utterance capable of being true or false, e.g. 'There are tigers in India'. (2.6; 6.3)

Assertion conditions The conditions in which a statement may correctly be asserted. (Compare 'truth conditions'.) (8.2)

Begging the question Assuming what is to be proved. (2.9)

Berkeleyan idealism The doctrine that there is no more to the so-called 'external world' than the fact that we have experiences or 'ideas' of appropriate kinds. (6.1)

Bivalence The 'principle of bivalence' is that every statement is either true or false. (8.5)

Cartesian dualism Descartes' thesis that we are composed of two very different 'substances': a material non-thinking body whose essence is to be extended; and an immaterial non-extended mind whose essence is to think. (10.1)

Circular argument An argument is circular if it depends on a premiss equivalent to its conclusion. (2.5)

Coherence theory of truth The theory that for a statement to be true is for it to fit into the whole system of statements accepted by a community. (2.9)

Concepts To have a particular system of concepts is to have certain particular ways of classifying things. (7.3)

Conceptual autonomy The thesis that to some extent it depends on us, not only on the world outside us, what concepts we have. (2.8)

Contingent truth Truth that is not necessary (see 'necessary truth'). (5.7)

Epistemology or 'theory of knowledge': the branch of philosophy concerned with questions of how, and how far, our claims to knowledge can be justified. (1.4)

Equivalent, equivalence Two statements are equivalent if they are either both true or both false. They are *logically* equivalent if they are equivalent for logical reasons.

Follows (logically) from; implies One statement B follows from another statement A if it is impossible for A to be true and B false. In other words, A implies B. To say B follows 'logically' from A is to emphasize that there is a logical basis for this relation.

Form of life In the sense relevant here, two people have the same form of life if they have the same natural predispositions and tendencies to find certain ways of behaving natural, given the same training. (4.9)

Forms, Platonic Plato held that what makes truth and knowledge possible is the existence of special eternal entities, the Forms, graspable only by a sort of intellectual perception. (4.2; 6.2)

Implies; follows from One statement A implies another statement B if it is impossible for A to be true and B false. In other words, B follows from A.

Intentionality Beliefs, desires and intentions, and also sentences, are 'about' things and have 'content'. In other words they have intentionality. (5.9)

Language-game Wittgenstein hoped to help us to see how words actually work by describing simple ways in which people might have used expressions. He emphasized analogies between these activities and games. (4.2–4.5; 6.3–6.4)

Metaphysics, metaphysical Traditional label for central philosophical doctrines and inquiries concerning the ultimate nature of reality. Scientific realism is an example of a metaphysical position. (6.1; 8.4)

Necessary truth A statement is necessarily true if it does not depend on how things happen to be, but would hold in any possible circumstances, any 'possible world'; e.g. '2 + 2 = 4'. (5.7)

Neurath's boat The point that if we want to revise our beliefs or concepts we have to use some of the ones we already have. We could not 'stand outside' all concepts, beliefs and theories, and face an unconceptualized reality. (7.6)

Ontological   Traditional label for philosophical doctrines and inquiries concerning what exists. (6.1)

Phenomenalism   Phenomenalists claim that statements about objects 'out there' can be 'analysed' in terms of statements about actual or possible experiences. (7.4)

Projection   The idea that what we take to be 'out there' in the world is really an effect of our own mental activity. (2.8)

Proposition   The word 'proposition' is used for what is supposed to be capable of being true or false. The idea is that the same proposition may be expressed by means of different sentences and need not be actually expressed at all. (5.8)

Realism   The word 'realism' applies to a range of philosophical positions. In this book it is mainly used for 'commonsense realism', according to which most of the things we confidently suppose to exist do exist, independently of what we may think or experience. (6.1)

Redundancy theory of truth   The view that the expression 'is true' is redundant, i.e. can be eliminated without significant loss (exploiting the seeming equivalence of 'It is true that p' and 'p'). (2.7)

Reference   To refer to something is to pick it out, typically by means of words. The name 'Socrates' refers to the individual Socrates. (2.6; 4.4)

Relativism   There are several varieties, but the underlying idea is that there is no such thing as truth independent of point of view. (Chapter 3)

Scepticism   The view that we can never know anything. (7.2)

Statement   To make a statement is to produce a spoken or written utterance of a kind which, in the context, is capable of being true or false. (2.6)

Strict implication   A strictly implies B if it is impossible for A to be true and B false. The idea is applied here to the relations between commonsense and scientific theories of the world. (10.5; 11.6)

Theory of the world   An account of the nature of the world, past, present and future. Attempted by the ancient Greeks and by modern science, and, up to a point, by all of us. (1.5)

Truth-conditions   The conditions in which a statement would be true. (8.1)

Truth value   For a statement to have a truth value is simply for it to be true, or false. (6.2)

BIBLIOGRAPHY

Armstrong, David M., *A Materialist Theory of the Mind* (London: Routledge, 1968).

Ayer, Alfred J., *Language, Truth, and Logic* (London: Gollancz, 1936).

Barnes, Jonathan, *Early Greek Philosophy* (London: Penguin, 1987).

Baudrillard, Jean, *The Gulf War Did Not Take Place* translated by Paul Patton (Bloomington and Indianapolis: Indiana University Press, 1995).

Bell, E. T., *Men of Mathematics* (London: Penguin, 1953).

Bennett, Jonathan, *Locke, Berkeley, Hume: Central Themes* (Oxford: Oxford University Press, 1971).

Berger, Peter L., and Thomas Luckmann, *The Social Construction of Reality: a Treatise in the Sociology of Knowledge* (London, Penguin, 1967).

Berkeley, George, *Dialogues between Hylas and Philonous* and *Principles of Human Knowledge*, both in his Philosophical Works etc., ed. Michael R. Ayers (London: Dent; Vermont: Tuttle, 1975).

Boswell, James, *Life of Johnson*, ed. R.W. Chapman (Oxford: Oxford University Press, 1953).

Burnyeat, Myles F., *The Theaetetus of Plato*, with a translation by M. J. Levett revised by M. Burnyeat (Indianapolis/Cambridge: Hackett, 1990).

Carter, Angela, *Nights at the Circus* (London: Pan, 1985).

Churchland, Paul M., *Scientific Realism and the Plasticity of Mind* (Cambridge: Cambridge University Press, 1979).

Churchland, Paul M., and Clifford A. Hooker (eds), *Images of Science: Essays on Realism and Empiricism, with a reply from Bas C. Van Fraassen* (Chicago and London: University of Chicago Press, 1985).

Cornford, F. M., *Principium Sapientiae* (Cambridge: Cambridge University Press, 1952).

Craig, Edward (ed.), *Routledge Encyclopedia of Philosophy* (London: Routledge, 1998).

Dalley, Stephanie (trans. and intr.), *Myths from Mesopotamia* (Oxford: Oxford University Press, 1989).

Dancy, Jonathan, *An Introduction to Contemporary Epistemology* (Oxford: Blackwell, 1985).

——*Berkeley: an Introduction* (Oxford: Blackwell, 1987).

Davidson, Donald, *Inquiries into Truth and Interpretation* (Oxford: Clarendon Press, 1984).

Davidson, Donald, and Jaakko Hintikka (eds), *Words and Objections* (Dordrecht: Reidel, 1969).

Dennett, Daniel C., *Consciousness Explained* (Boston: Little, Brown, 1991).

Descartes, René, *Discourse on the Method* and *Meditations*. Many editions (e.g. London: Penguin, 1968).

Devitt, Michael, *Realism and Truth* (Oxford: Blackwell, 1984; 2nd edn Princeton: Princeton University Press, 1997).

Dreyfus, Hubert, *Being-in-the-World: a Commentary on Heidegger's Being and Time, division I* (Cambridge, Mass.: MIT, 1991).

Dummett, Michael, *Truth and Other Enigmas* (London: Duckworth, 1978).

——*The Logical Basis of Metaphysics* (London: Duckworth, 1991).

——*The Seas of Language* (Oxford: Clarendon Press, 1993).

Dundes, Alan (ed.), *Sacred Narrative: Readings in the Theory of Myth* (Berkeley, Los Angeles, London: University of California Press, 1984).

Ellroy, James *American Tabloid* (London: Random House, 1995).

Evans-Pritchard, E. E., *Witchcraft, Oracles, and Magic among the Azande* (Oxford: Clarendon Press, 1937).

Feynman, Richard, *QED: the Strange Theory of Light and Matter* (London: Penguin, 1985).

Goodman, Nelson, *Ways of Worldmaking* (Indianapolis, Indiana: Hackett, 1978).

Grayling, A. C., *An Introduction to Philosophical Logic* (Brighton/Totowa, N.J.: Harvester/Barnes and Noble, 1982).

Grice, H. P., and Peter F. Strawson, 'In Defense of a Dogma', *Philosophical Review* 65 (1956), 141–58.

Grim, Patrick, *The Incomplete Universe* (Cambridge, Mass.: M.I.T. Press, 1991).

Haack, Susan, *Philosophy of Logics* (Cambridge: Cambridge University Press, 1978).

Hall, A. R., *The Scientific Revolution 1300–1800* (London: Longmans, 1962).

Hardin, C. L., *Color for Philosophers* (Indianapolis: Hackett, 1988).

Heidegger, Martin, tr. John McQuarrie and Edward Robinson, *Being and Time* (San Francisco: Harper, 1962).

Hollis, Martin, *The Cunning of Reason* (Cambridge: Cambridge University Press, 1987).

Hollis, Martin, and Steven Lukes (eds), *Rationality and Relativism* (Oxford: Blackwell, 1982).

Honderich, Ted (ed.), *The Oxford Companion to Philosophy* (Oxford: Oxford University Press, 1995).

Hookway, Christopher, *Quine: Language, Experience and Reality* (Oxford: Polity Press, 1988).

Hume, David, *An Enquiry into Human Understanding*. In *Hume's Enquiries*, ed. A. Selby-Bigge (Oxford: Oxford University Press, 1966).

——*A Treatise of Human Nature*, eds A. Selby-Bigge and P. H. Nidditch (Oxford: Clarendon Press, 1978).

Husserl, Edmund, *The Crisis of European Sciences and Transcendental Phenomenology*, tr. and int. David Carr (Evanston: Northwestern University Press, 1970).

James, William, *Pragmatism: a New Name for Some Old Ways of Thinking*, and *The Meaning of Truth* (Cambridge, Mass., and London: Harvard University Press, 1978).

Kenny, Anthony, *Wittgenstein* (London: Penguin, 1973).

Kerferd, G. B., *The Sophistic Movement* (Cambridge: Cambridge University Press, 1981).

Kirk, Robert, *Translation Determined* (Oxford: Clarendon Press, 1986).

——*Raw Feeling: a Philosophical Account of the Essence of Consciousness* (Oxford: Clarendon Press, 1994).

Koestler, Arthur, *The Sleepwalkers* (London: Hutchinson, 1968).

Kripke, Saul, *Wittgenstein on Rules and Private Language* (Oxford: Blackwell, 1982).

Kuhn, Thomas S., *The Structure of Scientific Revolutions* (2nd edn) (Chicago: University of Chicago Press, 1970).

Latour, Bruno, and Steve Woolgar, *Laboratory Life: the Social Construction of Scientific Facts* (Beverly Hills and London: Sage Publications, 1979).

LePore, Ernest (ed.), *Truth and Interpretation: Perspectives on the Philosophy of Donald Davidson* (Oxford: Blackwell, 1986).

Locke, John, *An Essay Concerning Human Understanding*, ed. P. H. Nidditch (Oxford: Clarendon Press, 1975).

Lowe, E. J., *Locke on Human Understanding* (London: Routledge, 1995).

Lyons, John, *Chomsky* (London: Fontana/Collins, 1970).

——*Semantics* (Cambridge: Cambridge University Press, 1977).

Malachowski, Alan R. (ed.), *Reading Rorty* (Oxford: Blackwell, 1990).

McFarland, David (ed.), *Oxford Companion to Animal Behaviour* (Oxford: Oxford University Press, 1989).

McGinn, Colin, 'Truth and Use', in M. Platts (ed.), *Reference, Truth and Reality* (London: Routledge and Kegan Paul, 1980).

McGinn, Marie, *Wittgenstein and the* Philosophical Investigations (London, New York: Routledge, 1997).

Miller, Alexander *Philosophy of Language*, (London: UCL Press, 1998).

Monk, Ray, *Ludwig Wittgenstein: the Duty of Genius* (London: Vintage, 1990).

Morton, Adam, *Philosophy in Practice: an Introduction to the Main Questions* (Cambridge, Mass. and Oxford: Blackwell, 1996).

Nagel, Thomas, *The Last Word* (New York and Oxford: Oxford University Press, 1997).

Nietzsche, Friedrich, *The Will to Power* (New York: Vintage, 1968).

Pears, David, *The False Prison: a Study of the Development of Wittgenstein's Philosophy*, vols. i and ii (Oxford: Clarendon Press, 1988).

Popper, Karl R., *The Poverty of Historicism* (London: Routledge, 1957).

——*Conjectures and Refutations* (London: Routledge, 1963).

——'Back to the Presocratics', reprinted in his *Conjectures and Refutations* (London: Routledge, 1963).

Putnam, Hilary, 'The Refutation of Conventionalism', in his *Mind, Language and Reality: Philosophical Papers vol. 2* (Cambridge: Cambridge University Press, 1975), pp. 153–91.

——*Pragmatism: an Open Question* (Oxford: Blackwell, 1995).

——*Realism with a Human Face*, ed. and int. James Conant (Cambridge, Mass. and London: Harvard University Press, 1990).

——*Reason, Truth and History* (Cambridge: Cambridge University Press, 1981).

Quine, W. V., *From a Logical Point of View* (Cambridge, Mass.: Harvard University Press, 1953).

——*Word and Object* (Cambridge, Mass., New York and London: MIT Press and Wiley, 1960).

——*Ontological Relativity and Other Essays* (New York and London: Columbia University Press, 1969).

——*Philosophy of Logic* (Englewood Cliffs: Prentice-Hall, 1970).

——'Mind and Verbal Dispositions'. In S. Guttenplan (ed.), *Mind and Language* (Oxford: Clarendon Press, 1975).

——*Theories and Things* (Cambridge, Mass., and London: Harvard University Press, 1981).

——*Pursuit of Truth*, rev. edn (Cambridge, Mass., and London: Harvard University Press, 1992).

——*From Stimulus to Science* (Cambridge, Mass., and London: Harvard University Press, 1995).

——'Two Dogmas of Empiricism' (*Philosophical Review* 60, 1951, reprinted in his *From a Logical Point of View*).

Rorty, Richard, *Philosophy and The Mirror of Nature* (Princeton: Princeton University Press, 1980).

——*Consequences of Pragmatism* (Brighton: Harvester, 1982).

——*Contingency, Irony, and Solidarity* (Cambridge: Cambridge University Press, 1989).

Ryle, Gilbert, *The Concept of Mind* (London: Hutchinson, 1949).

Saatkamp, Herman J. (ed.), *Rorty and Pragmatism: the Philosopher Responds to His Critics* (Nashville and London: Vanderbilt University Press, 1995).

Schacht, Robert, *Nietzsche* (London and New York: Routledge, 1983).

Schmitt, Frederick F., *Truth: a primer* (Boulder, San Francisco, Oxford: Westview Press, 1995).

Scruton, Roger, *Kant* (Oxford: Oxford University Press, 1982).

Searle, John R., *The Construction of Social Reality* (London: Penguin, 1995).

Sellars, Wilfrid, *Science, Perception and Reality* (London: Routledge, 1963).

Smart, J. J. C., *Philosophy and Scientific Realism* (London: Routledge, 1963).

Van Fraassen, Bas C., *The Scientific Image* (Oxford: Oxford University Press, 1980).

Warburton, Nigel, *Philosophy: the Basics* (London: Routledge, 1992).

Williams, Bernard, *Descartes: the Project of Pure Enquiry* (London: Penguin, 1978).

Winch, Peter, 'Understanding a Primitive Society', *American Philosophical Quarterly* 1, 1964, reprinted in *Rationality*, ed. Brian Wilson (Oxford: Blackwell, 1970).

Wittgenstein, Ludwig (ed. G. E. M. Anscombe and R. Rhees), *Philosophical Investigations* (Oxford: Blackwell, 1961).

——(trans. D. F. Pears and B. F. McGuinness), *Tractatus Logico-Philosophicus* (London: Routledge, 1961).

——(ed. G. E. M. Anscombe and G. H. von Wright; tr. D. Paul and G. E. M. Anscombe), *On Certainty* (Oxford: Blackwell, 1969).

Wright, Crispin, *Realism, Meaning and Truth* (Oxford: Blackwell, 1987).

INDEX

DATE DUE

GAYLORD

PRINTED IN U.S.A.

B 835 .K57 1999

Kirk, Robert, 1933–

Relativism and reality